1979 Proceedings of
The American Ethnological Society

The Development of Political Organization in Native North America

1979 Proceedings of
The American Ethnological Society

Elisabeth Tooker, Editor
Morton H. Fried, Symposium Organizer

THE AMERICAN ETHNOLOGICAL SOCIETY

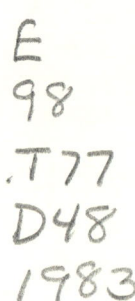

Copyright © 1983 by the American Ethnological Society
All rights reserved
Printed in the United States of America
ISSN 0731-4108

Library of Congress Cataloging in Publication Data
Main entry under title:

The Development of political organization in native North America.

(Proceedings of the American Ethnological Society; 1979)
 1. Indians of North America—Tribal government—Addresses, essays, lectures. 2. Indians of North America—Politics and government—Addresses, essays, lectures. I. Tooker, Elisabeth. II. Fried, Morton Herbert, 1923- . III. Series.
E98.T77D48 1983   323.1′197   82-24378
ISBN 0-942976-01-0

Copies may be ordered from:

 American Ethnological Society
 1703 New Hampshire Avenue NW
 Washington, DC 20009

Contents

Editor's Introduction vii

I

1 Tribe and State in the Sixteenth and Twentieth Centuries
   William C. Sturtevant 3

2 Ethnohistorical Investigation of Egalitarian Politics in Eastern North America
   Eleanor Leacock 17

3 Pueblo Councils: An Example of Stratified Egalitarianism
   M. Estellie Smith 32

4 Aboriginal Sociopolitical Organization in Owens Valley: Beyond the Family Band
   Robert L. Bettinger 45

5 On Steward's Models of Shoshonean Sociopolitical Organization: A Great Bias in the Basin?
   David Hurst Thomas 59

II

6 Aboriginal Tlingit Sociopolitical Organization
   Frederica de Laguna 71

7 Ecology and Political Organization on the Northwest Coast of America
   Philip Drucker 86

8	Seasonal Settlements, Village Aggregations, and Political Autonomy on the Central Northwest Coast	
	Donald H. Mitchell	97
9	Was Nuu-chah-nulth-aht (Nootka) Society Based on Slave Labor?	
	Leland Donald	108
10	Pre-contact Political Organization and Slavery in Aleut Societies	
	Joan B. Townsend	120
11	Warfare and Redistributive Exchange on the Northwest Coast	
	Brian Ferguson	133
12	Limiting Access to Limited Goods: The Origins of Stratification in Interior British Columbia	
	Charles A. Bishop	148

III

13	The Recognition of Leadership in Egalitarian Societies of the Northeast	
	Nan A. Rothschild	165
14	Moundville: Late Prehistoric Sociopolitical Organization in the Southeastern United States	
	Christopher S. Peebles	183
15	The Analysis of Prehistoric Political Organization	
	Fred Plog and *Steadman Upham*	199
16	Some Simple Measures for the Study of Prehistoric Political Organization	
	Frank J. Findlow and *Neil J. Goldberg*	214

Editor's Introduction

The last four decades have witnessed a renewed interest in the evolution of society among both ethnologists and archaeologists. After a dearth of such studies in the first four decades of the century, a number of books and articles have appeared suggesting what the course of social evolution has been, including that of political organization. One of the most widely noted of these along with those of White, Steward, Sahlins, and Service is that outlined by Morton H. Fried (1967), organizer of the sessions of the 1979 American Ethnological Society Spring meetings held in Vancouver, British Columbia, jointly with those of the Society for American Archaeology and the Canadian Archaeological Society.

It might be expected, then, that the papers presented at the 1979 AES meetings on the topic "The Development of Political Organization in Native North America" would have offered elaboration and refinement of ideas now widely current respecting the evolution of society. Such, however, did not prove to be the case. Although some of the papers used the conclusions reached in various studies of social and political evolution, others were critical of one or another contention of these admittedly somewhat programmatic expositions. Taken as a whole, the papers offer an opportunity not so much to measure recent advances in evolutionary theory as to evaluate how successfully such theories account for the data and to consider what future direction such studies might take.

The opportunity for evaluation this present collection offers is just that—an opportunity. The papers in this volume offer no systematic review of current anthropological theory regarding political development; rather, most are case studies using ideas drawn from this body of theory or treating issues those ideas present. Neither do they offer a systematic review of the variety of political organization to be found among the Indian peoples of North America. In fact, some of the imbalance is intentional: since the meetings were held in Vancouver, more papers were invited on the subject of Northwest Coast political organizations than those of other areas, and these papers taken together serve as a longer case study.

Any evaluation of the progress and success of various theories of political evolution must, of necessity, involve a number of questions, not all of which can be considered here. Nonetheless, several of importance are evident in this collection, and so warrant mention.

Of all these questions, undoubtedly the most basic concerns the validity of the typologies used in the study of social and political evolution. On this most fundamental of questions there is no particular agreement among authors. Some, if implicitly, regard the typology as valid and use it to interpret one or another body of data. For example, Rothschild, accepting the idea that in egalitarian societies as defined by Fried and others social distinctions are based on age, sex, and achieved leadership positions, uses data on mortuary treatment from two Northeastern Archaic period cemeteries both to confirm that these sites represent remains of egalitarian societies and to suggest that differences in respect to age, sex, and leadership position inferred from remains in these two cemeteries are linked to differences in environmental potential of the two areas. In a somewhat similar manner, Peebles uses data on settlement pattern as well as burial practice to trace changes in social and political organization in the Black Warrior River Valley, Alabama, from 900 A.D., suggesting that over a 600-year period societies in this region evolved from simple, egalitarian ones to more complex ones.

Others are more skeptical. Sturtevant, for example, suggests that such typologies as have been developed bear a rather ambiguous relation to the real world and may say much less, with much less certainty, than many suppose. Nor is this, Sturtevant suggests, merely a matter of academic interest. It is one that is of great concern to people living in the real world for the unanticipated grave social and political consequences it may have on them.

Not perhaps unexpectedly this difference of opinion respecting the validity of theories of sociopolitical evolution leads to differences of opinion respecting the validity of certain historical data. To mention only one instance: Peebles accepts as accurate descriptions in the accounts of the de Soto expedition. Sturtevant does not, as he illustrates through an example.

The question of validity of typologies is intimately bound up with the character of typologies and the methods used to construct them—as Sturtevant also suggests. This is a matter given, perhaps, too little attention, and surprisingly so—for it can be easily argued that it was the method employed, what may for convenience be termed the typological method, not the faulty use of it or the lack of sufficient data that brought down 19th-century evolutionary theory and now threatens comparable 20th-century evolutionary the-

Editor's Introduction

ory. Nineteenth-century anthropologists, like 20th-century evolutionists, supposed that through inspection of a body of data the correct classification of these data would suggest itself—the inductive method they labeled the Baconian (sometimes Newtonian and sometimes, simply, scientific) method—and that application of such a method would produce general laws. It did not. What it did produce were a number of evolutionary typologies, more or less contradictory, most of which are now forgotten, probably for the reason that there were no grounds on which to resolve the differences between them. None considered all the relevant data; each selected, almost unwittingly it would seem, certain features—characteristics or components—and certain principles that either often appeared to or might be expected to govern relationships between the factors. But opinion differed as to what features and what principles were the primary or the most fundamental ones, and there were no generally accepted criteria on which to base such a judgment. In fact, it may have been the impossibility of deciding which of the many theories was the better one that led Boas among others to espouse the methods and types of study he did, what evolutionists are apt to term "historical particularism"—a concern with the unique histories of the peoples of the earth.

Twentieth-century sociopolitical evolutionary theories may fare no better than 19th-century ones, and there are indications that such a process is now underway. Some of the differences of opinion involve disagreements regarding what *may* be the case, which are often transformed by a process that occasionally resembles legerdemain to statements of what *is* the case; that is, they are transformed from statements regarding factors that might be of significance in a particular case to statements of general law. One suspects, for example, that such is involved in the current disagreements regarding interpretation of burial practices or mortuary remains among archaeologists mentioned by Plog and Upham and by Sturtevant. Some, including Plog and Upham, Rothschild, Peebles, and Bettinger either argue or assume that because burial practices *may* reflect social status, these practices can be used as evidence of that status, which in practice becomes the statement of general law: because burial practices reflect social status, they are indicators of social status. Others, arguing that other factors *may* also be involved (the importance of these other factors also being subject to dispute), are not so certain that burial practices are as neatly correlated with social status. Other proposed correlations may—on examination—prove to be no less subject to dispute.

These considerations lead to another important question: the underlying basis of the typology, or classification, which in its turn may well rest on the personal predilections of the analyst. At least this seems to be the reason for disagreements respecting interpretation of type cases. Sociocultural evolutionary theory generally posits a change from simple to complex; on this there is little disagreement. What is disputed is what quality, what feature or characteristic, is to be regarded as "simple" and hence what cases are deemed type cases and what cases not. For example, Julian Steward took the family (properly, nuclear family) as the simplest unit of sociopolitical organization and so regarded multifamily aggregates such as the patrilineal band and the composite hunting band as more complex forms of society. This in turn apparently led him to regard the "simple" Great Basin Shoshonean Indians as a type case of the "family level of integration" (Steward 1955:101–121). Elman Service, however, regards not the nuclear family but the group based on a unilineal residence rule—the patrilocal band—as "the simplest, most rudimentary form of social structure" (Service 1962:107). All other forms of organization are more recent. He asserts, for example, that the composite band is a form of social organization "obviously a product of the near-destruction of aboriginal bands after contact with civilization"—although admitting that direct evidence that "the bands were patrilocal before disaster struck [is] not conclusive in every case" and that recourse to indirect evidence is necessary to support the supposition (Service 1962:108). Somewhat similarly he argues that Steward's "family level" Shoshonean case may merely represent "survivals of a earlier form of patrilocal band organization" (Service 1962:98–99) and so not be characteristic of pre-contact Shoshoneans.

This same case—the Great Basin Shoshoneans—is considered in the present collection in two papers. After examining the archaeological and the published ethnographic data including Steward's, Bettinger suggests that Owens Valley Paiute sociopolitical organization was quite unlike that indicated in Steward's characterization of Great Basin Shoshonean organization. Thomas outlines how Steward's model, which ignores regional variation in Great Basin habitat, culture, and society, grew out of his earlier field work, which did.

Some perusal of evolutionary typologies suggests that more complex forms of sociopolitical organization than Steward's "family level," Service's "patrilocal band," and Fried's "egalitarian society" invoke more complex arguments and more criteria—not always explicit and not always consistent. It may be this feature of the classifications that led authors of various papers on these more complex societies in this volume to question not the validity of the type cases but the terms used. Two frequently mentioned are "tribe" and "confederacy." Donald, for example, noting that the connotations of the term "confederation" used by Drucker in reference to Northwest Coast village (local group) aggregations do not fit well the actual case, uses the word "federation." Drucker himself observes that his and others' rather casual use of "tribe" and "confederacy" has led to a characterization of the Northwest Coast as an area of complex political systems and as having kinds of political institutions not indicated by the ethnographic data. Sturtevant offers some discussion of the term "tribe," including Fried's use of it, and suggests substituting a technical term borrowed from an exotic lexicon. And Smith, discerning "profound inequalities" in egalitarian societies and egalitarianism in even

Editor's Introduction

the most stratified ones, discusses councils as a type of "stratified egalitarianism."

As differences of opinion respecting the validity of evolutionary theories lead to differences of opinion respecting the validity of data in the historical documents, so also do these differences lead to differences of opinion regarding the validity of "conjectual history." This, too, is not a new question. Explicit or implicit in at least some evolutionary theories is the view that "simpler" societies have remained static over periods measured not in years but in millennia and such significant change as has occurred has been the result of recent contact with Western civilization, the history of which is familiar to us. And further, since that radical disruption by our civilization may have occurred before "trained observers" were there to record it, evolutionary theory may be used to disclose what these "broken" societies were like in the period just before "contact." Others (including the "historical particularists") would argue that the accumulated ethnographic, linguistic, and archaeological data indicate that the history of all the many peoples of the world is vastly more complex than this and that certain features of sociopolitical organization that might be expected to be found in certain types of societies are not, while features that might not be expected on the basis of comparison to our society and a knowledge of recent Western history are. Such questions may even arise when relatively good accounts exist in the historical documents. To mention only one of the papers in this volume to examine this issue: Townsend asks whether early historical reports of "slaves" and "classes" in the small scale Aleut societies are erroneous or are accurate accounts of an indigenous development, and one not in response to the fur trade.

A number of these papers also express concern that one or another taxonomy has given what Leacock characterizes as "a false sense" of understanding phenomena that are by no means well understood. Various suggestions for improving this understanding are made by various of the authors. For example, Leacock is concerned with better understanding political processes in egalitarian societies, suggesting that in such societies individuals who are responsible for carrying out a decision or who are directly affected by it must have a share in making it commensurate with their experience and wisdom and that those who do not agree with the decision are not bound by it. Smith is also concerned with how political decisions are reached in egalitarian societies, and particularly with how the politics of egalitarianism functions to support what might be termed a "stratified" structure.

Others are concerned with economics, broadly or narrowly construed, and not unexpectedly so, for current evolutionary theory is apt to stress the primary role of ecology and redistribution in determining forms of sociopolitical organization. Drucker, for example, discusses the interplay of ecologic factors on settlement pattern and political life on the Northwest Coast, although he does not limit his discussion to these features. Mitchell also discusses settlement pattern in one region of the Northwest Coast and relates one type of settlement to considerations involving whale hunting.

Plog and Upham give primary importance to managerial decisions, particularly those involving access to space, to human and natural resources, and to social resources including statuses, organization, and symbols, suggesting how these decisions might be inferred from the archaeological record. Findlow and Goldberg offer some programmatic measures based on Central Place Theory for inferring prehistoric political organization from data on settlement pattern.

Donald stresses the economic importance of slave labor in one Northwest Coast society, a matter also mentioned by Townsend. Ferguson argues that the emphasis on redistribution in Northwest Coast economies can be explained as a response to intensive warfare in the area. And Bishop sees the system of hereditary rank as first developing from exchange in non-essential goods and sees the source of the potlatch redistribution in validation rituals for maintaining privileged trade positions.

But even the primary role of economics in determining forms of sociopolitical organization does not pass unchallenged. Smith questions the idea that ranking and stratification have their basis in economic distribution of material goods, suggesting that the non-material "good" may be more important and be the source of social inequality.

Thus, perhaps, it remains to be demonstrated whether any or all of these factors can fully account for the various native North American attitudes and beliefs such as those described in de Laguna's masterful summary of Tlingit sociopolitical organization.

References Cited

Fried, Morton H.
   1967   The Evolution of Political Society: An Essay in Political Anthropology. New York: Random House.

Service, Elman R.
   1962   Primitive Social Organization: An Evolutionary Perspective. New York: Random House. 2nd ed., 1971.

Steward, Julian H.
   1955   Theory of Culture Change: The Methodology of Multilineal Evolution. Urbana: University of Illinois Press.

I

1
Tribe and State in the Sixteenth and Twentieth Centuries

William C. Sturtevant
Smithsonian Institution

Evolutionary typologies of sociopolitical organization proposed in recent years by Fried (1975, 1978) and others deserve to be seen as what they are: social anthropological models or ideal types, which have a rather ambiguous relation to the real world evidenced by archaeology, ethnohistory, ethnography, and jurisprudence. They are certainly useful as guides for investigating and understanding the real world, but they do not have the full status of testable scientific laws or generalizations.

Fried's method can be described, with only slight caricature, as the use of a logic of social evolution to develop a scenario of stages, labeled with familiar terms, that are then illustrated with a few ethnographic and historical examples that come readily to hand. Misunderstanding this method of argumentation can lead to at least two dangers. One, treated later in this discussion, involves the misinterpretation or misuse of social anthropological argumentation by lawyers, judges, juries, legislators, and bureaucrats. The other is that some historians and some archaeologists are misled into supposing that social anthropologists have established a typology such that, if a poorly known society can be placed into one of the types because it seems to have one or a few of the attributes of that type, then significant other, undocumented, cultural features can be attributed to the poorly known society by drawing on social anthropological characterizations of societies of that type. Thus some historians assume that calling 16th- and 17th-century New England Indian groups "bands" tells us things about their descent rules, political organization, and economic behavior that the available documents do not mention. Some archaeologists assume that certain patterned differences in grave goods imply the social ranking or stratification of the buried individuals when they were alive, that this implies a chiefdom or state, and from this follow many ideological, economic, and other characteristics of the societies to which the dead belonged for which no more direct archaeological evidence need be discovered. Good archaeology may provide data on interesting sociopolitical characteristics, but it may say less, with less certainty, than is suggested by much recent writing (see Chapter 15, this volume). If social anthropological argumentation were a bit more cautious, archaeologists might be less convinced of its relevance and might have begun earlier to develop typologies with attributes more directly discoverable through archaeological survey and excavation.

In *The Notion of Tribe* Fried (1975) lists a set of characteristics often said or assumed to be typical of social groups called "tribes," suggesting that possession of the full set is necessary and sufficient for any group to be properly so labeled. He then takes up the features or attributes one by one, and finds in the ethnographic literature several groups that lack each attribute yet are explicitly called tribes or might be so called because they evidently have most of the other attributes. From this he concludes that the concept "tribe" is useless or erroneous (although he might have suggested that the concept be defined polythetically rather than monothetically). Here (Fried 1975:ch. 12) and in a later paper (Fried 1978) he says that "all tribes are secondary, meaning by that that all known tribes, including those known to us only from the recesses of history . . . formed as a reaction to previously existing states. Before the first state there were no tribes." This hypothesis might be tested against the evidence on 16th-century southeastern North America. If we can identify tribes at the time of first European contact in this region—adopting the attributes discussed by Fried (1975, 1978) as the definition of tribe—then they are either pristine tribes, not caused by an impinging state (a type that Fried says does not exist), or they are secondary tribes, the results of reaction to a state. Yet the closest known states were in Mesoamerica, rather far away, so the mechanism of the influence becomes an interesting problem and furthermore this might be added to evidence, as yet vague but still convincing, for Mesoamerican effects on the prehistoric Southeast.

However, Fried's statement that all tribes are secondary may be impossible to test. All tribes known to ethnography or history are close enough to some state or states so that some indirect if not direct influence can have occurred. If enough details about a society are known to place it securely into one of the social anthropological typologies, those details come from literate observers, anthropologists or others, who originate (almost by definition) in a state. By the time they can get close enough to have informative contacts with the putative tribespeople, and there is an open channel of communication, so that they can learn enough about and convincingly record the attributes of the society that are criterial for classifying it as a tribe, the tribespeople will long since have been exposed to the impinging state or state system in which the observers originate. The only answer, then, will come from archaeology, and that can only be a very partial one so long as the attributes of tribe are so non-material.

The 16th-century Southeast provides an interesting example of the nature of documentary records made before the effects of an impinging state must be assumed (leaving aside possible Mesoamerican influence). In deducing the situation at that time one must abandon the ethnohistorical technique of "upstreaming" from later and therefore better ethnographic and historical evidence. The later societies of the region on which we have good written evidence, beginning in the 18th century, had certainly been drastically influenced in just those areas of interest by the heavy impingement of the European states from which the recorders came. Upstreaming presupposes that one can disentangle cultural persistences from the changes introduced in the intervening period. The specific forms of the 18th-century Southeastern secondary tribes (and a few chiefdoms and perhaps incipient states) were indeed changed outgrowths of their 16th-century predecessors. But one can hardly subtract the later changes in the very cultural features in which one is interested in order to discover a pre-existing sociopolitical system of the same type whose existence is precisely the question. One must, instead, examine the primary written sources of the 16th century in search of Fried's criterial attributes, without reading into them features we know to have been present among the tribes of the region in the 18th and 19th centuries.

To anticipate the test: the documents are simply not adequate to the question. One cannot conclude that most of the criterial attributes were either present or absent; whether or not tribes or secondary tribes existed in the 16th-century Southeast is not determinable from the documentary evidence. The observers were present in any one place for too short a time; or in the rare cases where we have more varied evidence on one locality we know almost nothing about the distribution of the cultural features, about the boundaries and networks that must be understood in order to apply Fried's definitions. There were almost always extreme difficulties in communication, on the basic level of language and even more on the level of European cross-cultural naïveté. The early sources are full of references to kings, nobles, tribute, empires, and provinces, yet these were certainly not empires, kingdoms, or theocratic feudal states. Unfortunately there was no Sahagún in the Southeast, and even Sahagún was no modern social anthropologist.

The first European contacts with the Indians of the interior Southeast occurred during de Soto's long march from 1539 to 1543. It is a priori unlikely that any of de Soto's men, or any other 16th-century Spanish or French observers, knew enough, understood enough, or wrote enough about Southeastern Indian societies to tell us whether the features by which Fried characterizes tribes (or secondary tribes) were present.

According to Fried (1975, 1978), a tribe is a loosely organized set of villages or migratory camps with some centralized leadership that has little or no coercive power. These communities participate in networks of the following sorts, that are largely congruent—their shared boundary delimits the tribe:

- there is a network of economic production and/or distribution and/or consumption;
- there is a kinship network, for the tribe tends to be an endogamous unit;
- the tribe is the largest defensive unit and the largest basic peace field;
- there is a basic unity of linguistic intelligibility, the tribe being a minimal speech community;
- there is a cultural network, including shared and exchanged ritual and religious belief, and a natural clustering of other cultural traits.

In addition, the tribe is an ideological group and has a distinctive name.

In all the de Soto narratives (most of them conveniently collected in Quinn 1979:90–188), there is no evidence whatsoever on most of these features, while for a few there are ambiguous hints that could be interpreted as implying such features but can easily also be interpreted otherwise (for example, as being merely reflections of European preconceptions). A fine example appears in Brain's recent, excellent discussion of late prehistoric settlement patterning in the Lower Mississippi Valley. After a sophisticated analysis of the archaeological evidence, Brain (1978:357) writes:

> A fascinating glimpse of the power and confidence of . . . a central authority is provided by the Cacique of Quigualtam. . . . In response to De Soto's typically arrogant demand for subservience, this chief (referred to in the narrative as "the greatest of that country") sent a marvelous message, which with equal arrogance bade De Soto mind his manners (Bourne 1922, I:154–155):
>
>> It is not my custom to visit anyone, but rather all, of whom I have ever heard, have come to visit me, to serve and obey me, and pay me tribute, either voluntarily or by force: if you desire to see me, come where I am; if for peace, I will receive you with special goodwill; if for war, I will await you in my town; but neither for you, nor for any man, will I set back one foot.
>
> This was supreme power, and apparently intimidating enough that the Spaniards never pressed their demands nor actually visited Quigualtam. A most unfortunate turn of events for this study, because Quigualtam was the proto-Natchez "province" of the Emerald phase; and the Emerald site itself was probably the seat of that great chief.

This incident is reported by one of the better sources on the de Soto expedition, that written by the Gentleman of Elvas, who was a participant (although evidently not the keeper of a diary). How did he know the content of the chief's message? When de Soto first landed in Florida he rescued near Tampa Bay a Spaniard, Juan Ortiz, who had been left by the Narvaez expedition 11 years earlier. In the interim he had become quite thoroughly Indianized and learned to speak the local language (perhaps a Timucua dialect). Although during his captivity he had never been more than 10 leagues from the place where he was rescued, he served de Soto as an interpreter all through the interior (Quinn 1979:104–105). There must usually have been a whole chain of interpreters, with Juan Ortiz at the end; there are a few hints to this effect (e.g., Quinn 1979:180–181), and the accounts often mention seeking and kidnapping Indians (who could have known no Spanish) to serve as interpreters. But Juan Ortiz had died at least several weeks before the incident quoted by Brain. The Gentleman of Elvas reports:

In Autiamque died Juan Ortiz, which the governor [de Soto] felt deeply, for without an interpreter, not knowing where he was going, he feared lest he enter a region where he might get lost. After that, a youth who had been seized in Cutifachiqui,[1] and who now knew something of the language of the Christians, served as interpreter. So great a misfortune was the death of Juan Ortiz, with regard to the exploring or trying to leave the land, that to learn from the Indians what he stated in four words, with the youth the whole day was needed; and most of the time he understood just the opposite of what was asked, so that many times it came about that the road they took [in] one day, and at times, two or three days, they would return on, and they would wander about lost from one side of those woods to the other (Robertson 1932–33: II:207, with the original Portuguese text in facsimile on I:cxx^r–cxx^v).

The proud speech by the Cacique of Quigualtam, transmitted by an Indian messenger, must have been explained to de Soto by the poor boy from Cofitachequi, a place perhaps 600 miles away as the crow flies. It is of no value as evidence on Southeastern sociopolitical structure.

Markedly contrasting with the fragmentary and usually problematical evidence from the de Soto expedition and other 16th-century Spanish *entradas* is our knowledge of the Calusa of southwestern Florida. The documentary evidence on Calos, the main Calusa town, is more complete than that for any other site in the East in the 16th century. Several Spaniards were in close contact with this community for two or three years in the 1560s; among them was an intelligent Jesuit, Juan Rogel, who wrote important descriptions in contemporaneous letters. The cultural data are particularly extensive and convincing because of the presence at Calos of several long-term Spanish captives who served as interpreters. No important documents on the Calusa have been discovered since Goggin and Sturtevant (1964) surveyed the historical sources. The following paragraph summarizes our findings.

The town of Calos had a population of perhaps 1,000. Here there was a chief with considerable authority, who wore special insignia of office and was entitled to particular forms of respect. An exception to the usual incest rules required that he marry his own full sister. When he or his wife-sister died, retainers were sacrificed. When his children or some other leading people died, children were sacrificed. There are quite convincing indications that the chief's town was linked to smaller satellite dependent villages (although the Spaniards did not visit them) and that these and some more distant settlements were tied to the high chief by marriages and owed him material tribute. There is both documentary and archaeological evidence for the flow of goods to the Calusa chief, especially gold and captives from Spanish shipwrecks on the opposite east coast of the peninsula. Warfare was important and the chief played a leading role in it. Military campaigns were interpreted by the Spaniards (who may here reflect their European preconceptions) as aimed at establishing and maintaining political and economic dominance. There are also statements that warfare yielded trophy heads and sacrificial victims essential for rituals. There is a little evidence (beyond mere Spanish summary statements) for social stratification into at least two classes. Some specific details are given on the attributes of occupants of several high-ranking statuses, who evidently had greater access to at least some economic resources, wielded some political authority, and had distinctive ritual knowledge and duties.

Even though many of Fried's criterial attributes have not been mentioned, on the above evidence the Calusa would probably be classified as a chiefdom rather than a tribe. But we know essentially nothing about the cultural networks in which Calos presumably participated (although Widmer 1978 has made some reasonable deductions from the distribution of archaeological sites and from modern ecological data), so we cannot say what the boundaries of its sociopolitical group may have been. Yet the congruence of such networks is an important feature of Fried's definition of tribe (and of chiefdom). Furthermore by the 1560s there had been at least 50 years of indirect European influence on south Florida societies, which is well illustrated by the presence at Calos of many Calusa-speaking Spanish captives and large quantities of Spanish gold and silver.

Documentary evidence appears to be inadequate to resolve whether or not "tribes" (in some special social anthropological sense) existed among North American Indians when they first met representatives of European states. However, we do know something of the real nature of eastern North American Indian polities in the 18th and 19th centuries, after they had been influenced drastically by European states. This understanding can be used to

Tribe and State 9

measure the shifting applications and implications of the labels used in European languages to refer to these (and other) societies.

No thorough study has been made of the meanings of labels such as "nation," "tribe," and "clan" in the English of ordinary conversation and writing, of legal, diplomatic, and treaty terminology, or of anthropological usage. It is well known that Lewis Henry Morgan shifted his usage between the *League of the Iroquois* (1851) and *Ancient Society* (1877)—the same units called "tribe" and "nation" in the earlier work were labeled respectively "clan" and "tribe" in the later one. But this shift seems to have been little related to earlier usage by others.

Thomas Jefferson's usage in his *Notes on the State of Virginia* (1972:92–107; first published in 1782 and 1787) was quite like the modern one. He wrote of "tribes," sometimes joined in "confederacies." "Nation" is rarer and usually synonymous with "tribe" (as for example when each of the Five Nations is listed in tables headed "tribes"); occasionally "nation" is used interchangeably with "confederacy." Jefferson's friend Charles Thomson, in an appendix to the *Notes*, is more systematic, speaking of a "nation" or "confederacy" (the Powhatan, the Delaware, the Iroquois), each consisting of several "tribes," each of which was "subdivided into towns, families, or clans, who lived together," with chiefs at each of these three taxonomic levels (Jefferson 1972:202–208). The usage of William Bartram around 1790 (Bartram 1853; 1958:306–332) was again different. Writing of Southeastern Indians, he often used "tribe," "town," "band," and "nation" interchangeably in different passages referring to the same social units (what modern anthropologists call "towns" and "tribes"). Bartram tended to use "tribe," "town," or "band" (indiscriminately) for a subdivision of a larger "nation," but was not consistent in this.

The texts of ratified federal treaties with Indians from 1778 to 1796 (Kappler 1904:3–50) usually refer to nations, which are sometimes subdivided into tribes or towns, although occasionally the subdivisions of nations are themselves referred to as "tribes or nations." Only once, in a 1794 treaty, is "tribe" applied to what would now be called "clan," and then only in identifications next to signatures (Kappler 1904:38–39). From 1797 through 1803 the treaties use only "nation," without any reference to "tribes." Thereafter, until at least the 1830s, "tribe" and "nation" are used interchangeably, often in the same treaty.

Thus the evidence exists on which a more thorough study might be based—one which would be useful for ethnohistorical interpretations (cf. Gagnon 1980), for the history of changing attitudes towards Indians, for the history of anthropology, and, almost certainly, for jurisprudence and other aspects of the current relations between Indian tribes and North American states.[2]

What Fried and others have accomplished in redefining "tribe" (and probably "band") is to introduce further terminological confusion in an area of discourse that has considerable significance beyond anthropological theory. Some probable consequences can be illustrated from a recent legal case.

In November 1977 I found myself under oath in a federal court, as an expert witness in the Mashpee case tried before a jury in Boston. I was asked to testify as to whether the Mashpee Indians of Cape Cod are a tribe at present and whether they were in 1790 and at several other significant dates. The question is important, and similar ones will be important for other Indian groups, especially in the East, because U.S. law gives to tribes rights that do not accrue to Indian communities that are not tribes. In the Mashpee case, as for others, it was a question of land ownership: the Indian Non-Intercourse Act of 1790 (as modified through 1834) reserved to the federal government the right to purchase land from what the act calls "any Indian nation or tribe of Indians."[3] If an Indian group can show that they lost land after 1790 in any manner except through a federal treaty (or an equivalent agreement after 1871), they have a legal claim to that land provided that they can also show that they were a tribe when they lost the land and have been a tribe ever since. For this and other legal purposes there is an accepted definition of "tribe": the Supreme Court in *Montoya* v. *United States* in 1901 defined a tribe as "a body of [1] Indians of the same or a similar race, united in [2] a community under [3] one leadership or government, and [4] inhabiting a particular though sometimes ill-defined territory" (Davis 1901:266=180 U.S. 266; numbering added). *Conners* v. *United States* (1901) and other decisions contrast a "tribe" with a "band," which has "a less permanent organization" based on temporary adhesion (Cohen 1942:270–271; Davis 1901:275=180 U.S. 275). *Montoya* also contrasts "tribe" with "nation"; the latter term "presupposes or implies an independence of any other sovereign power more or less absolute, an organized government, recognized officials, a system of laws, definite boundaries and the power to enter into negotiations with other nations. These characteristics the Indians have possessed only in a limited degree, and when used in connection with the Indians, especially in their original state, we must apply to the word 'nation' a definition which indicates little more than a large tribe or group of affiliated tribes possessing a common government, language or racial origin, and acting for the time being, in concert. . . . In short, the word 'nation' as applied to the uncivilized Indians is so much of a misnomer as to be little more than a compliment" (Davis 1901:265=180 U.S. 265).

Given the old-fashioned, even racist, implications of this last passage (especially of the section omitted in the quotation above), it is fortunate that legal precedent seems to focus on "tribe" rather than "nation" in the phrasing of the Non-Intercourse Act. Anthropologists should have little difficulty with the *Montoya* definition of tribe. The four attributes are clear and readily translatable into anthropological categories. One can testify as to whether the evidence indicates that at any given date any specific group had these attrib-

Tribe and State

utes. But as Fried's and other writings on social anthropological theory become better known, lawyers can easily muddy the waters and confuse judges and juries into believing that group X was not or is not a tribe, since according to prominent anthropologists (and ones not involved in the case) in fact tribes do not exist or may not exist.

The problem can be illustrated by extracts from the transcript of testimony in the Mashpee case (Mashpee Tribe v. Mashpee 1977:78, 182–183, 209–210). The quotation begins with an example of the difficulty of explaining a taxonomic classification under hostile cross-examination. ("Q" in all the following identifies James St. Clair, while "A" is the present writer.)

Q. [In 1969 you] referred to Mashpee as an Indian community, is that right?
A. That's correct.
Q. And today you say that they are a tribe?
A. A tribe and a community, yes.
Q. I thought you told me that a community was not a tribe?
A. That's correct, it's not. They're not synonymous.
Q. In '68 you thought they were a community; in '77 you think they are a tribe; is that your testimony?
A. Yes, surely.
Q. Now, before I leave this document, would you turn to page 17 on a different subject?
THE COURT [that is, the judge, interrupting]. Hold it, just stop there. Presently you say they are a tribe. Are they a community?
A. Yes, both.
THE COURT. So you say they are both a tribe and a community?
A. Yes.
THE COURT. You say they are not the same thing?
A. Many tribes consist of more than one community, that's the problem, I think.
THE COURT. This tribe consists of but one community?
A. Obviously, that's right, yes.
. . .
Q. Now this morning you testified, sir, I think with regard to some writings of a Dr. Fried, Morton Fried, is it?
A. Yes.
Q. And it was in connection with his writings that you testified that the word "tribe" may well be a white man's use of the word to facilitate—Do you recall this morning testifying about the word "tribe" perhaps being a white man's word?
A. Concept, I think, is the better word.
Q. White man's concept?

A. Yes, in a sense.
Q. And in your view of the matter as an anthropologist, I take it you did not accept the white man's concept of tribe as that word implies?
A. I *understand* it; what do you mean "accept"?
Q. Well, did you apply the white man's definition of the word "tribe"?
A. I believe that—you mean when I testified that the Mashpee were a tribe?
Q. Yes.
A. I believe I said that reflected my understanding from usage by anthropologists and Indians familiar with tribes in other parts of the United States. So in that sense I accept white man's and Indians', English-speaking Indians', usage—or some white people and some Indian English-speakers' usage of the term "tribe."
Q. Well, in this case, you know we are dealing with the word "tribe" as contained in the white man's law, don't you?
A. The white man's law? I thought it was American law.
[That reply drew applause from the audience, who were then reprimanded by the judge, and thus somewhat deflected St. Clair's attack.]

. . .

Q. Sir, we've seen some references in your testimony to Prof. Fried. Are you familiar with his paper entitled "The Myth of Tribe," published in the Natural History magazine, April, 1975?
A I read it once, but the reason I didn't cite it is because his book that was published at the same time is a more extensive treatment of the same topic.
Q. Would you agree with this statement that appears in his paper:

"Although many anthropologists have now become wary of the word tribe, it has steadily gained popularity in common speech and writing. But curiously, it did not become a general term of reference to American Indian society until the 19th century."

Do you agree with that?
A. I don't agree with that.
Q. Continuing,

"Previously, the words commonly used for Indian populations were nation and people. Indeed, even when the word tribe was used in the early 19th century, it was often coupled with the word nation, as in tribe or nation."

Do you agree with that?
A. I agree with that with the exception of the date at the beginning, the "previously" reference.

St. Clair then engaged in a line of questioning designed to show that there was no anthropology, and hence no anthropologists, in 1790, presumably having decided that he had sufficiently confused the jury over what anthropologists understand by "tribe."

The notion of tribe and tribal status is an important aspect of the relations between Indian communities and the American state (see Cohen 1942). The term is very common in the pre-1871 treaties that serve as charters for modern Indian societies and political groups and are the basis for many important rights. The governments and corporations set up in many parts of the U.S. under the Indian Reorganization Act (I.R.A.) of 1934 are legal entities officially denominated as "tribes" (United States Code 1977:1091–1092=25 U.S.C. §§476, 477). By 1978 requests for official recognition as tribes from groups not organized under the I.R.A. had become so frequent that the Bureau of Indian Affairs instituted complex "procedures for establishing that an American Indian group exists as an Indian tribe" (Code of Federal Regulations 1980:199–204=25 C.F.R. §54). Such labeling will make these groups eligible not only for various federal programs offered to federally recognized tribes but also for some available to other local governmental units such as cities and states.

Thus it ill behooves anthropologists now to suggest that tribes do not exist. Fried (1975:52), discussing anthropological testimony in Indian Claims Commission cases, comments that "claims for indemnification should not require post hoc creation of units compatible with the categories of the state." An appropriate response is that anthropologists should not redefine a word that has an established legal meaning, especially when such a shift will cause difficulties to anthropologists applying their specialized knowledge to practical situations.

The existence, indeed the importance, of the term and the concept of tribe in the English used by Indians as well as by the courts and by Congress is a further instance of the impingement of a state on non-state peoples. The state forces Indian groups to define themselves as tribes, and provides the characteristics to which they must conform—and, often, must show that their ancestors conformed—in order to negotiate with the state to preserve some rights, especially territorial rights. In this situation anthropologists should take care that their theoretical formulations are not used by the state to the disadvantage of the subjugated peoples.[4]

There is a solution that will not require the complete jettisoning of Fried's theoretical discussions of the notion of tribe (although, as indicated, there are some serious difficulties with his treatment even on the theoretical plane). Anthropological technical terms are often, like "tribe," ordinary English words redefined. But others are words borrowed from exotic or obsolete lexicons and defined as labels for specialized concepts. The words totem, taboo, mana, shaman, and potlatch have moved from technical anthropological use to common parlance, with rather different or at least less precise meanings. It is easier to explain such a change of meaning than it is to elucidate, especially under cross-examination, how it is that anthropologists do not always mean "tribes" when they write about "tribes."

According to Fried (1978), the term most frequently used in modern Chinese for "tribe" is 部落, in pinyin romanization *bùluò*. I propose that this term be borrowed into English with the pronunciation anglicized as [búlwɔ̃]. Then one can say that Fried (1975, 1978) has argued that buluos have in fact never existed, or that all buluos are secondary buluos, originating from the impingement of states. It has been claimed here that the historical documents on the 16th-century Southeast are inadequate to determine whether buluos, secondary or pristine, were present, and that archaeological evidence is unlikely to answer the question so long as Fried's definition of buluo is accepted. However, it should be possible to redefine the buluo so that archaeologically discoverable attributes are sufficient to identify its presence. Historical and ethnographic evidence can be used to determine whether the Mashpee and other Eastern Indian groups are buluos now, and whether they were at various dates in the past. Whether they are or were tribes are questions of a quite different nature.

Notes

1. This site, called Cofitachequi in other accounts, has been located at various places in South Carolina. DePratter, Hudson, and Smith (1980) place it at Camden; Baker (1974) thought it was at the confluence of the Wateree and Congaree Rivers; Swanton (1946:143) put it on the Savannah River below and across from Augusta, Georgia. Swanton thought it was a Creek town, while according to the other two interpretations it would be among the predecessors of the historic Catawba.

2. It is curious and probably significant that "reservations" in the United States normally belong to "tribes" recognized by federal law, whereas in Canada "reserves" belong to federally recognized "bands."

3. In the act of 1790 the wording was "any Indians, or any nation or tribe of Indians." In the 1793 act this was changed to "any Indians or nation or tribe of Indians," while in the act of 1834, still in force, the passage reads "any Indian nation or tribe of Indians" (Cohen 1942:269, 322, 326; United States Code 1977:985=25 U.S.C. §177).

4. For an interesting analysis of various concepts of "tribe" in U.S. Indian law, see Weatherhead (1980), whose discussion implies the relevance of anthropological evidence at many points. For example, the appellate court's characterization of the judge's instructions to the jury in *Mashpee* is quoted (Weatherhead 1980:24) to the effect that he depended on "an anthropological concept" in stressing the importance of the "boundary" of the Mashpee community. As I recall, that concept was at the least underlined (at the most introduced) by the anthropologist witnesses at the trial.

References Cited

Baker, Steven G.
 1974 Cofitachique: Fair Province of Carolina. M.A. thesis. History Department, University of South Carolina.
Bartram, William
 1853 Observations on the Creek and Cherokee Indians. American Ethnological Society Transactions, Vol. 3, No. 1, pp. 8–58.
 1958 The Travels of William Bartram. Naturalist's Edition, Francis Harper, ed. New Haven: Yale University Press.
Bourne, Edward Gaylord, ed.
 1904 Narratives of the Career of Hernando de Soto. . . . 2 vols. New York: A. S. Barnes.
Brain, Jeffrey P.
 1978 Late Prehistoric Settlement Patterning in the Yazoo Basin and Natchez Bluffs Regions of the Lower Mississippi Valley. *In* Mississippian Settlement Patterns, Bruce D. Smith, ed. pp. 331–368. New York: Academic Press.
Code of Federal Regulations
 1980 Code of Federal Regulations, Revised as of April 1, 1980. Containing a Codification of Documents of General Applicability and Future Effect as of April 1, 1980. [Title] 25: Indians. Washington: Office of the Federal Register, National Archives and Records Service.
Cohen, Felix S.
 1942 Handbook of Federal Indian Law. Washington: Government Printing Office.
Davis, J. C. Bancroft, rep.
 1901 Cases Adjudged in the Supreme Court at October Term, 1900. United States Reports, Vol. 180. New York: Banks Law Publishing.
DePratter, Chester, Charles Hudson, and Marvin Smith
 1980 Juan Pardo's Explorations in the Interior Southeast, 1566–1568. Paper read at the meetings of the Society for American Archaeology, Philadelphia, May 3, 1980.
Fried, Morton H.
 1975 The Notion of Tribe. Menlo Park, CA: Cummings Publishing.
 1978 Tribe to State or State to Tribe in Ancient China? *In* The Origins of Chinese Civilization, David N. Keightley, ed. pp. 467–493. Berkeley: University of California Press. (Published 1983.)
Gagnon, François-Marc
 1980 "Gens du pays" ou "Sauvaiges": Note sur les désignations de l'Indien chez Jacques Cartier. Recherches amérindiennes au Québec 10(1–2):24–36.
Goggin, John M., and William C. Sturtevant
 1964 The Calusa: A Stratified, Nonagricultural Society (with Notes on Sibling Marriage). *In* Explorations in Cultural Anthropology: Essays in Honor of George Peter Murdock, Ward H. Goodenough, ed. pp. 179–219. New York: McGraw-Hill.

Jefferson, Thomas
    1972   Notes on the State of Virginia. William Peden, ed. New York: W. W. Norton.
Kappler, Charles J., ed.
    1904   Indian Affairs. Laws and Treaties. Vol. 2. (Treaties.) Washington: Government Printing Office.
Mashpee Tribe v. Mashpee
    1977   Record, Twenty-second day. Mashpee Tribe v. Mashpee, 477 F. Supp. 940 (D. Mass. 1978) aff'd *sub nom.* Mashpee Tribe v. New Seabury, 592 F.2d. 557 (1st Cir. 1979). Typescript.
Morgan, Lewis H.
    1851   League of the Ho-dé-no-sau-nee or Iroquois. Rochester: Sage and Brother.
    1877   Ancient Society or Researches in the Lines of Human Progress from Savagery through Barbarism to Civilization. New York: Henry Holt.
Quinn, David B., ed.
    1979   New American World: A Documentary History of North America to 1612. Vol. 2. New York: Arno Press and Hector Bye.
Robertson, James Alexander, transl. and ed.
    1932–33   True Relation of the Hardships Suffered by Governor Fernando de Soto. . . . Now Newly Set Forth by a Gentlemen of Elvas. 2 vols. Publications of the Florida State Historical Society, No. 11.
Swanton, John R.
    1946   The Indians of the Southeastern United States. Bureau of American Ethnology Bulletin 137.
United States Code
    1977   United States Code, 1976 Edition, Containing the General and Permanent Laws of the United States, in Force on January 3, 1977. Vol. 6. Washington: Government Printing Office.
Weatherhead, L. R.
    1980   What Is an "Indian Tribe"?—The Question of Tribal Existence. American Indian Law Review 8(1):1–47.
Widmer, Randolph J.
    1978   The Structure of Late Prehistoric Adaptation on the Southwest Florida Coast. M.A. thesis. Anthropology Department, Pennsylvania State University.

2

Ethnohistorical Investigation of Egalitarian Politics in Eastern North America

Eleanor Leacock
City College, CUNY

I am one among many who uses the taxonomy of pre-state political organization offered by Elman Service—band, tribe, chiefdom—with uneasiness. Although helpful in ordering data at the time it was advanced, it assumes a neat progression in the formalization and centralization of political power that does not accord with historical reality. My own work on the band among the Montagnais-Naskapi of the Labrador Peninsula (Leacock 1954, 1969, 1978) convinced me that "bands" as relatively stable political and territorial entities are a product of colonization, and Fried (1968, 1975) has cogently argued that "tribes" as generally conceived are, in fact, products of relations with politically organized states. In a 1954 symposium on the Indian Claims Litigations, Kroeber wrote that the more closely one looks at aboriginal North America, the more largely does "our usual conventional concept of tribe . . . appear to be a White man's creation of convenience for talking about Indians, negotiating with them, administering them" (Kroeber 1955:313).

Conceptually, the band-tribe-chiefdom terminology allows no leeway for qualitative distinctions both in the organization and manipulation of political power in different kinds of societies and in the very nature of "politics" and "power" themselves. As a prime example of conceptual problems involved in speaking of bands and tribes, consider the term "chief." It is commonly pointed out that in egalitarian societies, chiefs have influence but no formal authority, and that they are no more than "firsts among equals." Sometimes the authoritarian implications of the term chief are avoided by using alternatives like leader or headman. Whatever the term, however, it becomes encrusted with connotations of an office with political power that, albeit ephemeral or extremely watered down, is nonetheless similar to that found in stratified state-organized society. Lurking behind the assumption of a chiefly "office" is the concomitant assumption that it is backed up by some kind of forceful sanction. The use of the term chief or some equivalent, then, causes questions about the actual nature of decision making in non-hierarchically ordered societies to be bypassed. The questions may not be asked: What kinds of decisions are important in such societies? Which of these are matters of "public" or formal concern? Who is responsible for making these decisions and how do they go about making them? In sum, in so-called bands and tribes, what are the processes subsumed under the rubric "political"?

The matter of political organization in egalitarian societies is of more than theoretical interest. It is of great practical importance to native Americans now engaged in battles for land rights and some measure of political autonomy, and anthropologists must be extremely sensitive to the fact that references to such events as the colonial decimation of a people, or to such traits as flexibility in group membership or non-individual ownership of lands, can be twisted and turned against them in legal disputes. Sturtevant (chapter 1, this volume) reveals the opportunistic way in which anthropological reconstructions of culture history can be used against native peoples.

However, the existence of legal chicanery in the interest of land grabbing should not lead anthropologists to back away from the reconstruction of culture history—far from it. Instead, peoples' histories should be dealt with the more fully and accurately, and special attention paid to the viewpoints of the people themselves. For example, it should be made clear that despite the decimation of many coastal Indian peoples, survivors united in mutual support, reformed their communities, and taught their own values and life styles to their descendants. Further, traditional flexibility in group membership helped make this possible. The fact that Indian groups hospitably and generously took in outsiders who wished to become full members of their communities made them if anything more, not less, culturally integrated. And as for collective ownership of lands, it was coterminous with inalienable rights to lands—rights so unquestioned that in Western terminology that are best called "sacred," despite the fact they have been so devastatingly violated during the last half millennium.

With respect to political organization, native North American societies for the most part did not invest their leaders with impersonal authority backed up by force, akin to the power of office in kingdoms or states. Nonetheless, as nations, peoples, or "tribes," they were well integrated politically, in that they had highly developed principles and practices for effecting group organization and cohesion. It appears to me that one way to serve the needs of Indians living in the United States who by historical happenstance were never formally recorded by the U.S. government as "tribes," and who consequently have been refused their legal rights, is to document this point. Robert Lowie (1929) long ago argued that egalitarian societies have universally been organized like hierarchical ones along political and territorial lines in what are in effect incipient states. The unfortunate implications of this erroneous assumption is that societies not so organized were not in fact societies. This implication continues to lurk behind legal disputes, and it would seem the best way to challenge it is to analyze and demonstrate the structure and complexity of actual Native American political forms.

Needless to state, the ethnographic and ethnohistorical record of political organization in eastern North America abounds in contradictions. Europeans were received with pomp and circumstance by persons who spoke with measured assurance and apparent authority. Hence they referred to sagamores, chiefs, kings, queens, and empresses with the assumption that these leaders held power over their people of a similar order to that held by European monarchs and their delegated deputies. However, other Europeans who came to know Indian societies well found that such persons held little or no formal authority over their presumed subjects. Americanists have resolved this contradiction by pointing out that chiefly people did not themselves have decision-making powers but were empowered only to carry out decisions made by some type of council. Yet in specific instances chiefly people held great power over others. To substitute parliamentary democracy for royal autocracy as a model for native American sociopolitical organization, while closer to the mark, still does not do justice to its distinctive complexities.

To break fully away from the band-tribe-chiefdom taxonomy and its implications, then, means taking a fresh look at questions about political processes such as those raised above, and moving beyond the limitations of early European reportage in a renewed search of the ethnohistorical record. It seems to me the appropriate focus of this search should be concrete analyzable events. The method used in field research of rounding out, qualifying, or even discounting statements about behavioral norms by assessing them in relation to specific incidents can be well adapted to ethnohistorical research. True, the vast majority of decision-making events referred to in historical materials pertain to relations with outsiders who were more predatory and threatening than any people most native North Americans had yet confronted. True, too, these outsiders introduced trade and corollary economic choices of a entirely new magnitude. Nonetheless, when the economic and political context of specific actions are defined, and the position and motives of the observer appraised (Hudson 1974), recorded events yield important clues as to how decisions within a group were arrived at. In addition there are valuable "inside" accounts by captives, missionaries, and others who lived close to American Indians and wrote about them. Finally, recent writings by native American political leaders and theorists, as well as ethnographic accounts of egalitarian politics in North America and elsewhere, furnish insights into how recorded events of the past might best be interpreted.

As examples of inquiry into political processes with a focus on events, I shall consider the Montagnais-Naskapi, a "band" society, as described by Champlain (Biggar 1922–36) and Le Jeune (Thwaites 1896–1901), and review the work done on "tribal" societies, the Delaware and other Eastern Algonkians by Grumet (1978a, 1978b, 1980), and the Cherokee by Gearing (1962) and Reid (1970). The inquiry reveals more similarities than differences between band and tribal politics in these Native American egalitarian societies where the authority accorded to chiefs in their dealings with outsiders contrasts with their lack of formal authority over their people. It also reveals, however, that this lack of formal authority did not keep American Indian leaders from moving with decisiveness and effectiveness in carrying out their delegated responsibilities.

Finally, the illustrations presented indicate the need for detailed ethnohistorical research to complement ethnographic studies of the complex decision-making and conflict-resolving processes that govern life in band and village egalitarian societies. It is not enough to repeat that in such societies the "political" sphere is scarcely separable from the social; it is necessary to go further. To spur discussion, I offer the proposition that the two basic sociopolitical principles that govern decision making in egalitarian societies are: first, the parties who are responsible for carrying a decision out or who are directly affected by it must have a share in making it commensurate with their experience and wisdom; and, second, those who do not agree to a decision are not bound by it. In my view, the nature of and economic foundation for political processes based on these principles must be understood—or if they are found lacking, refinements or alternatives must be suggested—before it will be possible to define with any precision the nature of the non-egalitarian political processes that begin to emerge in what are designated as "big man" and "ranking" societies. Only on such a basis, as I see it, can an adequate typology of political forms in non-stratified societies be developed.

The Montagnais-Naskapi of the Labrador Peninsula

If Champlain's accounts of his expeditions up the St. Lawrence River in 1603 and 1608–9 were the only available references to political life among the Montagnais-Naskapi of the 17th century, there would be no basis for questioning their governance by "grand Sagamores" or "grand Captains," advised by councils of elder men and the revelations of shamans (Biggar 1922–36:I: 98–118). However, Champlain's later experiences raise questions about this image, and it is thoroughly revised by the reports of Paul Le Jeune, Jesuit superior of the Residence of Quebec.

Champlains's first political act after his arrival at Tadoussac was to present himself, and two Montagnais who had traveled to France and been received by the French king, to Anadabijou, "grand Sagamore of the savages of

Canada" (Biggar 1922–36:I:98). The "grand Sagamore" along with "some eighty or a hundred of his companions" was preparing for a feast to celebrate the victory of a Montagnais, Algonkin, and Etchemin war party that had successfully attacked the Iroquois. One of the Montagnais with Champlain's party reported to the assembled group on what he had witnessed of life in France and on the desire of Henri IV "to people their country, and to make peace with their enemies . . . or send forces to vanquish them" (Biggar 1922–36:I:l00). Anadabijou received and responded to the speech. Champlain did not report on the language used or the translation process; after all his intent was to report that the "grand Sagamore" fully accepted the French program for colonization. Anadabijou listened, smoked, shared his pipe with Champlain and "certain other Sagamores who were near him." Then

> he began to address the whole gathering, speaking with gravity, pausing sometimes a little, and then resuming his speech, saying to them, that in truth they ought to be very glad to have His Majesty for their great friend. They answered all with one voice, *Ho, ho, ho*, which is to say, *yes, yes*. Continuing his speech, he said that he was well content that His said Majesty should people their country, and make war on their enemies, and that there was no nation in the world to which they wished more good than to the French. Finally, he gave them all to understand the advantage and profit they might receive from His said Majesty. [Biggar 1922–36:I: 100–101]

The interchange thus concluded, Anadabijou was recognized in ritual dancing (perhaps acknowledging his successful leadership in the killing of the enemy?). Meat for the feast was boiling in eight or ten kettles, placed some six paces apart along the communal lodge, and each man

> rose up, and took a dog, and went leaping about the said kettles from one end of the lodge to the other. When he came in front of the grand Sagamore, he threw his dog violently upon the ground, and then all with one voice cried, *Ho, ho, ho*. [Biggar 1922–36:I:102]

The next day Anadabijou led the some thousand people camped together to Tadoussac, albeit in the style of an egalitarian leader, not a chief of rank.

> At daybreak their grand Sagamore came out of his lodge, going round about all the other lodges, and crying with a loud voice that they should break camp to go to Tadoussac, where their good friends were. Immediately every man in a trice took down his lodge, and the said grand

Captain was the first to begin to take his canoe and carry it to the water, wherein he embarked his wife and children, and quantity of furs. [Biggar 1922–36:I:104]

Five years later, after exploring the coast of New England, Champlain returned to the Upper St. Lawrence. He accompanied an expedition of Montagnais, Algonkins, and Hurons who, aided by French firearms, successfully engaged the Iroquois at the edge of the lake Champlain chose to rename. By contrast with his first account, Champlain no longer referred to "grand chiefs" but instead to the several chiefs, each leading a different party of warriors, that joined for the occasion (e.g., Biggar 1922–36:II:68). Midway in the expedition Champlain encountered the now well-known of principle of autonomy among Native Americans with respect to the decision to go to war. The result of "some difference of opinion regarding the war," Champlain wrote, was that "only a part of them decided to come with me, whilst the rest went back to their own country with their wives and the goods they had bartered" (Biggar 1922–36:II:76). Nonetheless the leadership of the chiefs was respected by those who remained. Champlain described them laying out the campaign strategy on the ground, using a foot-long stick for each man and longer ones for "leaders" or "headmen." The warriors studied the layout, then rehearsed their order several times, so that there was no "need of a sergeant to make them keep their ranks, which they are quite able to maintain without getting into confusion" (Biggar 1922–36:II:89). Though not as elevated as the "grand Sagamore of all the savages of Canada," chiefs were apparently still chiefs.

By contrast with Champlain, the Jesuit missionary Le Jeune was not the head of an expedition interacting with parties of men at war. Le Jeune's mission was to help create a base for French colonization through converting, settling, and otherwise "civilizing" the native population. Shortly after his arrival in Quebec in 1632, Le Jeune spent the winter in a Montagnais lodge in order to master the language, religion, and culture of the people he sought to change. He gathered a core of followers around his mission, and his relations with them and their "pagan" relatives covered a wide range of practical and religious matters.

I have elsewhere elaborated at length on Le Jeune's plaints about a people who had "neither political organization, nor offices, nor dignities, nor any authority," who "cannot endure in the least those who seem desirous of assuming superiority over the others," but "who imagine that they ought by right of birth to enjoy the liberty of wild ass colts" (Thwaites 1896–1901:VI:165, 231, 243; Leacock 1958, 1977, 1980a, 1981). In addition to his direct statements, Le Jeune recounted in detail many examples of his difficulties introducing the Montagnais to European principles of chiefly authority over a group, male authority over women, parental authority over children, and jail or physical punishment for non-compliance. In 1640, two years after Le Jeune organized an election of chiefs (Thwaites 1896–1901:XVIII:99–123), a baptized woman was forced by the threat of imprisonment to return to the husband she had left. Le Jeune wrote proudly of his success that "among these peoples—where everyone considers himself from birth, as free as the wild animals that roam in their great forests—it is a marvel, or rather a miracle, to see a peremptory command obeyed, or any act of severity or justice performed" (Thwaites 1896–1901:XXII:81–85).

At first blush, Champlain's portrayal of the "grand Sagamore" Anadabijou seems wholly at odds with the anarchy described by Le Jeune. However, the contradiction between the two accounts disappears as soon as one abandons a search for hierarchical principles of empowerment and deals with leadership in the context of what can be called "consensus polity" (Silberbauer 1982). Reading between the lines of early accounts, it would seem that those called chiefs by the French were able and influential people who in some part initiated actions and in some part were accorded leadership in organizing warfare, in speaking to outsiders for their people, and in guiding the formulation of foreign policy. However, they did not have authority either to insist on the making of a policy decision or to enforce any that might be made. Champlain came to know this well in later years, and described with some irritation the complexities of negotiating with the Montagnais and his attempt to resolve his difficulties by making a chief of an Indian close to the French (Biggar 1922–36:V:1–19). As for Montagnais attitudes, Le Jeune recounted a revealing plea of a young man to his father.

> Although thou hast no sense, thou wishest to act the Captain; this is why they make fun of thee, and I am humiliated by it. . . . Give up this vain idea of being a captain, since thou hast neither the ability to make speeches nor to be a leader. (Thwaites 1896–1901:XI:249)

Behind the "Sagamores" or "Captains" who negotiated with the Europeans and led war parties lay the many ways in which individual initiative and influence interacted with measured discussions and ritual mediation (especially scapulamancy, dream divination, and the shaking tent) in the making of decisions about group movements and activities. Those who agreed upon a course of action acted effectively and in unison; those who disagreed apparently simply withdrew. Misconduct was prevented or sanctioned through teasing and ridicule; fear of disapproval was a strong deterrant to antisocial behavior. If attempts to avoid open confrontation between two antagonists failed and anger erupted and led to physical injury or death, a person's kin might retaliate immediately. If the wrongdoer escaped, compensation was negotiated (Biggar 1922–36:I:179; Thwaites 1896–1901:V:219, XXII:81–85).

Like men, women might influence decisions on the basis of their prestige as individuals, as epitomized by the account of a powerful female shaman exhorting her people to fight the Iroquois (Thwaites 1896–1901:IX:113–117), and evidenced in much later times by Lips' account of the Mistassini and Lake St. John bands in 1935. Lips described Maggy Moar, a highly respected woman who acted as translator for summer church meetings and whose advice was sought and followed by men and women alike, and he referred to two then dead women who were considered by some to have been band chiefs (Lips 1947:385–386,400–401). Seventeenth-century Montagnais women also made decisions concerning their own interests by meeting together in council (Thwaites 1896–1901:VII:175). Women had a major share in "the choice of plans, of undertakings, of journeys, of winterings" (Thwaites 1896–1901: LXVIII:93), while experienced men took a lead in making decisions about local moves in search of game (Thwaites 1896–1901:VII:109). Expediency necessarily entered in, however. When Le Jeune set off in a Montagnais canoe on his winter trip, the final decision as to which direction his party should take was made after learning the plans of other Indians encountered on the way (Thwaites 1896–1901:VII:97).

Some of the chiefs elected under the supervision of the Jesuits adopted the French role of meting out punishments rather than the Montagnais practice of adjudicating compensation for injury (Thwaites 1896–1901:V:219: XXII:81–85; XXVI:117). In 1935, Lips' Mistassini informants also reported punishment as a chief's responsibility, although the Mistassini band, despite Canadian government regulations, had chosen to get along without a chief for seven years when Lips was there, and he had difficulty eliciting actual examples of punishment (Lips 1947:399, 403–404). Lips was, however, focusing on "the chief." At Natashquan in 1950 I found a distinction being made between informal chiefs seasonally responsible for specific hunting parties—experienced people who usually had large family networks and could be expected to play an important role in conflict resolution—and the formally elected "outside" or "government" chief (Leacock 1958:205–206). The responsibility of the latter was negotiation with outsiders, as it had long been— primarily with the French in the early years, later with Hudson's Bay Company factors (Bailey 1937:91–94; Leacock 1980b; Lips 1947:402–404; Rogers 1963:25; Rogers and Leacock 1981).

Returning to the subject of aboriginal political orgainzation, to say that the chiefs who dealt with outsiders served purely as negotiators with no actual power does not mean that the role has not changed over the years. The problems that must be dealt with by contemporary Montagnais-Naskapi councils who are confronted by and negotiate with multinational corporations and the Canadian government (Charest 1982; Feit 1982) throw two long-term developments into sharp relief: first, the bounding of political units, both in terms of lands and of people; and, second, the concomitant creation of an economic base for politics in the sense of negotiating impersonal power. The latter undercuts the principle that no authority of office should supersede the wisdom, commitment, and ability of specific incumbents; and the former vitiates the principle of individual and group autonomy—the freedom to choose whether or not to act in concert. Both these principles, it should be noted, were probably so taken for granted in aboriginal society that they were not stated as such.

Hudson's Bay Company records of 19th-century "principal men" (Lips 1939:149–186; 1947:405–412) corroborate early data indicating that chiefs were made by the consensus of those who chose to follow and unmade when followers simply withdrew their support. And a compilation of all references made to specific Montagnais groups and movements in 17th-century records (Leacock 1969:8–12) reveals that the Montagnais-Naskapi were organized in a series of levels, each of which could choose whether to act under the direction of a leader or leaders. The basic units were multifamily lodge groups of 10 to 20 individuals (who were free to change their affiliation as they chose); the next level was of several lodge groups, some 35 to 75 people, who kept together or in close touch over the winter; aggregates of these, 150 to 300 or more people, were probably the named units associated with particular territories; and, finally, large summer gatherings were made up of several such "bands," and often some neighboring peoples as well (Labrecque 1978).

In sum, descriptions of specific individuals, groups, and events, as seen in specific contexts, indicate that leadership through consensus and according to ability—and not through formal authority or economically based power—could and did occur at any level of Montagnais-Naskapi society, commensurate with the task at hand and the need or desire to carry it out. Furthermore, I would argue that in this respect leadership among egalitarian villagers to the south did not differ from that of the Montagnais-Naskapi, despite the more elaborated relations of production and distribution required by horticultural economies. The Cherokee, whose egalitarianism contrasts with the ranking found among many other Southeastern cultures, and the Delaware both exemplify this point.

Leadership and Decision Making among the Cherokee and Delaware[1]

Gearing's study of the Cherokee transformation from a "jural community" to a "state" (Gearing 1962:83–84) and Reid's (1970) interpretation of Cherokee law, both largely based on the analysis of specific historical events, offer rich data on leadership and decision making. For the Dealware, a methodologically innovative study of northern New Jersey and southeastern New York groups (Grumet 1978a, 1978b) affords an unusual example of how sociopolitical processes can be revealed through the partial reconstruction of actual situations. Grumet culled over 4,000 references to Delaware individuals from some 700 archival documents, mostly deeds, that dated from the 17th and 18th centuries. During this period the Delaware were negotiating their relations with the colonists through the systematic sale of their lands in return for money, goods, and earnests of ongoing reciprocal ties. The names of about 300 persons kept reappearing in the documents, and by gathering information on the roles these individuals played in policy making, Grumet was able to reveal something of the ways in which the little-understood Delaware polity functioned.

The picture of leadership and decision making that emerges from Reid's and Gearing's studies of the Cherokee, and Grumet's as well as other recent resumes of the Delaware (Goddard 1978:216) is similar to that of the Montagnais-Naskapi in three ways. First, leadership was based on personal influence and ability, not formal office. Second, decisions were made by those who would be carrying them out and were not binding on those who did not agree. Third, autonomy was unquestioned both for individuals and groups. Autonomous units could and did act separately, although—a point sometimes slighted—they also could and did come together and act effectively under the leadership of respected and able individuals.

The arena for the formulation of Cherokee policy was the town council, "an assembly of all the men and women, who met every night except during the hunting season" (Reid 1970:30). Consensus was achieved, "not by the minority acknowledging that it was constitutionally bound to yield its views to majority rule," but "with the disappearance of opposition, through compromise or withdrawal" (Reid 1970:50). De facto headmanship fell to the one who expressed majority opinion or won majority support. Opponents of an agreed-upon policy "were neither rebels nor outlaws, they were merely potential headmen" waiting to replace a leader who might fail (Reid 1970:54).

The importance of Cherokee consensus was soon learned by James Glen, governor of South Carolina from 1743 to 1756. Soon after his arrival, when told that some three to five hundred Cherokee were converging on Charles Town, he ordered that none but "the King or the Chief of the Nation with Six of His assistants be allowed to come and one man from Each town." However, Glen's more experienced advisors persuaded him that he not only had to receive "each Cherokee who wished to attend the council, but that he had to treat all with equal respect." Glen learned the lesson well.

> By 1755 when he sought to purchase land for a fort, Glen knew better than to think he could deal with a few chiefs. Instead he asked the Cherokees to convene a national council and drafted the instrument of sale in words implying that the entire population was party to the transaction. [Reid 1970:59]

Grumet's data indicate that a similar lesson was learned by the Dutch to the north in relation to purchasing land from the Delaware. Although in the latter 17th and in the 18th centuries small plots of land were transferred to the Europeans by a few Delaware individuals, early contracts for land transfer generally involved large plots and were signed by many parties. The Delaware did not sell their lands outright, but negotiated deeds that ensured them some continuing use of lands (such as for hunting or for houseplots); they called for periodic renewals of contracts to bind the colonists in ongoing relations of reciprocity; and they sometimes maintained that non-use by the purchasers (such as when lands changed hands or were abandoned due to warfare) invalidated a contract. The last had happened to Staten Island, signed over to the Dutch in 1657, but temporarily abandoned by them. When they wished to gain permanent control over the land in 1670, "much care was taken to ensure that the . . . deed would be the last for Staten Island." In addition to obtaining signatures from the surviving signers of the 1657 transaction, therefore, "children as young as five or six years old affixed their marks to the document" (Grumet 1978a:177).

Among the Cherokee, principles of individual autonomy and of leadership based on effective influence rather than on formally ascribed status pertained to towns as well as individuals. Gearing and Reid (1970:17–24) differ on some points, but both agree that, despite the assumptions of 18th-century Europeans and of later historians, there were no Cherokee "capitals." Instead it was probably "the actual influence of a village" that tended, over time, "to make it a mother village" (Gearing 1962:81; Reid 1970:17–27). Reid points out that Chota, the "beloved town" and reputed Cherokee capital of the mid-18th century, had been unimportant earlier in the century and that it lost its ascendant position later during the wars of the 1770s. During a critical period in Cherokee history, Chota won leadership because "the headmen of Chota were politically active, and the actions they took politically successful." They seized the initiative and "attempted to formulate a new national policy." However, the Chota headmen "did not order, decree, direct, or legislate." Instead, "they conferred, discussed, proposed, and conciliated, with more energy and greater conviction than did their rivals in other towns" (Reid 1970:26).

Grumet (1980:46–48) discusses leadership among the Delaware and other Middle Attlantic Coastal Algonkians in similar terms. He defines five levels at which groups might function autonomously, or, as the situation required, might unite for action under the leadership of chiefs and councils. Successively, these were the level of the clan, the village, the district, the tribe, and the confederacy. At each level, consensus was necessary for action. "Unable to arbitrarily order any action, those in leadership positions were provided an opportunity, rather than a mandate, to authority; power depended upon the power of persuasion rather than the persuasion of power." However, this did not mean that leaders were not effective. "It is clear that astute, subtle, and facilitative civil leaders possessed considerable authority so long as they were not authoritarian."

Despite formal statements to the contrary, women as well as men could become leaders among the Delaware and neighboring Algonkians (Grumet 1980:49), just as they could among the Cherokee. The best known Cherokee example is the influential Nancy Ward, commissioned by her people to negotiate with an American army invading Cherokee lands in 1781 (Reid 1970:68–69, 187–188). Grumet documents a number of important women chiefs among the Delaware and their neighbors (Grumet 1980:46–53). Women also could and did act in unison to press or assert their political and economic interests. In 1664, the Esopus women allied with the Esopus young men (the "barebacks") to force their war leaders to make peace with the Dutch and end five years of fighting. Among the Cherokee, Reid (1970:67) describes a situation in 1760 when women chose to trade with the British garrison in Fort Loudoun at the very time Cherokee warriors were attempting to capture it. When the Cherokee captain, Willenawah, threatened the women, they merely laughed; "they knew he was legally impotent" and unable to stop their activities.

However, Cherokee society was not controlled purely by the desire for approbation and the fear of ridicule and social ostracism. Powerful though these motivations are in such societies (Gearing 1962:30–36; Reid 1970:70–71), an additional principle was also at work—the principle of responsibility for kin. In its sharpest form this principle appears in the historical record for the Choctaw and Chickasaw as well as the Cherokee in relation to homicide. If compensation could not be negotiated, murder required the execution of either the murderer or a clan relative (Reid 1970:233). This was not blood feud; murder did not set off a retaliatory cycle of killing. Instead the killing of the murderer or a non-guilty relative was accepted by all as ending the matter.

The acceptance of responsibility for the behavior of kin among the Cherokee was so profound that, to the puzzlement of European observers, a man could be relied upon to appear at his appointed execution rather than endanger a kinsman, or a kinsman might offer himself for execution in place of the guilty one (Reid 1970:75–84). The holding of corporate authority over kin was perhaps implied, for a clan could "officially" shed responsibility for a perpetual troublemaker. However, responsibility for kin was the principle stressed. The important roles of mother's brother and older brother were defined not in terms of rights, for example, but in terms of duties: "the honored position of the elder brother was not one of privilege . . . but of responsibility" (Reid 1970:40–41, 114).

Further research is needed both to follow through on the ramifications of responsibility for the behavior of kin as a governing principle in Cherokee and similar societies (Moore 1972) and to ascertain whether a similar principle is at work among the Montagnais-Naskapi and other Subarctic hunting peoples. In any case, Montagnais-Naskapi hunting "bands" and Cherokee and Delaware horticultural "tribes" do not differ with respect to the structure of leadership and decision making. In so stating, however, I am not suggesting a simple return to the 19th-century insight that governance through "kinship" was qualitatively different from governance through recourse to formal power and authority. I am suggesting instead that the band-tribe-chiefdom taxonomy has given a false sense that we understand processes that are by no means well understood; and that serious attention should be given to the ways in which egalitarian societies did in fact arrive at decisions, resolve conflicts, and solve problems.

Note

1. I follow *Handbook* usage (Goddard 1978) but Grumet and others prefer Delawaran.

References Cited

Bailey, Alfred Goldsworthy
    1937   The Conflict of European and Eastern Algonkian Cultures, 1504–1700. Publications of the New Brunswick Museum, Monographic Series, No. 2.

Biggar, H. P., ed.
    1922–36   The Works of Samuel de Champlain. 6 vols. Toronto: Champlain Society.

Charest, Paul
    1982   Hydroelectric Dam Construction and the Foraging Activities of Eastern Quebec Montagnais. *In* Politics and History in Band Societies, Eleanor Leacock and Richard Lee, eds. pp. 413–426. Cambridge and New York: Cambridge University Press.

Feit, Harvey
    1982   The Future of Hunters within Nation States: Anthropology and the James Bay Cree. *In* Politics and History in Band Societies, Eleanor Leacock and Richard Lee, eds. pp. 373–412. Cambridge and New York: Cambridge University Press.

Fried, Morton H.
    1968   On the Concepts of "Tribe" and "Tribal Society." *In* Essays on the Problem of Tribe: Proceedings of the 1967 Annual Spring Meeting of the American Ethnological Society, June Helm, ed. pp. 3–20.
    1975   The Notion of Tribe. Menlo Park, CA: Cummings Publishing.

Gearing, Fred
    1962   Priests and Warriors, Social Structures for Cherokee Politics in the 18th Century. American Anthropological Association Memoir 93.

Goddard, Ives
    1978   Delaware. *In* Handbook of North American Indians. Vol. 15: Northeast, William C. Sturtevant and Bruce G. Trigger, eds. pp. 213–239. Washington: Smithsonian Institution.

Grumet, Robert Steven
  1978a "We Are Not So Great Fools": Changes in Upper Delawaran Sociopolitical Life, 1630–1758. Ph.D. dissertation. Anthropology Department, Rutgers University.
  1978b An Analysis of Upper Delawaran Land Sales in Northern New Jersey. *In* Papers of the 9th Algonquian Conference, William Cowan, ed. pp. 23–35. Ottawa: Carleton University Press.
  1980 Sunksquaws, Shamans, and Tradeswomen: Middle Atlantic Coastal Algonkian Women During the 17th and 18th Centuries. *In* Women and Colonization: Anthropological Perspectives, Mona Etienne and Eleanor Leacock, eds. pp. 43–62. New York: Praeger.
Hudson, Charles M.
  1974 The Historical Approach in Anthropology. *In* Handbook of Social and Cultural Anthropology, John J. Honigmann, ed. pp. 111–141. Chicago: Rand McNally.
Kroeber, A. L.
  1955 Nature of the Land-holding Group. Ethnohistory 2(4):303–314.
Leacock, Eleanor
  1954 The Montagnais "Hunting Territory" and the Fur Trade. American Anthropological Association Memoir 78.
  1958 Status among the Montagnais-Naskapi of Labrador. Ethnohistory 5(3): 200–209.
  1969 The Naskapi Band. *In* Contributions to Anthropology: Band Societies, David Damas, ed. pp. 1–17. National Museum of Canada Bulletin 228.
  1977 Women in Egalitarian Society. *In* Becoming Visible: Women in European History, Renate Bridenthal and Claudia Koonz, eds. pp. 11–35. Boston: Houghton Mifflin.
  1978 Women's Status in Egalitarian Society: Implications for Social Evolution. Current Anthropology 9:247–255.
  1980a Montagnais Women and the Jesuit Program for Colonization. *In* Women and Colonization: Anthropological Perspectives, Mona Etienne and Eleanor Leacock, eds. pp. 25–42. New York: Praeger.
  1980b Les Relations de Production parmi les Peuples Chasseurs et Trappeurs des Regions Subarctiques du Canada. Recherches Amérindiennes au Québec 10 (1–2):79–89.
  1981 Seventeenth Century Montagnais Social Relations and Values. *In* Handbook of North American Indians. Vol. 15, Subartic. William C. Sturtevant and June Helm, eds. pp. 190–195. Washington: Smithsonian Institution.
Labrecque, Marie-France
  1978 La Mobilité comme Élément de l'Infrastructure? Remarques Exploratoires à Partir de Données Ethnohistoriques, Recherches Amérindiennes au Québec 7(3–4):91–99.
Lips, Julius E.
  1939 Naskapi Trade, a Study in Legal Acculturation. Journal de la Société des Américanistes, n.s. 21.
  1947 Naskapi Law. Transactions of the American Philosophical Society, Vol. 37, Part 4, pp. 379–492.

Lowie, Robert
   1929   The Origin of the State. New York: Harcourt.
Moore, Sally F.
   1972   Legal Liability and Evolutionary Interpretation: Some Aspects of Strict Liability, Self-help and Collective Responsibility. *In* The Allocation of Responsibility, Max Gluckman, ed. pp. 51–107. Manchester: Manchester University Press.
Reid, John Phillip
   1970   A Law of Blood: The Primitive Law of the Cherokee Nation. New York: New York University Press.
Rogers, Edward S.
   1963   The Hunting Group-Hunting Territory Complex among the Mistassini Indians. National Museum of Canada Bulletin 195.
Rogers, Edward S. and Eleanor Leacock
   1981   Montagnais-Naskapi. *In* Handbook of North American Indians. Vol. 15: Subartic. William C. Sturtevant and June Helm, eds. pp. 169–189. Washington: Smithsonian Institution.
Silberbauer, George
   1982   Political Process in G/wi Bands. *In* Politics and History in Band Societies, Eleanor Leacock and Richard Lee, eds. pp. 23–36. Cambridge and New York: Cambridge University Press.
Thwaites, Reuben Gold, ed.
   1896–1901   The Jesuit Relations and Allied Documents. 71 vols. Cleveland: Burrows Brothers.

3
Pueblo Councils: An Example of Stratified Egalitarianism

M. Estellie Smith
SUNY-Oswego

The last decade has seen a renewed interest in problems of governing—that broad process of secular, deliberately rational, and pragmatically oriented management of matters explicitly related to the public interest. There has been revived questioning about such problems as the origin of the state, the evolution of political organization, the basis for shifts from the posited initial egalitarianism of human society to the inequality we increasingly recognize pervades much of modern society. Despite this renaissance, one critical area has received relatively little attention: though councils are found at all "levels" of sociocultural organization, have a peculiarly uniform structure, functioning, and function, and show great durability despite organizational changes in other sociocultural features, our data are skimpy and analyses of governing often minimize their role. Seemingly ubiquitous, there has been no broadly based study of them (the volume edited by Richards and Kuper, 1971, with one exception, deals with African societies).

Councils range in type from the elder-led "open assemblies" of bands, through the formally designated councils of larger polities (including those councils within councils in highly complex societies, e.g., privy councils and presidential cabinets), to the paranational councils of such confederations as the United Nations and the European Economic Community. Their primary characteristic is that they consist of some few people who are recognized as possessing public authority to consider problems relevant to the well-being of the commonweal. More often than not, councils have no explicit decision-making rights; yet the sense of their deliberations can determine further actions by others and even the most autocratic ruler or powerful legislative body cannot long ignore or defy the policy stance of a cohesive council. Thus, even when not actually empowered to make decisions directly, councils often structure decisions de facto. In "relatively" egalitarian societies, it is a select group of elders that calls for public debate, channels the course of the discussions, and announces (not always accurately) the consensus of those assembled. Whether informally or by charter, elders or council members may use their positions of prestige and/or authority to extend or curtail debate, silence dissent, skew summations of discussions (especially the contributions of those who, if allowed to participate at all, are not "of the council" but, rather, "of the gallery"), and define the format for implementing further action. Not only events but apparently also council members themselves control the council process; new members, no matter how critical of council management prior to their own accession to membership, rarely function much differently from their predecessors. In short, this significant forum for community decision making has the capacity to guide the lives of all in the society.

It is important to note that cross-cultural data indicate that, statistically, mature or senior males dominate such groups. They control access to community goods and Good by others. Even in the most "egalitarian" of societies, junior males—however cadet status is culturally defined and regulated—and females, generally, play at best secondary roles in public life. It is true that certain statuses (queen mother, the inherited crown of an infant king, or the collective role of "asexual" sodalities of virginal or post-menses females) can be claimed to give evidence against this position. I argue, however, that such variants do not alter the formal, technical, and informal criteria that favor the selection of mature males for priority of access to public authority and, as a result, privileged access to goods and Good. As occupants of two general categories, "the young" and "females" are, *a priori*, considered less competent than "adult" males to decide on matters of public import. Systems of authority that develop from this usually carry on such a distinction.

There is a peculiar unwillingness to accept that a hierarchy based on age and sex—treat it how you will—is a system that generates the same inequalities as any other hierarchy. Service (1975:49) shrugs off "such distinctions of elder-younger, male-female statuses," despite admitting that they are "profoundly inequalitarian," because "all societies have such hierarchical age-sex statuses" and such status are, after all, only domestic, "not *political* systems of authority and hierarchy" (italics his). There are several obvious flaws in Service's logic, not the least being that it is not always easy to differentiate the domestic from the political (cf. Finley 1973:17–22). Is, for example, marriage a domestic and never a political matter? Further, Plotkin (1978:280) is not alone in maintaining that "the political" exists only in class societies. Finally, the ramifications of such a distinction expand as societies grow and the political positions become increasingly restricted.

If "profound inequalities" can be found in all societies and can become the basis for all later patterns of ranking and stratification, then egalitarianism may also be found in all societies, even the most stratified, and play a formative role in the ideational dimension of the sociocultural system. This is my rationale for referring to councils as a type of "stratified egalitarianism." Councils represent stratification in action because, on the whole, they consist of senior males; young men and women are rarely allowed even to observe council deliberations let alone participate in them. Even mature males who are deemed lacking in certain culturally defined qualities of "the superior man" may be excluded from participation. Yet, for all this, relations among council members are marked by a pronounced emphasis on equality; all members are claimed to hold parity with all other members. Indeed, much of the dynamics of council decision making revolves around the attempt among members to validate this equality of status and role. It is also important to note that, in many societies, councils are held to be bodies that serve society and speak for rather than at the people. Exclusivity of membership is claimed to signify only relative differences in ability (due to natural, innate differences among individuals) and not to indicate any inequality between councilmen and nonmembers. Yet in the ethnographic literature it is clear that such elders do exercise an extraordinary amount of power over the affairs of the society.

One might wonder why so little material on councils is available. A partial explanation may be found in observing the members at work. The deliberative process can be complex, even Byzantine, obscured by deliberate secrecy, behind-the-scenes discussions, and the lack of reference to information that "everybody knows." Even in public meetings only a portion of the relevant factors are made explicit. It is the essence of such a management process that transactions in this arena are usually most effective when various details are obscured from general view. In more complex societies, where councils are only part of governing, the process becomes even more veiled.

Illustration of all this is given in the material on Tiwa councils that follows. The data are drawn from fieldwork (1962 to the present) among the Tiwa-speaking Pueblo Indians of the Rio Grande Valley, New Mexico. The Tiwa, together with the Tewa and Towa speakers, constitute one of the main Indian groups in the American Southwest—the Tanoans. There are four autonomous Tiwa villages and their populations range from less than 100 (Picurís) to over 2,500 (Isleta). Taos and Picurís are the two northernmost of the Rio Grande pueblos while, some 80 miles south, Isleta and Sandia are the most southern of the seventeen Pueblo villages. Though altered by Hispanic and American rule over almost 400 years, linguistic evidence (Smith 1972: 487–501) indicates that the positions discussed below were present in the precontact period. Though my presentation differs (at times sharply) from the traditional ethnographic statements, it is consonant with the Tiwa view of their governing system, and is in line with ethnohistorical and linguistic evidence.

Tiwa Governing

In order to understand the role of councils specifically it is necessary to review the overall governing system of the Tiwa. The structure consists of four levels or aspects: (1) the Societies; (2) the Governor, the War Captain, and their staffs; (3) the Council; (4) the *t'aykabede* (initially glossed by the Spanish, and by successive generations of outsiders since then, with the Arawakan word *cacique*). Levels 1, 2, and 4 will be briefly discussed before that of level 3—the Council.

The *first level* of governing is contained within the ceremonial Societies (glossed in English by native and outsider alike as "clans" or "corn groups"). Individuals are assigned to such groups at birth on the basis of the personal preferences of their parents, and it is not uncommon for siblings to belong to different Societies among the four to fifteen in any particular village. Males are expected to play an active role in Society affairs but women form an auxiliary group of "Corn Mothers" with a separate set of rituals. The latter are much less active and tend to limit their participation to mundane matters of food preparation or the making of ceremonial costumes for males. Most women say they have too many (secular) duties to become involved in the time-consuming rituals and less than a handful fulfill their complete role as Corn Mothers. Male members are gradually trained in an increasingly complex ritual system and failure to give evidence of fully comprehending training at one level bars them from moving on in the system.

The Societies perform a variety of secular functions in addition to their ceremonial duties, the latter of which validate the consociate and moral standing of the Society within the community (despite their perceived potential for creating cleavages). Each has a leader who will be succeeded by one of his assistants. Members should be "right-thinking" if the rituals of the Society are to function successfully. To ensure this state of affairs, leaders are expected to correct individual wrong-doing of their members, settle disputes among members, and settle disputes between members of two or more Societies through consultation among the leaders. Leaders also give counsel and aid to members on personal problems. Leaders derive their authority from their acknowledged possession of ceremonial wisdom, not because they are viewed as priests but because the positions they hold could not have been attained if they had not been mature men, capable of thoughtful action.

Certain rituals are believed part of the general Good of the community and must be performed in concert with the rituals of other societies on community feast days. The esoteric inventory unique to each group cannot, however, be shared with outsiders because it is believed that the ritual power is finite and the wider its distribution, the weaker it becomes. As one member explained it: "You know, like the brown-outs we always have in the village because too many people are running things at the electric current at the same time." The problem of how to have an integrated and logically sequential pan-Societal performance without weakening the power is solved by each Society's sharing its knowledge with the *t'aykabede*, who thus becomes the repository of the cumulative wisdom of pueblo members.

The *second level* of governing is in the hands of the pueblo's Governor, its War Captain, and their staffs. In some villages these two men and their assistants are appointed by the Council; in others, they are chosen by a limited electorate from a slate prepared by the Council and submitted annually in December, a practice that seems to have been a Spanish innovation.

Daily order within the village is maintained by the Governor and his staff. Today, a large portion of his duties is directed towards dealing with matters initiating outside the village (relations with the state and federal agencies, business contracts, etc.), but he still performs his traditional duties of caring for the elderly, correcting the young, keeping the pueblo in good repair, and acting as representative for the Council with outsiders. To be chosen Governor one must be "mature" (i.e., married and in good standing in one's ceremonial Society). A Governor is never a Society leader though he may become one later in life (at which time he is no longer eligible for the position of Governor).

The War Captain is chosen for his ability to make quick but sound decisions. Today, his major function is that of range boss and policeman of public affairs. Traditionally, he was in charge of defense and hunt parties, and he is still expected to keep watch for unusual or strange events outside the immediate environs of the village. He is the only leader who can "give orders."

Though the Governor and War Captain appear to function quite differently from the Society heads, officials at both levels are seen as dealing with matters "in their household." At the first level, "households" are the "extended families" of Society membership; at the second level, the Governor controls affairs in the village, which is considered to be "the people's house"; and the War Captain manages "the fields of the house"—farmlands and hinterlands (which include sacred locales such as springs, lakes, and wild onion patches).

Setting aside for the moment consideration of the third level of government, the Council, we turn next to the *fourth level*, "the household of all things," which is headed by the *t'aykabede*. He is the ritual integrator and caretaker of the sphere in which nature/man/natural/supernatural all become one. The *t'aykabede* has knowledge of all that is necessary to and is a part of the production of goods and Good. The most knowledgeable figure in the village, he is accepted as the final arbiter on basic questions of rule, law, and axiomatic guidelines. He attends Council meetings only on special occasions since one of the few explicit directives concerning his role is that "he is not to be involved in fights or problems, in everyday things, because it would be bad for his thoughts." As one person put it: "If he was involved with trouble, how could his mind stay in harmony with the balance of things as they are naturally?" Thus, the *t'aykabede* is called upon only when events have led to the Council's defining the issue as one related to an ignorance of the proper underlying and fundamental principle of natural law, "the right of it." When the *t'aykabede* issues his pronouncement there can be no disagreement; his words carry the same authority as a papal encyclical or a Supreme Court decision; anyone who would question it would be expected to surrender community citizenship. (This is the ideal and, rarely, *t'aykabedes* have been deposed just as have the popes.)

This is the traditional statement of the role of the *t'aykabede*. Today, his position varies considerably among the pueblos. Isleta has none because of a dispute some years ago as to which of two claimants was legitimate. Under their new constitution, three judges attempt to fill the vacuum. At another pueblo, the holder of the position is old, infirm, and frequently drunk—mocked at by children and often manipulated by certain Councilmen for their own advantage.

The *third level* of governing is the Council, whose members are called "house heads." The Council deals with any matters that are concerned with land allocation, village residential rights, long-range water management, village-threatening disputes, foreign negotiations, and, in general, any matter that affects the lives of all in the pueblo. The "household" of the Council is comprised of the several Societies, individual households, and private/public fields and hinterlands. Unlike the two "lower" levels, each of which consists of cooperative and co-equal but autonomous units, level 3 (and 4) synthesizes the constituent elements into a single entity. Isleta is the only pueblo in which the Council consistently holds public meetings; this is provided in their constitution (which the Bureau of Indian Affairs had a large hand in designing). But even there the majority of meetings are private.

Originally, the Councils may have included all male family heads—as they still do in the smaller pueblos. In larger villages, however, the Council consists only of the symbolic house heads—Society leaders, as well as present and past Governors and War Captains—and, of course, the *t'aykabede*. Those Council members who are also Society leaders have more influence in Council matters than do other members. In some pueblos, Councilmen serve for life but in other villages their positions are reaffirmed annually. Those who serve repeatedly and/or are the most influential speakers are usually men mature in years (the average age for Tiwa Councilmen is 57), have been concerned to learn the traditions, have been promoted through ceremonial and/or junior staff positions, and are "respected citizens." They are expected to be prosperous, since prosperity is taken as evidence of competency and industry, to be active in community affairs at the informal "neighboring" level, and to be family heads whose wives and children reflect well on them.

No Tiwa pueblo has any female Council members and, in point of fact, it is only at Isleta that women are even allowed to participate in the electoral process. Participation of junior males is almost as restricted, though they are eligible to serve in staff positions. Regardless of age, "young men" are those who are unmarried or have only minimal knowledge of the traditional lore. The Council has found it increasingly necessary to call on such individuals as involvement in the outside world intensifies. Personal qualities required for advancement are work skills and job diligence, an ability to speak well (i.e., have a sound grasp of the native language and its formal oratorical stylistics), and a modest demeanor. Until post-World War II times, the increasing population of the pueblos forced some Councils to control the number of participants "democratically" by increasing the level of ritual competency required to qualify for Governor and War Captain. Thus, membership was gradually decreased relative to the population. When returning veterans called for the right to participate in the government since they had "fought for democracy and wanted it in the village," the number of junior staff positions was increased (e.g., some Councils created staffs of their own rather than use that of the Governor). This has allowed greater participation by younger men, including some lacking extensive ritual training but possessing modern skills useful in managing the business affairs of the pueblo. Some few who perform well in junior positions (and are willing to undergo the requisite additional training in ritual matters to make them eligible for senior positions) will have a greater opportunity to achieve the prestigious posts than in former times.

Despite my definition of governing as centered on public management and decision making, Council members, like other governing personnel, are not regarded as making decisions or managing; rather they announce what their collective discussions have led them to understand is "the right of it." As one Councilman explained: "The accountant who does my taxes doesn't *decide* what I owe; he figures it out and then tells me. That's how we work on the Council."

In their deliberations the Council aims for consensus. Authority, in the sense that any individual or group can give directives, does not (in theory) exist. Even the *t'aykabede* is viewed as a judge who "reveals the truth." The ideal of consensus, however, is far from the reality and authoritative pronouncements are made and accepted—whether all agree or not. Consensus by proclamation is one device for creating an artificial unanimity, but can be used only by the most senior, long-established members. The technique consists of "summing up" what is declared to be the sense of the discussion thus far. The time for doing this must be right, e.g., when people are tired and want to go home (as at the culturally defined, maximal closure point of the meetings, about 11 P.M.), or when a skilled leader intuits that people are baffled by the discussion and can be led into "understanding" what has been happening. I have often heard Councilmen remark after a meeting that "I didn't think that was what was happening," or, "I wasn't ready to sum up to that position."

When I asked why they didn't object, some answers were: "I didn't want everybody mad at me for being the one to hold things up," "I thought maybe I was the only one confused," "I thought maybe I had missed something."

Whether real or stage-managed, when group unanimity is reached the decision is announced within a few days by public crier. If, on the other hand, consensus is not reached, renewed discussion may or may not be scheduled, and days, weeks, or months may elapse before the matter is again raised. Not uncommonly, events will simply peter out or run their course without any resolution by the Council. Some issues are never settled and one or another event may revive the festering irritation, resulting in factual disputes.

Most villagers believe the Councils are representative and democratic, the members working for the community and giving their labor so that all may benefit. Ideally, Councilmen are seen as voluntarily taking on the extra burden of Council work for the good of all and not for any personal advantage.

Governing Overview

Despite the introduction of wage work and the influence on pueblo life that outside work increasingly exerts, pueblo leaders still govern in terms of the traditional lifestyle. This is not as anachronistic as it might at first appear. Despite a growing reliance on wage income, most villagers still rely heavily on home-produced foodstuffs, but hunting, gathering, agriculture, and stock raising serve ideological as well as economic and nutritional needs. The most prosperous individual at one pueblo (a certified public accountant with a large non-pueblo clientele) continues, with his family, to farm, maintain stock, gather, and hunt because "it's expected of a good community member—and that's the difference between us and White people." Agriculture especially interrelates with the governing system and continues to serve as the primary focus for pueblo life. The communal joint action required by such features as the annual village-wide spring cleaning of the irrigation ditches, the blessing of the water, or membership in the Water Conservancy District validates the cooperative principles, synergistically basic to village life.

The same communal principles are demonstrated when members of the governing system, especially Councilmen, work to produce the Good Life for pueblo residents—sharing their efforts with those who lack the necessary practical or managerial skills and knowledge. Conversely, the participation of the less knowledgeable is also necessary. The more expert (especially the elders because of their age) cannot perform taxing physical labor in addition to their demanding governing and ceremonial duties. Ideologically, this is seen as a balanced inequality between those who have the knowledge—which is more to be husbanded because scarcer—and those who perform the commonplace chores.

There are those, of course, who complain about the system and/or maintain that leaders are not performing competently. Most, however, blame this on outside influences, corruption of native patterns, or temporary aberrations. Councilmen themselves, however, are inclined to argue that such assessments are simply unfair.

> Sure we "make a lot of decisions" that we didn't use to make. It used to be that we would talk things out, help each other see different points, and that way come to the right of it. That wasn't "deciding" anything. It was just figuring out the way things really were. And then we would let everyone know. Not *tell* them to do this or that because that's what we wanted but *explain* to them.
>
> But now, you've got all these people who haven't been taught—kids and all, with nothing in their heads but everyday things. They got all this junk and they can't sit quiet and sort things out because they're into this and that after a few minutes of trying to think. That woman last night [a member of the audience at a Council meeting], she kept talking about what her kids did, and how much her grocery bill was—stuff like that. These aren't the kinds of things to consider when you have an important problem. How can she come to the right way for the *community* if her own personal problems are all she sees? And see how those people applauded her? None of them know how to do these the right way. So we got to be more firm than in the old days when these kinds of people had more respect and understanding [and listened to us].

Another said:

> Before that B.I.A. [Bureau of Indian Affairs] made us have that constitution—and now that all those kids and women can vote and put their own people on the Council and make them Governors and like that—well, we didn't have all this trouble. That proves that our way, the old Indian way, was right.

As may be gleaned from the above, Tiwa Councilmen believe that those who reject the results of the Council's deliberations are immature, ignorant, narrow, or of unclear mind. Such people are interfering with the balance of things. To know is to have learned how things are—and to have the tools to learn still more. An individual may have the capacity to learn, or he may have to be protected from the consequences of his ignorance, but no person can be forced to accept and work diligently for a goal that is beyond his comprehension. The capable must be taught so that they can mature and share the burden, but the incapable must be led. As one Governor put it:

You must help people see the right . . . but you can't make them do it. . . . [T]hat never makes a person's heart change. Can you squeeze a cloud to make it rain?

You have to show people that there is no way to change the way things are. That's why they have to accept what we tell them is right. You know, the strongest man in the village couldn't push that tractor over there and move it. But my grandson [age 10], he knows how to work it. I taught him how to get in, turn the key in the ignition, steer it, and work the field.

Conclusion

Despite the claim of egalitarianism, the Tiwa governing system—particularly the Council—functions to support a stratified structure. Women are excluded, out of hand, from all but peripheral participation; they are seen as having power that is dangerous because women are not capable of fully comprehending how to channel such resources. Males, unless meeting the standards for "right thinking" (according to criteria established by the senior males), cannot advance through either the ceremonial or the governing system. They are deemed lacking in the full range of attributes ascribable to truly mature humans—and may even, in some cases, be permanently categorized as "young men" no matter what their age or marital status.

From this fundamental stratifying principle the Tiwa have been able to construct a system of ranking—introducing new positions for young men that, while seeming to expand the number of governing positions, in fact only makes it more explicit that some are never capable of maturing. When Council members discussed the expanded staff positions they indicated that they saw the following effects: Firstly, junior positions allow further but seemingly democratic exclusion from senior positions since, while some may never advance beyond those minor positions, they cannot claim to have been denied the opportunity. Secondly, expansion of the governing system actually enhances the authority of those at the senior level since leaders gain prestige by comparsion with those performing more menial tasks. Both the responsibilities and the pronouncements of the elders carry more weight because the community is given de facto evidence that there are differences in the quality of governing skills that one is capable of attaining. Thirdly, those jealous of preserving the status quo may train their successors, apprentice leaders advancing only as the latter give evidence of "mature, right thinking," and allowing the weeding out of those who might pose a threat. Fourthly, the new staff positions confirm the egalitarian aims of leaders while also promulgating greater participation and encouraging the community cooperation needed for implementing actions. Fifthly, staff personnel provide useful services to senior

Councilmen by gathering information, acting as a kind of "data bank," and giving greater visibility to the governing system in an expanding population. I would also add that junior personnel can serve as scapegoats, carrying the blame for unfavorably received actions and protecting the myth that senior males rarely err in their performance.

Coda

I have suggested that those who wish to decide and interpret usually believe that they and other like-minded individuals are better equipped and more capable of serving the best interests of the society by limiting the decision-making ability of those unfit to assume the responsibility for polity affairs. Those who have "the right of it" believe others are wrong-headed, prone to ill-considered, hasty acts and folly, and lacking in experience or knowledge. But perhaps we should not argue that particular historical dynamics produced centralization or "spontaneously generated" stratified, superordinate positions like these until we have addressed such basic questions as "Why does anyone want power to redistribute benefits, manage groups, and make decisions?" and "Why do people wish to relinquish control over their own lives?"

It is true that leaders often accrue certain personal material privileges and advantages but that, for many, is frequently irrelevant. The really powerful and authoritative "accept the burden of stewardship" when they already possess great material advantage over others in the society. There are, of course, some in authority who are job seekers, sycophants, figureheads, and leaders as a result of a quirk of fate. These are not the leaders of whom I speak; they are partakers rather than participants, not uncommonly achieving their positions by deliberate planning on the part of true leaders. Even in the most open-ended governing systems, power may be increasingly concentrated through the appearance of diffusing it, or by putting weak and malleable individuals into key positions.

The distinction, then, between egalitarian, ranked, and stratified societies may, at best, have only narrow analytical utility, particularly if it rests on such ethnocentrically materialistic criteria as access to real goods. Evolutionarily, non-egalitarian distribution of goods may be an effect not a cause, the outcome of a more fundamental inequality involving differential access to such Good as differential access to valued sacred and secular knowledge employed in the making of decisions affecting an individual's own life as well as the lives of others in the society.

I would argue that inequality rests not merely on material differences but on non-material elements such as prestige, honor, respect, and the ability to obtain a masterful postion in life—whether over others or simply over one's own destiny. "Managers" have enticed many into surrendering their real equality in exchange for material goods. The former gain their own Good (control, authority, power over the actions of others so that "things are done right") by giving to others the goods of this world; they risk impoverishing themselves on the material level to gain on the non-material level—a transformation that often goes unrecognized by their fellows (and scholars as well). Folk and scientist alike sometimes argue that because there is material parity among members the society must be egalitarian, but this may be missing the point of what constitutes sociocultural inequality.

It also can be argued (contra Fried [1967] and others) that stratification can and often does precede ranking evolutionarily. Increasing limitations on and ultimate, outright exclusion of some to positions of decision making have positive structural advantages from the leaders' perspectives. The trend in Tiwa communities in the last thirty years or so, for example, has been that, as the populations have grown, the number of positions at the junior or apprenticeship level has been expanded. Introducing a ranking mechanism appears to open up a stratified system, especially for those who, by previous criteria, were formally ineligible. It has not lowered the standards or implied they were false or unfair, yet the system has opened up.

Sociocultural systems must always contain the potential of generating those who believe in preserving both the socioculture and its fundamental truths (Smith 1982). A great tragedy that almost inevitably arises from this is that inequalities are generated by the desire to promote the common good. The more fundamentally "true" and close to historical fact knowledge is believed to be, the less others are permitted to challenge it and the greater the likelihood that some will be defined as incapable or unworthy of exercising alternative options—of having the right to make decisions and reaping the benefits or suffering the consequences. Those with access to canonical wisdom will reserve the right to protect the less competent. The process of excluding some (the immature, incompetent, or irrational) and forming coalitions with like-minded others breeds a "class ideology," which, I suggest appeared long before the differential distribution of material goods or a developed technological system gives explicit evidence of inequality. There is pitifully little evidence for this "software" inventive phase in the archaeological record and we are therefore presented with the illusion, but only the illusion, of great sociocultural stability over hundreds of millennia—especially by those who have allowed the technological dynamic in hardware inventiveness during recent centuries to color their analyses.

But we should not ignore what is the essence of humanity, our symboling capacity—especially as that allows, perhaps compels, us to classify and evaluate, to rank and stratify, as well as determine what are equivalents. Those who look at artifacts only have concentrated on the most trivial of human skills, one that fundamentally we share with many other species—birds who make nests and beavers who build dams. Until only recently (a handful of centuries and even then in only a few societies) humans have chosen to concentrate on what modern scholars often choose to ignore—non-material aspects of culture. We humans have indeed been tool makers but mentifacts, not artifacts, have been the primary, most basic, and most economically crucial products of humans. Knowledge and ideas are the crux of productive control; the distribution of goods is *a* consequence, not *the* cause, of that inequality that excludes some from the real wealth of humans—knowledge and the freedom to use it.

References Cited

Finley, M. I.
   1973   The Ancient Economy. Berkeley: University of California Press.
Fried, Morton H.
   1967   The Evolution of Political Society: An Essay in Political Anthropology. New York: Random House.
Plotkin, Vladimir
   1978   Ritual Coordination and Symbolic Representation in Primitive Society: The Evolution of Kinship. Dialectical Anthropology 3:279–314.
Richards, Audrey, and Adam Kuper, eds.
   1971   Councils in Action. Cambridge Papers in Social Anthropology, No. 6. Cambridge: Cambridge University Press.
Service, Elman R.
   1975   Origins of the State and Civilization: The Process of Cultural Evolution. New York: W. W. Norton.
Smith, M. Estellie
   1969   Governing at Taos Pueblo. Eastern New Mexico Contributions in Anthropology, Vol. 2, No. 1.
   1972   Notes on an ethnolinguistic Study of Governing. *In* Studies in Linguistics: Papers in Honor of George L. Trager, M. E. Smith, ed. pp. 487–501. The Hague: Mouton.
   1982   The Process of Sociocultural Continuity. Current Anthropology 23:127–142.

4
Aboriginal Sociopolitical Organization in Owens Valley: Beyond the Family Band

Robert L. Bettinger
University of California, Davis

Although our knowledge of aboriginal Great Basin culture remains imperfect in both broad outline and specific detail, the organizing principles of this lifeway have never been thought of as mysterious. Recurrent characterizations of it as "pragmatic," "eclectic," "close to the vest," "no nonsense," and so on indicate the thrust of current interpretations. Steward (1938a:46), however, probably put the case best when he described Great Basin culture as "gastric." He meant, of course, that human existence in the Desert West was so irrevocably tied to the subsistence quest that the resulting culture was essentially a product of the local environment and the primitive extractive technology at the disposal of its native inhabitants.

Steward's well-known summary of Great Basin man/land relationships developed this "gastric orientation" in a more elegant and straight forward fashion (Steward 1938a:256–257). In particular, his interpretation draws heavily on what he saw to be environmental limitations posed by the Great Basin, an area of chronic moisture deficits and severely restricted subsistence potential. Productive resources were few in number, thinly spread, and unpredictable with respect to the timing and abundance of their crop yields. Accordingly, subsistence patterns were eclectic and unspecialized, emphasizing the exploitation of virtually all available resources sufficiently productive to repay collection. As a further response, the aboriginal population was sparse and deployed in small, highly mobile groups that traveled and made critical decisions largely without reference to other social units. In keeping with this adaptive pattern, the autonomous nuclear family—or the slightly larger *kin clique* with a nuclear family serving as its core (Fowler 1966)—was the primary social, economic, and political unit (Steward 1955). More complex organizations were impossible to maintain because family units were unable to anticipate or regulate their seasonal movements in such a way as to permit the development of compositionally stable social aggregates larger than the nuclear family (Steward 1938a:246–248). More to the point, such organizations would have been disadvantageous because of their potential for creating social or territorial barriers that would impede free access to resources—this being an essential precondition to successful human adaptation in the Great Basin according to Steward (1970).

On close inspection, then, Steward's model of Great Basin human ecology assigns a dual role to sociopolitical organization as manifested in the family band unit. First, viewed as a tool of subsistence adaptation, it underscores the overriding economic bias that governed aboriginal life in the Great Basin. Second, distinguished by its elemental simplicity, the family band illustrates the primitive character of Great Basin cultural development vis-à-vis more advanced developments in adjacent regions.

Although Steward clearly intended his model to apply only to ethnographic contexts (Steward 1970), it has been of great service in archaeology, and it is archaeologists who have been primarily responsible for exploring its implications and ramifications in specific situations, both within the Great Basin (Jennings 1957; Thomas 1973) and in other areas (MacNeish 1964; Flannery 1968). Significantly, this research has not tended to address directly the problem of sociopolitical organization—despite its signal importance to the Steward model—but has instead stressed the investigation of subsistence and settlement patterns with the explicit assumption that, where economic patterns are approximately equivalent to those recorded for the historic Great Basin, the family band organization is most likely to have been present (e.g., Thomas 1974).

Archaeologists operating within this interpretive framework have furnished a good deal of support for the notion that the adaptive pattern described by Steward is broadly applicable over long periods of time throughout much of the Desert West (Jennings 1957, 1972; Thomas 1973; Aikens 1970; Heizer and Baumhoff 1962:7). In turn, this has led to almost unquestioned acceptance of the family band as *the* sociopolitical unit throughout the Great Basin without its ever having been actually studied first hand (e.g., O'Connell 1975).

It is true, of course, that this basic interpretation recently has undergone a good deal of scrutiny since prehistoric data from several parts of the Basin have persuaded archaeologists that the precise environmental constraints pictured in the Steward model are not universal. For example, in certain localities, lacustrine resources supported subsistence adaptations more reliable than Steward thought possible (e.g., Heizer and Napton 1970; Weide 1974; O'Connell 1975); and in some of these same localities, settlement patterns feature permanent, year-round occupation of large village sites (e.g., O'Connell 1975), rather than the short-term shifting settlements that play a key part in Steward's model. Obviously, adaptive postures of this kind must hold some implications for sociopolitical organization. Despite this, however, most investigators continue to endorse the universality of the family band unit by arguing that the residential permanence and subsistence security reflected archaeologically in these localities would probably increase the size and stability of local groups and the regularity with which they used certain resource areas, but ultimately would not change the fundamental emphasis on the egalitarian, aterritorial family band (O'Connell 1975). This is essentially the same position Steward (1970) himself took when confronting adaptive anomalies of this sort among historic groups. In sum, present archaeological thinking continues to hold in favor of Great Basin sociopolitical uniformity with some minor variation due to circumstances of local environment.

An Alternative Case

On the one hand, I am disinclined to dismiss this generally accepted interpretation of Great Basin sociopolitical organization out of hand, if for no other reason than because it makes good common sense and because technology and environment do place some obvious limitations on the potential for cultural evolution in the area. On the other hand, however, it should be recognized that a very good case can also be made that there existed in the Great Basin sociopolitical forms wholly incompatible with the family band model and that these forms are difficult to explain solely with reference to the native environment and technology.

Owens Valley, a long, steep-sided fault trough in central eastern California occupied by the Mono-speaking Owens Valley Paiute, provides us with an opportunity to explore this possibility, as the region has been traditionally singled out by Steward (1938a) and others as being unusually well endowed with natural resources, encouraging reduced aboriginal movements and other related cultural developments uncharacteristic of Great Basin groups as a whole.

What makes Owens Valley an ideal case for study is that Steward left us with an abundance (relatively speaking) of ethnographic data bearing on the issues of subsistence adaptation and sociopolitical organization (Steward 1930, 1933, 1934, 1938a, 1938b, 1955, 1970) and numerous other sources (e.g., Chalfant 1933; Parcher 1930; Earl ms.), including a local newspaper—the *Inyo Independent*—offer additional information. Given these data, it is surprising that neither Steward nor those after him ever took the time to examine or discuss Owens Valley Paiute organization in much detail. They were content, rather, to sketch its rough outlines and argue that its more anomalous features—specifically, more regular social interaction and quasi-territoriality (Steward denied that it was true, i.e., exclusive, territoriality)—were only weak developments out of a pattern that was on the whole compatible with the Shoshonean family band system (Steward 1970).

Such an interpretation, however, would not seem to comport with the situation as Steward (1933, 1938a) himself described it.[1] On the contrary, a detailed consideration of Owens Valley organization shows it to be substantially at odds with the family band model. Owens Valley sociopolitical organization exhibits sharply curtailed family autonomy, exclusive resource ownership and control at several levels, and comparatively powerful positions of leadership based on ascribed status distinctions in contrast to the family band model of unchallenged family autonomy, lack of resource ownership, and almost exclusively egalitarian status distinctions based on age, sex, and achievement.

Owens Valley Paiute sociopolitical organization and the data relevant to the interpretation of that organization are too complex to be discussed in detail here, but a brief description can be offered to illustrate in more specific terms the nature of the contrast between it and the family band. These differences are perhaps most readily perceived if it is understood that while the Owens Valley Paiute family was of clear economic and social importance, its influence was eclipsed by two higher levels of organization, the village and the district, that assumed roles and responsibilities that elsewhere in the Great Basin were the sole jurisdiction of the family band or kin clique.

Villages were exogamous residential units of stable composition, varying in size from 25 to 150 individuals, most of them considered relatives (Steward 1933:294, 1938a:51–52, 234, 236, 251; Chalfant 1933:45; Earl ms.). In the southern part of the valley, below the modern town of Big Pine, a strong preference for matrilocal residence combined with the rule of local exogamy to produce villages that closely approximated matrilineal clans in Steward's terms (Steward 1933:294–296, 1938a:57; cf. Eggan 1968). This seems to have been tied to matrilineal inheritance of seed lands, irrigated plots, and piñon groves (Steward 1938a:52, 256). In the northern part of the valley, patrilineal inheritance of resource areas appears more prevalent (Steward 1938a:52; but see Steward 1933:305), but whether such inheritance indicates the presence of unilocal residence groups is uncertain, although it is possible it does. The point here is that Owens Valley marriage and residence practices were couched in terms of the village unit rather than the family, thus reducing the autonomy and importance of the latter.

Further, the autonomy of the village itself was commonly superseded by the still higher district level of organization, which in turn further minimized the potential for family individualism. Districts might be coextensive with either isolated villages or very large ones, i.e., those consisting of perhaps more than 100 members (Steward 1933:304; 1938a:50–51). However, villages that were smaller or more closely spaced were often politically allied within districts (Steward 1938a:51, 251). The district organization is clearly at odds with the family band model for it was a well-defined political entity that owned and made exclusive use of a sharply circumscribed subsistence territory (Steward 1933:305; 1938a:50–54, 233–234, 236, 251, 255–256), which, if

Aboriginal Sociopolitical Organization in Owens Valley

need be, it defended against trespass (e.g., Chalfant 1933:78, 191). These territories generally included fishing beats, seed plots, irrigated plots, piñon groves, communal hunting areas, and salt sources (Steward 1933: map 2).

Its character as the largest land-holding unit of reference also made the district the primary arena for sociopolitical affairs and decision making—matters that to a large extent came under the immediate authority and direction of the chief (Steward 1933:304–305; 1938a:55–56, 251; Chalfant 1933:46). This influential leadership position was inherited by males from their fathers, paternal uncles, or, less frequently, maternal uncles (Steward 1938b). In contrast to the position of headman in the family band organization—a position more frequently earned rather than inherited that carried strictly advisory powers (Steward 1938a:246–253), the chief in the Owens Valley Paiute district system had a considerable range of roles and duties and was vested with the power to carry them out. He directed communal construction projects—particularly fish and irrigation dams and sweathouses. He also saw to the maintenance and operation of irrigation systems and the planning and direction of communal drives, piñon expeditions, and annual fiestas or fandangoes—the latter being especially important since they provided regional resource distribution that permitted the population to remain more locationally stable than would have been possible in their absence (Bettinger and King 1971; Steward 1933:320–322; 1938a:54; Chalfant 1933:87; for examples see *Inyo Independent* 28 Dec. 1872, 26 April 1873, 29 Nov. 1873, 8 July 1876).

The chief submitted some matters to the general district populace for vote (Chalfant 1933:46; Steward 1933:304), but most he decided himself, although he frequently sought council from a standing advisory group made up of high-status individuals he appointed (Chalfant 1933:46). Significantly, the chief had the authority to settle at least some disputes between individuals and in doing so often enlisted the aid of much feared witches or shamans (Steward 1933:304–305; but see Steward 1938a:56), whose lives were under his express protection (Steward 1938a:56; 1938b:193). The more or less constant threat of reprisal by his clients or their relatives (Chalfant 1933:31–34; Inyo Independent 7 Oct. 1871, 30 Dec. 1871, 23 May 1874, 24 July 1875, 19 Aug. 1876, 2 Sept. 1876, 9 Sept. 1876, 11 Nov. 1876) probably made the shaman a willing tool of the chief, who alone could prevent such reprisals. This pattern of chief/shaman collusion is reminiscent of much of California, where such practices were widespread in aboriginal times (Gayton 1930; Bean 1978; Blackburn 1974). In summary, it is clear that Owens Valley Paiute chiefs had both the power and the prerogative to make and enforce unpopular decisions,[2] a kind of behavior that would be out of the question in a family band organization.

What limited information is available suggests that the influence and importance of individual families within the village/district hierarchy varied greatly according to their history and membership. The family ownership and inheritance of such important resources as seed plots, irrigated plots, and piñon groves mentioned earlier, as well as inheritance of chieftainship itself, would seem to have fostered substantial inequalities in the wealth and influence of different families. Long-distance trade for the purpose of wealth accumulation (Steward 1933:257–258; 1938a:44; Chalfant 1933:81; for specific examples see Steward 1934:431, 437–438; 1938b:188, 191) and preferential consideration in redistributive practices and communal endeavors (e.g., irrigation) might have further accentuated these contrasts. Steward (1938b) mentions one very powerful Owens Valley Paiute family that in three generations produced three chiefs and two doctors and was wealthy enough to meet the brideprice for five different wives for one of its members—a staggering sum by all accounts and far beyond the means of most families. As with the chief/ shaman collusion already discussed, the concentration of chiefs and shamans in the same descent group was commonplace in aboriginal California west of the Sierra Nevada (Bean 1975, 1978).

Early historic Owens Valley Paiute sociopolitical organization, then, presents a stark contrast to the Great Basin family band, particularly with respect to its extensive use of territoriality and resource ownership, its investment of substantial political authority in chiefs with ascribed status, and its restrictions on family autonomy. In all such respects, Owens Valley Paiute sociopolitical organization much more closely resembles aboriginal patterns found in California than it does those observed anywhere in the Great Basin.

Archaeological Implications

This ethnographic model of aboriginal Owens Valley sociopolitical organization can be criticized on the grounds that it was never observed first hand by any ethnographer. The data on which it is based were recounted to Steward and others by a few elderly informants who frequently contradicted each other, and, therefore, it quite possibly is highly idealized or infused with exotic elements. But, even if we accept the validity of the ethnographic interpretation, this tells us little about how this organization developed. Obviously, the case would be stronger if some solid archaeological data independently offered some rough estimate of its antiquity and confirmed the presence of the district organization in aboriginal times.

Most archaeological investigations of sociopolitical organization have dealt with mortuary data, attempting to distinguish egalitarian societies, where funerary ritual is thought to emphasize rank distinctions that are determined primarily by age, sex, and personal achievement, from ranked and stratified societies, where, in terms of rank, distinctions of age, sex, and achievement are superseded by membership in descent groups (Fried 1960; e.g., King 1976; Saxe 1970; Rothschild 1975).

At first glance, this approach does not appear particularly promising for most of the Great Basin, where cemetery sites are virtually absent (but see

Riddell 1960). Nevertheless, even this is evidence of a sort since the social fragmentation so prominent in the family band organization would likely discourage the development of specific mortuary sites reflecting corporate unity.

Thus it is of some significance that cemeteries are documented both ethnographically and archaeologically in Owens Valley (Steward 1933; Lanning 1963), suggesting the presence of at least some degree of social cohesion such as that of the district organization described above. In addition, there is at least some hint that burial ritual was an expression of group unity that tended to emphasize membership of the individual in the district organization (Steward 1933:296–299, 1938a) and was most elaborate for members of powerful or wealthy families (Kroeber 1925:589; Chalfant 1933:37). This pattern may have been present as early as 1500 B.C.; three Middle Rose Spring phase burials from the Rose Spring site, just south of Owens Valley, appear to be of two kinds, one characterized by utilitarian burial furniture—suggesting ranking based on some combination of age, sex, and personal achievement, the other by non-utilitarian wealth items—suggesting ranking based on membership in a high-status descent group, especially since the single individual of this latter kind was immature and probably would have been unable to earn personal distinction commensurate with its lavish burial accompaniments. Unfortunately, Owens Valley mortuary data are too fragmentary to furnish more than these few ambiguous suggestions about prehistoric social organization—a situation not likely to improve in the near future given current legal sanctions against the archaeological study of aboriginal cemeteries in eastern California.

Even without such data, however, it should be possible to study something of Paiute district organization in prehistoric contexts: the territorial character of the district organization would likely be reflected archaeologically by spatially restricted distributions of certain decorative styles or raw materials. We have recently explored this possibility by examining the distribution of Fish Springs obsidian—a readily identified olive green volcanic glass with feathery brown flow bands—whose source is located near the center of the area formed by combined Fish Springs and Big Pine Paiute districts in central Owens Valley (Bettinger 1982; Steward 1933:map 2). The study consisted of visually sourcing the obsidian debitage from 109 archaeological sites located by surface surveys in a study area roughly conterminous with the combined Fish Springs/Big Pine districts (cf. Bettinger 1977). The expectation was that if the Owens Valley Paiute district organization existed prehistorically, it would be reflected by a compact and sharply bounded distribution of Fish Springs obsidian, the obsidian of easy access to the prehistoric occupants of central Owens Valley, especially in comparison to other glass sources, which are on the order of three to five times more distant (Steward 1933: map 2). It was also expected that the compactness of the distribution and the crispness of its boundaries would be directly related to the degree to which territories were recognized and respected and to the antiquity of the territorial district system; the older and more well developed the system, the sharper and more discrete the boundaries.

The results of this analysis revealed three things (Bettinger 1982). First, the distribution of Fish Springs obsidian does not vary for different settlement types, i.e., regardless of their other characteristics, sites in the same survey units (sample tracts) tend to have very similar percentages of this glass. Thus, obsidian distribution crosscuts such variables as length of occupation, seasonality, and economic activity, as would be expected with a territorial system (Bettinger 1982). Second, when plotted against distance from its source, the percentage of Fish Springs obsidian in individual sample tracts holds at a frequency of between 60% and 90% for tracts within about 18 km. of the source; the frequency declines sharply to between 0% and 45% for tracts lying more than about 20 km. from the Fish Springs source. This abrupt break at a more or less precise distance threshold is entirely consistent with a territorial system; in the absence of territories, one would expect that the frequency of Fish Springs obsidian would gradually decline as distance from the source increased. Finally, when these sample tract percentages are actually plotted on a map, they disclose a sharp, boundary-like fall-off in the distribution of Fish Spring obsidian that corresponds to the eastern and, to a lesser extent, northern edges of the combined ethnographic territories of the Fish Springs and Big Pine Paiute. The southern boundary of these ethnographic districts lies outside our survey area, so we cannot be sure that it exhibits the expected break in Fish Springs obsidian distribution, although data presently available are consistent with this interpretation (Bettinger 1982; Ericson 1977). The western Fish Springs/Big Pine district boundary is defined by an unoccupied stretch of the Sierra Nevada crest (Steward 1933: map 2) rather than by contact with territory of an adjacent social group. Here, high frequencies of Fish Springs obsidian were found in tracts right up to the fringes of the unoccupied zone, supporting the notion of preemptive territorial use of the area by inhabitants of the Fish Springs/Big Pine districts.

Taken together, these data suggest that some sort of distict system was present in prehistoric times in central Owens Valley, the territory of which corresponded to that of the combined ethnographic Fish Springs and Big Pine Paiute districts and which is archaeologically defined by a line enclosing the area in which Fish Springs obsidian makes up more that 50% of all obsidian debitage. Furthermore, that this boundary is so well defined, at least on its eastern edge, suggests that the territorial system it apparently reflects is not of recent origin but has existed in the area for some time.

Two ancillary lines of evidence lend additional weight to the possibility that a territorial district-like system quite similar to that of the historic Paiute might have developed quite early in central Owens Valley. One of these is the mortuary data mentioned above that may point to the presence of ascribed

Aboriginal Sociopolitical Organization in Owens Valley 53

status distinctions at least as early as 1500 B.C. A second line of evidence comes from previously published archaeological interpretations of Fish Springs/Big Pine subsistence and settlement patterns from 3500 B.C. to ethnographic times. As it is presently understood, during this time aboriginal groups were primarily reliant on highly concentrated plant and animal resources that occur in great abundance within the prehistoric Fish Springs/Big Pine district as identified above, making this district a viable (i.e., self-sufficient) subsistence territory for the period in question (Bettinger 1977). Further, throughout this time span several settlements appear to be permanent, year-round occupied villages, the presence of which would be a necessary (but not sufficient) condition for the development of the village/district system.

In short, there is a good deal of evidence (albeit fragmentary) in favor of the conclusion that Owens Valley is a Great Basin region characterized by a sociopolitical organization fundamentally different from the family band and that this organization is not recent but may date from the earliest intensive occupation of the region. Admittedly, given our present knowledge, the case that can be made for occurrence of the district organization in Owens Valley is far from conclusive; nevertheless, it is stronger than the case that can be made for the family band in this area.

Reconsidering the Role of Local Environment

Ultimately, the above discussion brings us back to the more basic question regarding whether we can fully explain fundamental contrasts between the Owens Valley Paiute district organization and the family band organization as resulting from similar adaptive responses to dissimilar local environments. That is, can we treat them as different local manifestations of the same adaptive system, as Steward and others have held?

I do not deny the potentially important role of environment here, but two considerations make it unlikely that we can explain Owens Valley sociopolitical organization in these terms alone. First, as I have indicated, so far as we can tell the characteristic territorial system seems to show no developmental history in Owens Valley but appears virtually full blown from the earliest periods for which we have data. This is more consistent with the notion that the system developed elsewhere and simply moved to central Owens Valley or is a reaction to such movements (Fried 1960) than with the notion that it is a response to locally unique environmental conditions (Bettinger 1978). Second, if the distinctive character of Owens Valley Paiute organization were simply a response to local environment, one would expect to find a continuum of variability in Great Basin social organization ranging from that of family band at one extreme to that of district at the other, a continuum paralleling the range of environmental conditions from marginal (family band) to optimal (district). In fact, no such gradual continuum appears to exist. Rather, there seems to be a basic dichtomy between the family band and the district systems with no obvious intervening forms. To explain this on purely environmental grounds would require the argument that Owens Valley is far and away the most favorable environment in the Great Basin—an untenable view since the environmental qualities of Owens Valley are virtually indistingishable from those in certain other Great Basin localities (cf. Bettinger 1978).

Even disregarding the situation in Owens Valley, I think there is good reason to question the conventional wisdom that Great Basin sociopolitical organization must be regarded as a dependent variable that only follows the lead of environment and subsistence-settlement patterns. Perhaps most obvious in this regard is that, as I have pointed out elsewhere (Bettinger 1978), Great Basin adaptive strategies (i.e., the combined patterns of subsistence, settlement, and sociopolitical organization) seem very conservative and change little through time; the strategy found in many areas was brought by early or late colonizing groups (Bettinger and Baumhoff 1982). Since it makes sense to believe that the maintenance of a pre-existing social and political order might be a primary goal of such immigrant populations, it follows that these groups might well adjust their subsistence and settlement patterns to accommodate their sociopolitical organization rather than the other way around as is commonly assumed (cf. Schwartz 1970).

A second point, also made elsewhere (Bettinger 1978, 1980), is that any Great Basin locality would seem to encompass sufficient environmental complexity to be able to sustain two or more very different adaptive solutions given the same level of technology (a similar view has been expressed by Downs 1966; see also Bettinger and Baumhoff 1982). If one accepts this argument, it would follow that, within the range of viable adaptive choices, the effect of local environment on sociopolitical organization (and even subsistence adaptation) is indeterminate.

Implications

The current model of Great Basin sociopolitical organization has stood for more than four decades and up to this point has always worked very well. Given this, the Owens Valley data presented above are neither so definitive nor so unambiguous to require that we discard the model out of hand; they do, however, indicate that a thorough review of it is in order. It is symptomatic of the problem that this first requires that we reconsider the entire question of Great Basin man/land relationships, recognizing the strong materialist theoretical bias of many interpretations. One step in this direction would be to recognize that, for students of Great Basin human ecology, "the environment" has come to be defined operationally as the local subsistence area—an unnecessarily narrow view. While it is true that most, though by no means all, subsistence products were obtained locally, other aspects of aboriginal Basin life were set in much broader regional contexts. Among the more important of these were access to potential mates (Wobst 1978), procurement of raw materials, presence of markets for resource surplus and craft products, and open areas into which excess population might be budded. These are largely ignored in Steward's model: the distribution of surplus food and the budding of excess population are hardly relevant to groups barely able to eke out a living.

Nevertheless, the potential influence exerted by broad regional demographic and economic systems is readily apparent in Owens Valley. As I have said, the Owens Valley environment is not unique, there being numerous other equally productive areas in the Great Basin. On the other hand, in a larger spatial context, its access to the markets and products of central California to the west and to scarce and valuable raw materials such as salt and obsidian in the eastern Sierra and deserts to the east, as well as its socially and environmentally circumscribed setting, are rather unique in the Desert West. Detailed examination of these regional and interregional networks, rather than continued preoccupation with the local subsistence environment, would appear to be one promising avenue for explaining sociopolitical developments in Owens Valley. And this probably applies to other parts of the Great Basin as well.

Notes

Acknowledgments. I am greatly indebted to Julie Abraham, Michael Delacorte, and Kathy Riley for their participation in laboratory and library research connected with this project.

1. Steward's interpretation of Owens Valley sociopolitical organization changed over the years. For example, compare Steward (1933) with Steward (1970).
2. The *Inyo Independent*, 29 Nov. 1873, describes an incident involving an unpopular, but apparently powerful, Paiute chief.

References Cited

Aikens, C. Melvin
   1970   Hogup Cave. University of Utah Anthropological Papers, No. 93.

Bean, Lowell J.
   1975   Power and Its Application in Native California. Journal of California Anthropology 2:25–33.
   1978   Social Organization. In Handbook of North American Indians. Vol 8: California. William C. Sturtevant and Robert F. Heizer, eds. pp. 673–682. Washington: Smithsonian Institution.

Bettinger, Robert L.
   1977   Aboriginal Human Ecology in Owens Valley: Prehistoric Change in the Great Basin. American Antiquity 42:3–17.
   1978   Alternative Adaptive Strategies in the Prehistoric Great Basin. Journal of Anthropological Research 34:27–46.
   1980   Explanatory/Predictive Models of Hunter-Gatherer Adaptation. In Advances in Archaeological Theory and Method, Vol. 3, M. B. Schiffer, ed. pp. 189–255. New York: Academic Press.
   1982   Aboriginal Exchange and Territoriality in Owens Valley, California. In Contexts for Prehistoric Exchange, J. E. Ericson and T. K. Earle, eds. pp. 103–127. New York: Academic Press.
Bettinger, Robert L., and M. A. Baumhoff
   1982   The Numic Spread: Great Basin Cultures in Competition. American Antiquuity 47:485–503.
Bettinger, Robert L., and Thomas F. King
   1971   Interaction and Political Organization: A Theoretical Framework for Archaeology in Owens Valley, California. University of California Archaeological Survey Annual Report 13:187–195.
Blackburn, T.
   1974   Ceremonial Integration and Social Interaction in Aboriginal California. In Antap: California Indian Political and Economic Organization, Lowell J. Bean and Thomas F. King, eds. pp. 93–110. Ballena Press Anthropological Paper 2.
Chalfant, William A.
   1933   The Story of Inyo. 2nd ed. Los Angeles: Citizens Print Shop.
Downs, James F.
   1966   The Significance of Environmental Manipulation in Great Basin Cultural Development. In The Current Status of Anthropological Research in the Great Basin: 1964, Warren d'Azevedo et al., eds. pp. 39–56. Desert Research Institute Social Sciences and Humanities Publication 1.
Earl, Guy C.
   ms.   Unpublished Notes on the Owens Valley Paiute. On file at the Anthropology Department, University of California, Santa Barbara.
Eggan, Fred
   1968   Discussions, Part III. In Man the Hunter, Richard B. Lee and Irven Devore, eds. pp. 161–162. Chicago: Aldine.
Ericson, Jonathan E.
   1977   Prehistoric Exchange Systems in California: The Results of Obsidian Dating and Tracing. Ph.D. dissertation. Anthropology Department, University of California, Los Angeles.
Flannery, Kent V.
   1968   Archaeological Systems Theory and Early Mesoamerica. In Anthropological Archaeology in the America, B. Meggers, ed. pp. 67–87. Washington: Anthropological Society of Washington.
Fowler, Don. D.
   1966   Great Basin Social Organization. In The Current Status of Anthropological Research in the Great Basin: 1964, Warren d'Azevedo et al., eds. pp. 57–73. Desert Research Institute Social Sciences and Humanities Publication 1.

Fried, Morton H.
　1960　On the Evolution of Social Stratification and the State. *In* Culture in History, Stanley Diamond, ed. pp. 713–731. New York: Columbia University Press.
Gayton, Anna H.
　1930　Yokuts-Mono Chiefs and Shamans. University of California Publications in American Archaeology and Ethnology, Vol. 24, No. 8.
Heizer, Robert F., and Martin A. Baumhoff
　1962　Prehistoric Rock Art of Nevada and Eastern California. Berkeley: University of California Press.
Heizer, Robert F., and Lewis K. Napton
　1970　Archaeology and the Great Basin Subsistence Regime as Seen from Lovelock Cave, Nevada. Contributions of the University of California Archaeological Research Facility, No. 10.
Inyo Independent (newspaper)
　Independence, California.
Jennings, Jesse D.
　1957　Danger Cave. Society for American Archaeology Memoir 14.
　1972　Prehistory of North America. 2nd ed. New York: McGraw-Hill.
King, Thomas F.
　1976　Political Differentiation among Hunter-gatherers: An Archaeological Test. Ph.D. dissertation. Anthropology Department, University of California at Riverside.
Kroeber, A. L.
　1925　Handbook of the Indians of California. Bureau of American Ethnology Bulletin 78.
Lanning, Edward P.
　1963　Archaeology of the Rose Spring Site, Iny-372. University of California Publications in American Archaeology and Ethnology, Vol. 49, No. 3.
MacNeish, Richard S.
　1964　Ancient Mesoamerican Civilization. Science 143:531–537.
O'Connell, James F.
　1975　The Prehistory of Surprise Valley. Ballena Press Anthropological Paper 4.
Parcher, F. M.
　1930　The Indians of Inyo County. Masterkey 4:146–153.
Riddell, Francis A.
　1960　Archaeology of the Karlo Site, Las-7, California. University of California Archaeological Survey Report 53.
Rothschild, Nan A.
　1975　Age and Sex, Status and Role, in Prehistoric Societies of Eastern North America. Ph.D. dissertation. Anthropology Department, New York University.
Saxe, Arthur A.
　1970　Social Dimensions of Mortuary Practices. Ph.D. dissertation. Anthropology Department, University of Michigan.
Schwartz, Douglas W.
　1970　The Postmigration Culture: A Base for Archaeological Inference. *In* Reconstructing Prehistoric Pueblo Societies, William A. Longacre, ed. pp. 175–193. Albuquerque: University of New Mexico Press.

Steward, Julian H.
- 1930 Irrigation Without Agriculture. Papers of the Michigan Academy of Science, Arts, and Letters, Vol. 12, pp. 269–276.
- 1933 Ethnography of the Owens Valley Paiute. University of California Publications in American Archaeology and Ethnology, Vol. 33, No. 3.
- 1934 Two Paiute Autobiographies. University of California Publications in American Archaeology and Ethnology, Vol. 33, No. 5.
- 1938a Basin-Plateau Aboriginal Sociopolitical Groups. Bureau of American Ethnology Bulletin 120.
- 1938b Panatubiji, an Owens Valley Paiute. Bureau of American Ethnology Bulletin 119:183–195.
- 1955 Theory of Culture Change. Urbana: University of Illinois Press.
- 1970 Foundations of Basin-Plateau Shoshonean Society. *In* Languages and Cultures of Western North America, Earl H. Swanson, ed. pp. 113–151. Pocatello: Idaho State University Press.

Thomas, David Hurst
- 1973 An Empirical Test for Steward's Model of Great Basin Settlement Patterns. American Antiquity 38:155–177.
- 1974 An Archaeological Perspective on Shoshonean Bands. American Anthropologist 76:11–23.

Weide, Margaret
- 1974 Northern Warner Subsistence Network. Nevada Archaeological Survey Research Paper 5:62–79.

Wobst, H. Martin
- 1978 Archaeo-ethnology of Hunter-gatherers or the Tyranny of the Ethnographic Record in Archaeology. American Antiquity 43:303–309.

5
On Steward's Models of Shoshonean Sociopolitical Organization: A Great Bias in the Basin?

David Hurst Thomas
American Museum of Natural History

The Great Basin Shoshoneans have been of interest to anthropologists for decades, not only because of the readily available, well-documented raw data, but also because of the significance of the Shoshonean case in the development of ecological and evolutionary thought. Regardless of how one fabricates a cultural evolutionary sequence, the Shoshoneans almost inevitably end up on the bottom rung of the ladder. A recent study by Lomax and Arensberg (1977), for instance, begins a scale of worldwide modes of subsistence with the Basin Shoshonean case, then works up to more complex subsistence systems. At least a dozen similar scales could be cited.

Prehistorians also commonly employ the Shoshonean analogy when attempting to interpret the social organization of relatively simple extinct societies; examples that come immediately to mind include the work of Richard MacNeish (1964, 1972) and Kent Flannery (1966) in the Tehuacan Valley, Flannery and Joyce Marcus (1976) in Oaxaca, and Edwin Wilmsen (1970) for the Paleo-Indian period in North America.

Despite the reputation of what Lomax and Arensberg (1977:669) refer to as "those famine-ridden nomads," it is clear that the Shoshoneans practiced neither the world's most primitive technology (witness the Tasmanians) nor inhabited the world's harshest environment (let us not forget the Sahara). So why all this attention? Robert Murphy (1970:154) was probably correct when he attributed the theoretical importance of the Shoshoneans to the fact that "there are but few known societies in the world that have had to live so close to the margin of survival as the Shoshone." I suspect that this relatively nononsense ecological adaptation, coupled with relatively late Anglo contact and a well-documented ethnographic record, have combined to establish the Great Basin Shoshoneans as one of anthropology's standard "textbook societies."

The traditional view of Basin-Plateau sociopolitical organization has been repeatedly set forth by Julian Steward, and this brief paper will examine some foundations of his assertions. Briefly stated, Steward's interpretation of the Great Basin Shoshoneans emphasizes the ecological and sociopolitical importance of the nuclear family. The Shoshoneans are best characterized by a long list of *absences*, what Steward (1955:102) termed a "quantitative simplicity": the absence of sharp dialectical, cultural, and political boundaries, the absence of well-defined groups larger than the village, the absence of men's institutions and secret societies, the absence of clans, moieties, and lineages, the absence of age grades, women's societies, and warfare. In short, the Shoshoneans lacked any significant sociocultural groupings above the level of the simple family cluster. According to Steward's (1970:115) final analysis, "the small family cluster . . . was the inevitable response to areas of meager resources, low population density and an annual cycle of nomadism."

But was it?

Steward's views have assumed almost monolithic proportions, particularly to general anthropologists working *outside* the Great Basin. This is understandable and at least in part due to Steward's overall reputation as a cultural ecologist. There exists, however, a surprising amount of disagreement among ethnographers who have actually worked with Great Basin aboriginal peoples. John Wesley Powell, for instance, felt that Great Basin family band structure resulted from recent acculturation: "formerly, the Shoshoneans were organized into nations, or confederacies, under the influence of great chiefs . . . the original political organization had a territorial basis" (Powell and Ingalls 1874:3). Although Steward (1970:138) rejected this interpretation—remarking on Powell's "incredible ethnographic naïveté"—Elman Service (1962) has resurrected the Powell argument by suggesting that the Shoshoneans *devolved* from full-blown patrilocal bands into the well-known ethnographic family bands. The research of Omer Stewart (1939, 1966) and Isabel Kelly (1934, 1964) also emphasizes the territorial basis of Basin-Plateau sociopolitical organization.

Although we still lack the data necessary to resolve the issue, re-analysis of Steward's Great Basin research reveals a subtle, yet critical, evolution in Steward's own thinking. Steward's interest in the Great Basin was fostered when he attended the Deep Springs Preparatory School, near Owens Valley, California. While at Deep Springs, Steward became acquainted with local Paiute and Shoshone people, and his early papers dealt with the archaeology and ethnology of the Deep Springs area. Steward's formal Great Basin ethnographic research lasted almost exactly twelve months, conducted primarily during the 1930s.

In reading Steward's later publications dealing with the Great Basin—particularly chapter 6 in his influential *Theory of Culture Change* (1955)—one acquires a largely unconscious impression that Steward worked throughout the entire Great Basin, and that his family band model applies to Great Basin Shoshonean society as a whole. Both impressions are incorrect. A close examination of his ethnographies indicates that Steward worked with about sixty Shoshonean informants: 40 Western Shoshone, 14 Owens Valley Paiute, 4 Mono Lake Paiute, 3 Southern Paiute, and a single Northern Paiute.

In other words Steward's first-hand information relates almost exclusively to two groups: the Owens Valley Paiute and the Western Shoshone. It is particularly critical to note that Steward never worked with the lakeshore-adapted Northern Paiute groups, such as the Pyramid Lake or Walker River Paiute. In fact Steward's classic *Basin-Plateau Aboriginal Sociopolitical Groups* (1938) does not even include a sketch of these societies, an extremely important omission. It seems entirely likely that the microenvironments of these large inland lakes fostered a significantly different settlement pattern and probably more complex social organization than Steward's "typical" family band (see Fowler 1977).

Although the lacustrine groups were most heavily impacted by early Anglo settlers, mere acculturation cannot explain Steward's consistent omission of such groups. While Steward was conducting his Owens Valley and Western Shoshone reconnaissance, both Omer Stewart (1939, 1941) and Willard Park (1941) were simultaneously doing research among the Pyramid Lake and Walker River Paiute. Perhaps Steward simply assumed that, when published, the Stewart and Park material would have filled the gap (Fowler 1977). But this never happened. Steward consistently debunked Stewart's interpretations of territoriality and band structure among the Northern Paiute, and Park's research is available in only extremely truncated form (although C. Fowler is currently preparing Park's material for publication).

This is an important lapse in Shoshonean ethnography, and I suspect that a major bias has been introduced in the meantime. Part of this bias results from sampling error, pure and simple: the Western Shoshone are relatively overreported and the Northern Paiute are virtually ignored. But Steward himself must shoulder at least part of the burden. His early publications always emphasized just which Shoshonean group he was discussing and his most influential work on the Shoshoneans—*Basin-Plateau Aboriginal Sociopolitical Groups* (Steward 1938)—was never intended to be a general Great Basin ethnography. The 1938 monograph was, as Catherine Fowler (1977:19) put it, "a theoretical statement on the relationship of social and political groups to their environments." Emphasis was squarely on the Western Shoshone, and Steward was quite explicit about this. This fundamental synthesis left plenty of room for regional variation within the Great Basin, although it is clear that Steward always preferred the more general approach.

Not long after the publication of his 1938 volume, Steward's career took him in other directions, and he did not publish a single Basin-related article for nearly fifteen years. During this interval Steward acquired an impressive ethnographic and theoretical breadth, particularly through his efforts on the *Handbook of South American Indians*.

Steward's intellectual growth is evident in *Theory of Culture Change* (1955), which encapsulated his ideas on cultural ecology and evolution. The Shoshonean case was critical to the argument because it typified the rudimentary family band level of sociocultural integration. Although chapter 6 of this influential volume was billed as "essentially a condensation of 'Basin-Plateau Sociopolitical Groups' [sic]" (1955:101), a careful reading reveals otherwise. The earlier publications of the 1930s always emphasized specific Shoshonean groups, particularly the Western Shoshone and the Owens Valley Paiute. But after almost fifteen years away from the data, Steward returned to speak only in generalities. Chapter 6 bristles with Basin-wide references to "Shoshonean habitat," "Shoshonean culture," and "Shoshonean society." We must, of course, grant Steward a certain measure of poetic license, for it is clear that he was using the common didactic technique of illustrating the general by the specific. But I think there is more involved.

In *Theory of Culture Change*, we can detect a transformation in Steward's thinking. Through the years the Western Shoshone came to dominate Steward's view of the Great Basin. More and more, Steward glossed over intra-Basin variability: by the mid 1950s the Western Shoshone family cluster was taken as typical of Great Basin Shoshoneans in general. The "less typical" groups—traditionally slighted in Great Basin ethnography anyway—all but disappear from Steward's view.

This is what I mean by a "bias in the Basin." What began as a fundamental ethnographic description of a few very simple hunter-gatherers ultimately escalated into a theoretical statement of major anthropological importance. This evolution is particularly critical because of Steward's stature in the discipline. Despite the popularity of the Great Basin Shoshoneans in comparative studies, too few contemporary investigators bother to return to Steward's actual data, namely the publications of the 1930s. Steward's work is generally taken as "typical" of Great Basin ethnography, and chapter 6 of *Theory of Culture Change* is often taken as "typical" of Steward's views. Both views are incorrect. Steward's field work was not Basin-wide and his 1955 synthesis does not do his field work justice.

The bias is clearly present. Whether or not this is a *great bias* remains to be determined. As Catherine Fowler (1977:38) has put it, we simply do not know the subsistence and settlement strategies of the lacustrine groups; her re-analysis of Park's key ethnographic notes may shed some light in this direction, and perhaps even serve to counterbalance Steward's well-known Western Shoshone data.

The mere recognition of the bias should have some impact on anthropological research outside the Great Basin. Steward's classic Shoshonean case is *de rigueur* in cultural evolutionary and ecological studies. Reinterpretation of

On Steward's Models

the Steward model—or, more properly, a recognition that multiple models are really necessary—has obvious implications for such processual studies.

This is doubly true for anthropological research within the Great Basin, and the archaeological evidence illustrates the point. For the last couple of decades the Great Basin archaeologist has occupied a somewhat enviable position: the archaeological record seemed to reflect a relatively stable environmental and cultural adaptation, and Steward's synthesis provided the clues necessary to flesh out the sociocultural correlates. As Jennings (1957:8) put it, Steward's classic 1938 monograph is a "vivid contemporary description of the [prehistoric] Desert culture lifeway." And Jennings was correct—at the time.

But both the tenor and the tempo of research have shifted within the past few years. Emphasis is currently away from a theme of stability and conservatism, and toward an emphasis on regional variability and particularly on relative degrees of sociocultural complexity within the Great Basin.

This trend is well illustrated by two examples from my own archaeological field work. The Reese River Ecological Project was initiated in 1968 as an "empirical test" of Steward's model of Western Shoshone sociopolitical organization, particularly as it contrasted with Service's (1962) proposals. Steward's data for the Reese River Shoshone were computer modeled in the attempt to generate artifact-level archaeological expectations from the ethnographic settlement pattern: *If* this Western Shoshone group behaved as Steward suggested, *then* the artifacts should enter the archaeological record in *such and such* a density and distribution. These expectations were then tested by means of a large-scale regional random sample of the Reese River Valley, Nevada. We need not belabor the field work or the findings here (see Thomas 1972, 1973, 1974).

The upshot of the Reese River research is that Steward's model did seem to account for the observable prehistoric patterns, and the degree of correspondence was surprising (at least to me). At the time I concluded that a Western Shoshone-like pattern was quite consistent for the archaeological past, perhaps spanning the last 4,500 years (Thomas 1973:172–173). Additional work in the area has sharpened the chronological controls to such an extent that we should probably extend this estimate to about 7,000 years, *in this area*.

These findings were complemented by Bettinger's (1976, 1977) archaeological research in Owens Valley, California. Bettinger modified the Reese River methodology somewhat in order to examine Steward's model of Owens Valley Paiute settlement patterning and concluded that, although the Steward model seems to fit reasonably well for the later prehistoric period, certain discrepancies appear as one moves back in time in the Owens Valley. O'Connell (1971, 1975) also examined the relevance of Steward's model, this time for the Surprise Valley Paiute of northern California. Once again the Western Shoshone pattern corresponded reasonably well to the archaeological data, but the earlier periods seemed to reflect a somewhat more stable series of settlements (and perhaps a somewhat more complex mode of sociopolitical organization).

This is hardly a surprising conclusion, as archaeologists have long recognized the existence of alternative subsistence strategies within the prehistoric Great Basin (see Weide 1968 for a comprehensive discussion of this issue). But only within the past few years have archaeologists generated data of the quality necessary to attempt the systematic reconstruction of overall subsistence and settlement patterns (see Thomas 1979, chs. 8 and 9). It now seems clear that Steward's explanations work best for areas of the Great Basin that support only rather sparse and variable resources. The Steward model holds up rather well for the prehistoric Reese River area, which is located in ethnographic Western Shoshone territory. Steward's interpretation fares less well in the Surprise and Owens Valleys, both differing in some important respects from "typical" Western Shoshone habitat.

Even more serious problems arise when the resource base is more concentrated, as best exemplified near some of the large inland desert lakes and their tributaries. It is entirely possible that the relatively rich zones near Pyramid and Walker Lakes, for instance, could have supported a largely sedentary population throughout much of the year. While the family band probably still functioned as the primary social referent in such areas, the question does arise as to the importance of the suprafamilial organizations, which almost certainly increase in proportion to the overall degree of sedentism.

Steward's model may be singularly inappropriate for interpreting such adaptations, whether prehistoric or historic. We know that extensive systems of large inland lakes were present well after the arrival of man in the Great Basin, and remnants of these lakes survive within ethnographic Northern Paiute territory. It has been known for years that most Great Basin Paleo-Indian occupations tend to be associated with these now-extinct Pleistocene lakeshores. But finding a few large lakeside sites is, in itself, insufficient evidence for defining an overall settlement pattern and socioeconomic system. While it seems clear that the early settlement systems were indeed tethered to major inland water systems, almost no systematic archaeological research has been conducted on this issue. The on-going American Museum of Natural History work at Pleistocene Lake Tonopah is, however, suggestive in this regard (see Thomas 1979: ch. 9; Kelly 1978; Pendleton 1979). Despite nearly ten years of systematic regional sampling in the central Great Basin, we have been unable to locate an upland Paleo-Indian manifestation. Although scattered Paleo-Indian finds occur in the uplands, the artifacts never appear in any concentration, and never in systematic distribution. In other words we have been unable to find a non-lacustrine Paleo-Indian complement in the central Great Basin—and we have indeed been looking. (This is a major advantage of the systematic, randomized approach—we can say, with some degree of confidence, what archaeological remains did *not* occur in certain ecozones.) Based on a very different field strategy, Davis (1964) noted the similar lack of Paleo-Indian exploitation in the uplands throughout much of the southwestern area of the Great Basin.

At present we lack the seasonal counterbalance to the lacustrine/delta occupations during Paleo-Indian times. Perhaps this is sampling bias; perhaps significant upland components remain to be discovered. Or perhaps regional geomorphological processes are such that upland Paleo-Indian components have been eroded or buried, making their detection difficult (or impossible), even with a systematic regional approach. These certainly are possibilities.

But I think it is not unlikely that the Paleo-Indian pattern is significantly more sedentary than the better-known Western Shoshone settlement pattern. As I stressed earlier Steward's interpretation applies only to the Western Shoshone, not to great Basin Shoshoneans in general. This means that the hypothesized lacustrine adaptation—what Heizer (1967) once called limno-sedentism—is without a documented ethnographic counterpart; perhaps some of the ethnographic lakeside-adapted Northern Paiute groups had a similar settlement pattern; but at present, the data are simply lacking. Perhaps the high-altitude, quasi-lakeside orientation of the Washo may be relevant. Or maybe we will even have to turn to other areas, such as the prehistoric highlands of Mexico to see how such early lacustrine systems operated.

The problem of variability and diversity within Great Basin aboriginal societies can be approached from another angle. Fred Eggan (1980) recently presented a paper at the International Congress in Delhi in which he reanalyzed the kinship terms and marriage practices for Great Basin Shoshoneans. Eggan came up with what he called "unexpected results" and suggested that the simpler forms of kinship relate to the underlying environmental variables in the Great Basin in ways previously unrecognized. According to Eggan's interpretation Great Basin kinship systems functioned specifically to provide a network of relatives to pass on information concerning the availability of food—particularly grass seeds, piñon nuts, and game—plus the occurrence of fall festivals. In other words the kinship terminology in the sparser areas of the Great Basin maximized this information exchange. In more favorable environments, such as the Reese River Valley and the area immediately south of the Humboldt River, the need to disperse information on available food resources became relatively less important; the Western Shoshone of these areas developed a series of social institutions that increased local integration. Specifically, Eggan sees cross-cousin marriage, the sororate, and the levirate as continuing, but no longer obligatory, and the kinship terminology was modified accordingly. This situation was modified still further north of the Humboldt River, and those groups of Eastern Shoshone who ventured onto the Plains (to become the Comanche) gradually adjusted their Great Basin kinship and marriage practices to Plains-like models.

Eggan's analysis is not yet complete, and the next step will be to include the Mono-Paviotso sequences from the western Great Basin. This will be particularly interesting, since these sequences include the lakeside-adapted groups discussed earlier; in particular, I will be interested to see the degree of variation that exists within kinship terminology and marriage practices relative to the degree of environmental variability.

We seem to be left with a paradox. This paper began by emphasizing the heavy reliance of anthropological theory on the Shoshonean case. The Great Basin Shoshoneans have been used literally dozens of times to illustrate (and explicate) various schemes of cultural ecology and cultural evolution. But perhaps Steward's Shoshonean case has been forced to carry too large a burden. For the great Basin specialist, this means that we must be more cautious about accepting all of Steward's interpretations, particularly his later syntheses. The well-known Shoshonean model really applies only to the Western Shoshone, and the Western Shoshone are simply not "typical" of all Great Basin aboriginal peoples. While the anthropological world has often turned to the Shoshoneans as a prime example of classic egalitarian society, the existing Shoshonean model seems itself insufficient to explain the overall variability within the Great Basin.

Note

Acknowledgment. I wish to acknowledge with thanks the editorial assistance of Ms. Jane Epstein and Ms. Margo Dembo.

References Cited

Bettinger, Robert L.
 1976 The Development of Pinyon Exploitation in Central Eastern California. Journal of California Anthropology 3:81–95.
 1977 Aboriginal Human Ecology in Owens Valley: Prehistoric Change in the Great Basin. American Antiquity 42:3–17.
Davis, Emma Lou
 1964 The Desert Culture of the Western Great Basin: A Lifeway of Seasonal Transhumance. American Antiquity 29:202–212.
Eggan, Fred
 1980 Shoshoni Kinship Structures and Their Significance for Anthropological Theory. Journal of the Steward Anthropological Society 11:165–193.
Flannery, Kent V.
 1966 The Postglacial "Readaptation" as Viewed from Mesoamerica. American Antiquity 31:800–805.
Flannery, Kent V., and Joyce Marcus
 1976 Evolution of the Public Building in Formative Oaxaca. *In* Cultural Change

and Continuity: Essays in Honor of James Bennett Griffin, Charles E. Cleland, ed. pp. 205–221. New York: Academic Press.

Fowler, Catherine S.
  1977 Ethnography and Great Basin Prehistory. *In* Models and Great Basin Prehistory: A Symposium, Don D. Fowler, ed. pp. 11–48. Desert Research Institute Publications in the Social Sciences, No. 12.

Heizer, Robert F.
  1967 Analysis of Human Coprolites from a Dry Nevada Cave. University of California Archaeological Research Facility Report 70:1–20.

Jennings, Jesse D.
  1957 Danger Cave. University of Utah Anthropological Papers, No. 27.

Kelly, Isabel
  1934 Southern Paiute Bands. American Anthropologist 36:548–560.
  1964 Southern Paiute Ethnography. University of Utah Anthropological Papers, No. 69.

Kelly, Robert L.
  1978 Paleo-Indian Settlement Patterns at Pleistocene Lake Tonopah, Nevada. Senior thesis, Anthropology Department, Cornell University.

Lomax, Alan, and Conrad M. Arensberg
  1977 A Worldwide Evolutionary Classification of Cultures by Subsistence Systems. Current Anthropology 18:659–708.

MacNeish, Richard S.
  1964 Ancient Mesoamerican Civilization. Science 143:531–537.
  1972 Summary of the Cultural Sequence and Its Implications in the Tehuacán Valley. *In* The Prehistory of the Tehuacan Valley, Vol. 5, Richard S. MacNeish et al., eds. pp. 496–504. Austin: University of Texas Press.

Murphy, Robert F.
  1970 Basin Ethnography and Ecological Theory. *In* Languages and Cultures of Western North America, Earl H. Swanson, ed. pp. 152–171. Pocatello: Idaho State University Press.

O'Connell, James F.
  1971 The Archaeology and Cultural Ecology of Surprise Valley, Northeast California. Ph.D. dissertation, Anthropology Department, University of California, Berkeley.
  1975 The Prehistory of Surprise Valley. Ballena Press Anthropological Paper 4.

Park, Willard Z.
  1941 Culture Succession in the Great Basin. *In* Language, Culture and Personality: Essays in Memory of Edward Sapir, Leslie Spier, A. I. Hallowell, and Stanley S. Newman, eds. pp. 180–203. Menasha: Sapir Memorial Publication Fund.

Pendleton, Lorann S. A.
  1979 Lithic Tools as an Aspect of Regional Analysis at Pleistocene Lake Tonopah, Nevada. M.A. thesis, Anthropology Department, California State University, Long Beach.

Powell, John W., and G. W. Ingalls
  1874 Statement of Major J. W. Powell Made before the Committee on Indian Affairs as to the Condition of the Indian Tribes West of the Rocky Mountains. House of Representatives Miscellaneous Documents, No. 86, 43rd Congress, 1st Session, 1873, pp. 1–11.

Service, Elman
  1962 Primitive Social Organization. New York: Random House.
Steward, Julian H.
  1938 Basin-Plateau Aboriginal Sociopolitical Groups. Bureau of American Ethnology Bulletin 120.
  1955 Theory of Culture Change. Urbana: University of Illinois Press.
  1970 The Foundations of Basin-Plateau Shoshonean Society. *In* Languages and Cultures of Western North America, Earl H. Swanson, ed. pp. 113–151. Pocatello: Idaho State University Press.
Stewart, Omer C.
  1939 The Northern Paiute Bands. University of California Anthropological Records 2:127–149.
  1941 Culture Element Distributions; XIV: Northern Paiute. University of California Anthropological Records 4:361–446.
  1966 Tribal Distributions and Boundaries in the Great Basin. *In* The Current Status of Anthropological Research in the Great Basin: 1964, Warren L. d'Azevedo et al., eds. pp. 167–238. Desert Research Institute Social Sciences and Humanities Publications, No. 1.
Thomas, David Hurst
  1972 A Computer Simulation Model of Great Basin Shoshonean Subsistence and Settlement Patterns. *In* Models in Archaeology, David L. Clarke, ed. pp. 671–704. London: Methuen.
  1973 An Empirical Test for Steward's Model of Great Basin Settlement Patterns. American Antiquity 38:155–176.
  1974 Predicting the Past: An Introduction to Anthropological Archaeology. New York: Holt, Rinehart and Winston.
  1979 Archaeology. New York: Holt, Rinehart and Winston.
Weide, Margaret L.
  1968 Cultural Ecology of Lakeside Adaptation in the Western Great Basin. Ph.D. dissertation, Anthropology Department, University of California, Los Angeles.
Wilmsen, Edwin N.
  1970 Lithic Analysis and Cultural Inference: A Paleo-Indian Case. University of Arizona Anthropological Papers, No. 16.

II

6
Aboriginal Tlingit Sociopolitical Organization

Frederica de Laguna
Bryn Mawr College

This essay attempts to picture Tlingit social life and political development in the late 18th century, when these people were first encountered by Europeans, and in the early 19th century, during the florescence of native culture. It will also suggest how the Whites' expectations of what they would find and their misunderstandings of Tlingit culture were important factors of change. In describing Tlingit sociopolitical organization in the remote past I shall use the historical present, partly because many of the fundamental Tlingit attitudes and values that persist even today were derived from this past, and because a number of customs, to a greater or lesser extent, have been practiced in modern times.

Clan and Tribe

The Tlingit are not (and never were) a single political unit or tribe, but rather a nationality, united through conscious possession of a common language and culture and by the name, *łingí·t,* by which they call themselves.

The 18 to 20 local groups among the Southern, Northern, Gulf Coast, and Inland Tlingit[1] are not political units, either, though we may call them "tribes" for convenience. The Tlingit designate the people as -$q^wá·n$, "inhabitants of Such-and-such a place," like *Sitka-$q^wá·n$*. Their internal ties are only those of propinquity and frequent intercourse, with perhaps recognition of their own dialectical or cultural peculiarities, and fondness for their common country or town, *ʔa·n*.

The real unit of Tlingit society is the exogamous, matrilineal descent group, the clan, *na·*. It is the clan that owns the most important natural resources and wealth; the tribe owns nothing. And it is in the clan that political legal authority is vested, and in it personal loyalty, or "patriotism," is centered.

The "tribe" is only a local or geographical grouping, sometimes temporary, of several sovereign clans. Although there are perhaps some 60 to 70 clans scattered throughout Tlingit territory, the smallest tribes (Auk and Sumdum) are each composed of just two or three clans, and, correspondingly, many clans are restricted to a single tribe. Some of the most important clans, however, are represented in several tribes. Since such localized clan segments are more or less independent of each other, I have called them "sub-clans." The clan name usually refers to its supposed place of origin, such as *Ga·nax̲ʔádi*, literally "things (or beings) of *Ga·náx̲* (Security Bay)."

Houses

Each clan or sub-clan is likely to have several matrilineages or "houses" (*hít-ta·n*), although some very small "one-house" clans do (or did) exist, to create disagreement among ethnologists and among the Tlingit themselves as to their status and how they should be designated. Just as clans may grow and split, so a house may grow and bud off "daughter houses," too often because of internal dissension. It is through the establishment of a house in a new locality that the clan to which it belongs acquires a place in that tribe. Then begins the process whereby that branch in turn becomes a new clan.

The names of a number of clans refer to their origins as houses. Thus, the *Ka·gwa·nta·n*, an important clan among several Northern Tlingit tribes, traces its origin to the "burned down house" (*ka·waga·ni-hít*) in an 18th-century Hoonah village.

The house is the smallest unit in Tlingit society, possessing its own head or owner, *hít-śa·tí*, "master of the house," its own territories within or subordinate to larger plots owned by the clan as a whole, its own crests in addition to, or as variants of, the totemic crests of the clan, its own set of personal names, its own ceremonial prerogatives, and its own history. The name of the house refers to a crest, or to some distinctive feature of its location or construction, such as "Wolf House," "End of the (Beaver) Trail House," or "Fort House."

The master of the house is the maternal uncle or great uncle of the lineage (in principle or in fact); his subordinates are his younger brothers and the sons of his sisters. The women of the line, though married to husbands living in other houses (perhaps in other towns) are as much members of their "own" house line as their brothers, and usually as fiercely loyal to it. The women and children who live in the house belong to other houses and other clans.

Moieties

Tlingit society is based upon the fact that every Tlingit born into this world alive is—to paraphrase Sir William Schenck Gilbert—either a little Raven or a little Wolf, depending upon the affiliation of the mother, and his or her spouse must come from the opposite moiety or "side." These moieties, Ravens and Wolves, are not real social groups in themselves, for they never meet as a whole, own no property, have no moiety chief or leader, and have no function other than to arrange clans and their members into two groups of "opposites" (*gune·tkaná·yi*), that intermarry and perform services for each other.

There is one exception to this otherwise universal arrangement: the *Ne·x̣ʔádi* clan of the *Sanya-qʷá·n* call themselves neither Wolves nor Ravens, but Eagles, and marry into both the moieties, thereby creating situations that the other Tlingit find anomalous and confusing, and the *Ne·x̣ʔádi* themselves sometimes slightly embarassing. The *Ne·x̣ʔádi* are probably of foreign derivation, introduced through marriage with a Tsimshian Eagle woman.[2]

Like the members of one clan, the members of one moiety regard each other as brothers and sisters, observing the same deference avoidance shown between true brothers and sisters, except for those whose age obviously puts them in a grandparental or grandchild generation.

Marriage and the Family

Marriages linking houses and clans in opposite moieties are alliances between politically independent bodies. For chiefs and their heirs, and for their sons and daughters, marriages are planned with an eye to social, political, and economic advantage (just as were contemporary marriages among the crowned heads of Europe). Individual preferences are often set aside, as when a young girl is married to an old man for the sake of gaining for her house, as bride price, some valuable heirloom or when a young man has to marry his maternal uncle's old widow in order to inherit his title and position.[3] Successful alliances are not supposed to lapse; the sororate and levirate (extended to clan "brothers" and "sisters," if necessary) replace a deceased spouse, and men are as much subject to these obligatory unions as are women, unless they have enough wealth to buy their way out. Of both men and women it is said that they have married into the whole clan when they take a spouse: he is "husband of *Ka·gwa·nta·n*," or she, "wife of *Kiksʔádi*," for example.

Ideally, all the wives in one house are sisters, or "clan sisters," less likely to quarrel than unrelated women. Ideally, too, the two houses in opposite moieties are continually linked in marriage, to continue established ties. On the other hand, unions with several clans may well carry social and political advantages of creating friendly unions with several groups in different tribes.

All these are considerations to be weighed—for example, domestic tranquility against foreign ties—and one can say of sons-in-law, just as aptly as of that valuable commodity—women—that they are exchanged in marriage.

Marriages are between those who consider themselves to be cross-cousins (near or remote), and are therefore already "relatives" through descent from common ancestors: on the one side via the maternal line, on the other through the father.

The conjugal family and its branches, combining as it does representatives of both moieties, furnishes the basic pattern on which is built the social, political, and ceremonial life of the Tlingit. Each marriage unites through reciprocal affinal ties the members of two maternal lines, to each of which their chief stands as "uncle." The birth of offspring to his "sisters" provides junior members to his line; the children of his "brothers" are relatives in an opposed lineage. Thus the web of paternal and affinal bonds creates the fabric of Tlingit society, and *all* social intercourse is consciously conceived as between relatives of different categories, just as if they were members of an extended conjugal family. So strong is this notion that immigrant foreign Indian groups, no matter what their internal structure, are transformed by the Tlingit into clans like their own, trading partners are given a fictious kinship status, modeled on clan lines, and even the Whites are made kinsmen by the gift and exchange of personal names or wholesale "adoption." Kinship is extended even to the living animals represented as clan totems.

A sense of permanence to this system is given by the belief that every Tlingit is the reincarnation of the deceased maternal relative whose name he or she now bears. The house and clan are, therefore, not simply self-perpetuating through the birth of new members to replace those who have died, but, in theory, retain their original composition through the rebirth of the same individuals. Barring extinction through disaster or absorption by another clan, eventualities that have occurred, clans are immortal.

Rank

Tlingit society is graded, but lacks fixed classes. Those of the highest rank, the aristocrats, the chiefs and the wealthy, (*ʔa·nyádi, ʔa·nqá·wu*), have a status determined by birth, wealth (inherited and acquired), personal accomplishments, and character. Age adds to their prestige. There is no class of "commoners," for such people are the junior relatives of the chiefs, some of whom bear lesser inherited name-titles, or are noted as chief's speaker, song leader, war captain, dancer, artist, craftsman, or shaman. Such distinctions, except perhaps those of speaker and war leader, may belong to women as well as men; and some women seem to have been accomplished in both oratorical and warlike enterprises. A number are house chiefs. Lastly, there are the ne'er-dowells (*niška-yádi*), bastards or those abandoned by their relatives, and the so-called "dried-fish slaves," dependent upon the charity of others.

True slaves (*guˑxʷ*) are outside of Tlingit society. Slaves are Tlingit captives taken in war, or southern Indians (such as Kwakiutl, Nootka, or Salish) purchased from the Tsimshian and Haida, or the children of slaves. Though a slave may escape or be freed, it is a disgrace to marry such a person, and the taint of slave ancestry is remembered for generations.

Just as the occupants of the house are ranked from the master (*hít šaˑtí*) and his wife, who live in the place of honor at the rear, down to the lowly whose place is near the door, so the houses within the clan are ranked. The master of the leading house in the clan (or sub-clan) is a chief or "big man" (*ɬingít ⱡeˑn*). The heads of the other houses and the clan elders form his council. There is no village or tribal chief, although the head of the most prestigious clan in the community may appear to have such a position.

Clans are also graded within the moiety, within the local tribe, and between moieties and tribes, but on no exact scale. Some clans are said to be definitely "low class," like the foolish people who remained poor because they were afraid to trade with the Athabaskans. Other clans are very high, because of their wealth, their numbers, their many crests, their past victories in war, and the splendor of their recent potlatches. For example, it is said of the Raven *Ga̲ˑnaxteˑdí* and the Wolf *Ka̲ˑgwaˑntaˑn* of Klukwan that they are so high class they can use any crest they wish and that they cannot sleep nights for thinking of their greatness. (Since aristocrats are supposed to marry those of equal rank, these two clans are interlocked in a series of marriages with the result that the chief of the one is often the father, or son, of the other.)

Without formal grades, ranking is inexact and subject to dispute and re-evaluation. It is ultimately tested in the publicity of the potlatch, an occasion on which the chief of the host clan reaffirms his claims to inherited titles or other prerogatives, assumes new ones and bestows name-titles on junior members of his clan. All members of the host clan (subject to his approval) may give honorable names to their "clan-grandchildren," i.e., to members of another clan in their own moiety who are the grandchildren (son's children) of their clans*men*.

All this is witnessed, and thereby approved, by the two clans of the opposite moiety who come as guests. The relative status of the guests, too, is tested in the potlatch, for it is indicated by the size of the gifts they receive in payment for ceremonial services performed for their hosts, and for individual displays of dancing and singing, or prowess in gluttony. And there would be trouble if the host does not treat them and their chiefs as of equal rank.

Crests

The clan and its houses each own several crests. If two groups claim the same, this may be because they are closely related. Or, it may be considered an attempt on the part of one to usurp the exclusive rights of the other. Crests include celestial objects, natural features, mythical beings, and legendary heroes, but the most important are the totemic animals, including birds, fish, and other creatures. There is no notion of descent from these, and yet in some way the living members of the species are felt to belong to the same social and moral universe as the human members of the clan that owns the crest.

Crests are represented in concrete objects, such as houses, mortuary poles, canoes, hats, and other ceremonial garments. These objects have proper names referring to the crests (Eagle House, Killerwhale Canoe), and are decorated with crest designs. Inherited names and titles, especially of aristocrats, usually refer to crest animals; their faces are painted and, in addition, the women's hands are tattooed with totemic symbols. Crest-related prerogatives include the most sacred clan songs to mourn their dead and cries uttered when facing death.

The legendary history of house or clan justifies not only rights to certain territories, because the ancestors "discovered" them or were the first settlers, but also their claims to the crests, because the ancestors "discovered" the original entities. Such histories are themselves clan or house "copyrights," and crest designs may illustrate the story.[4]

Crest objects, including the garments and paraphernalia of the potlatch, are made for members of one clan by their "opposites," that is, by paternal or affinal relatives in the opposite moiety, who are handsomely rewarded when the objects are first displayed in the potlatch. Without such payment the beautiful things would have no value at all. And all Tlingit potlatches, directly or indirectly, honor the memory of the dead, who, like the living members of the line, are symbolically represented by their house and clan crests.

The most important potlatch is given when a new master of a house has it rebuilt or restored in memory of his deceased predecessor, whose title he now assumes. All the members of the host clan use this occasion to pay *their* funeral debts and/or to honor the memory of close relatives. Thus all the dead of the clan are remembered in the potlatch, and the house stands for them all as the supreme crest object.

To have the house built, the new head has called on all his chiefly "brothers-in-law," leaders in the opposite moiety, to pity and to help him, appealing in the name of their "grandfathers of old." During the previous funeral ceremonies for the deceased, the "opposites" have not only cared for the corpse but tried to assuage the grief of the bereaved by offering them, metaphorically, the comfort of their own crests.[5] All of these persons, of course, receive most at the potlatch for the new house.

What is important on these great occasions is not so much the affinal ties that may exist between hosts and guests, but the belief in their descent from common ancestors, including those in the host's line whose crests are now

Aboriginal Tlingit Sociopolitical Organization

displayed. Crests thus not only designate or define single lines but, through association with funeral and potlatch, can be made to express symbolically the close ties between lines in opposite moieties. This makes them effective instruments of social control in preventing and settling disputes.

Settling Trouble Cases

Quarrels may break out at potlatches, for at any major one there are always two groups of guests: one from the home village, the other from another tribe, representing two clans or two sub-clans, both in the same moiety. These pairings are traditional and the groups supposedly equal in rank. They are in theory "clan-grandparents" and "clan-grandchildren" to each other, and especially friendly on other occasions. But now they are jealous rivals who come "to dance against each other." For the potlatch is a warlike occasion (McClellan 1954), and involves much of the crest-related symbolism employed in a true feud or war and in the making of peace.

The foreign guests come like a war party, to be met and challenged on the beach in front of the host's house by the resident group of guests. But like two parties in a feud who have decided to make peace, they sing specially composed peace songs to each other, referring affectionately to each other's clan crests and to each other's "clan-children" (children of the men of the clan), thus appealing to the fathers' love for their children and to their pride of ancestry. Since the hosts are among the "children" of the guest clans, this also flatters them.[6] And during the potlatch each group is protected by their "clan brothers-in-law," men of some rank who are married to the women of the clan they are to represent and protect—the traditional neutral go-betweens.

Despite precautions, quarrels between guests sometimes break out. Then the host leader, or any man or woman of his clan, may step between the rivals, displaying some heirloom and uttering the cry of the hosts' totemic animal, and so prevent bloodshed. For this is an appeal to the revered ancestors of all present, symbolized by their crests and the objects they had once used.

Other disputes between clans are what we would call "legal cases," though the Tlingit call them "wars" and settle them as if they were such. This formal peace making is conducted almost exclusively between clans in opposite moieties, for intramoiety disputes are more apt to be "settled out of court." Although an habitual trouble-maker may be banished or even killed by his own clansmen, an injury or slaying within the clan cannot be settled by law. The only recourse is for one party to move away (cf. Oberg 1934; De Laguna 1952).

Quarrels over women (the unfaithful wife whose husband slays her lover) are traditionally cited as causes for the splitting up of a clan and the emigration of one faction. In cases of witchcraft practiced by a jealous clan member against a clan mate—the ultimate treason—a shaman from another clan is called in to detect the witch. No fellow clansman may defend the accused for fear of also becoming a victim of his or her evil spells.

Before a legal case can be settled or peace made after a war, there must be an evening up of the score by payments of blankets, slaves, or even human lives. The winners of the feud are the ones who must pay. Since the victims on both sides must be of equal rank, the killer is not necessarily the one to pay for his deed, but it should be someone from his house, if possible. Aristocratic women have volunteered themselves and been killed in such situations (Willard 1884:80–81), for all the members of a clan are responsible for the acts of any member. Those who are to die are usually designated by the injured clan, through go-betweens. They are expected to don their crest-decorated helmets and armor, and to go to their deaths, unarmed and fearless, singing their clan songs.

When a case is settled, each clan seizes one or more predetermined aristocratic hostages of equal rank from the other side, men being matched against men, and women against women. The hostages are given special names or peace titles referring to their captor's crests, and dance to songs especially composed for them, in which they are affectionately mentioned as children of their fathers' clan, which is certain to please. This is especially effective if the hostages are the "clan-children" of their captors.

If satisfactory compensation has not been paid, the injured clan may seize a crest of the offenders and use it as if it were their own until the debt is settled. This is equivalent to holding for ransom a noble war captive. the debtors *must* redeem their crest or their clan mate, or suffer eternal disgrace.

In all these solemn occasions, the crest is not only like the clan's "flag," arousing "patriotic" sentiments, but is used to evoke reverence for the dead, within and outside the clan, the love between father and child, and the religious or mystical sense of kinship with the totemic entity.

It is for all these reasons that the crest is so effective as a political device for unifying what might be a highly divided society.

Wars and Alliances

Wars, as we would distinguish them from feuds, are fights between clans in different tribes. Motives for warfare are to secure revenge and, secondarily, to obtain booty, especially slaves. Although wars may produce shifts in territorial ownership, they are not fought for territorial gain. Wars are more savage and much more difficult to settle than local, intratribal feuds, probably because there are few or only remote ties of relationship between the groups involved, so the crest symbolism of the peace ceremony is less effective.

Each clan decides independently upon matters of war and peace, and while indiscriminate killings might embroil all the clans of a tribe, yet each fights to avenge its own dead.[7] There are no *tribal* wars, as such. Sometimes several clans, in the same or opposite moieties, become allies in war, as when brothers-in-law, or a man and his father-in-law, leaders of their respective clans, fight side by side, supported by their fellow clansmen. But such alliances seem to be only temporary. (Even the major alliances, formed to destroy the Russian posts at Sitka [1802] and Yakutat [1805], and involving almost all the Tlingit tribal groups, did not include all their clans. Some Sitkans simply absented themselves from the fight, and remained friends of the Russians; victorious clans at Yakutat fought over the booty taken.[8] There were no long-term stakes to support a political union.)

Territorial Rights

The clan and house own territorial rights, which include rights to natural resources. The larger fishing streams, berrying or hunting grounds, beaches, firewood, and fresh water are owned by the whole clan, just as it might have the exclusive right to a "grease trail" into the interior and to trade with the Athabaskans (Olson 1936:211; Oberg 1973:106–107). Specific fishing places (small streams, or spots along a river) are owned by houses, the house chief acting as trustee for his group. Ownership often involves the right of the clan or of its chief to enjoy the first products of the season, frequently shared at a feast, and then to "open" the place to others.

In actuality, once the season is open, *any* person can hunt, fish, or pick berries at *any place*, provided he or she appeals to a member of the owning clan. Such a request acknowledges the rights of the owners, and they cannot refuse a "relative," whether that be a fellow clansman from a foreign town, a spouse, a "brother-in-law" or "sister-in-law," a "clan-child," or "clan-grandchild."

The Tlingit do not think in terms of whole tracts of land, or of ownership over whole territories, as we do, with the boundary of one area the boundary of the next, and no blank space in between. Rather, the country is conceived in terms of particular places, like landfalls or coves on a sailing chart. These specific spots are owned, but the terrain or waters between them are simply the relatively undifferentiated landscape through which one travels in going from one to the other, and are open to anyone, Tlingit or foreign, to "discover" and claim. In this way, the Kaigani Haida could settle on sites that the Tongass had deserted and the latter could move to Annette and Tongass islands, within what *we* would interpret as Sanya country, without the Tlingit regarding such movements as "invasions" (Olson 1967:70 and n.121).

Yet the early explorers of the 18th century got into trouble when they tried to help themselves to game, fish, or even to wood and water, in places that *they* considered to be wild, that is, "ownerless." But it is evident that these resources *were* owned, and the Tlingit wanted the Whites to acknowledge their rights and pay for what they took (see summary in De Laguna 1972:I:119).

The more limited the resources of house or clan, the more jealously they are guarded, it is said. Yet I have the impression that Tlingit country was aboriginally a land of plenty, with a relatively small population that did not press upon resources. This would permit both lavish hospitality and the existence of many unclaimed areas, as well as, perhaps, the lack of incentive to form organized political units to defend clan or tribal territories.

Chiefs

The Europeans and Americans who met the Tlingit in the 18th century expected to encounter organized tribes under "head chiefs." As sea captains and officials, they were used to dealing with the heads of hierarchical bodies. When they did not find the chiefs of their expectations, they created them, consciously or unwittingly.

The authority with which captains issued orders to their crews, the protocol and ceremony aboard naval vessels, and the deference shown to the officials of the Russian-American and Hudson's Bay companies, all offered models for the Tlingit aristocrats to emulate, even as they adopted uniforms with avidity.

Moreover, the Europeans and Americans *treated* the Tlingit "chiefs" as if they were really the autocrats they imagined them to be: Witness the honors paid by Ismailov and Bocharov to a Chilkat clan chief whom they met on a trading trip to Yakutat, and whom they assumed to be the "ruler" of the region (Coxe 1803:324–325, 330–332; De Laguna 1972:I:134–135). Or witness the futile attempts by the Russians to woo the Tlingit by creating a "head chief" of the Sitkans, or even of all the Kolosh (Khlebnikov 1861:41; Lisiansky 1814:I:231; Markoff 1862:52; Okum 1951:209–210). Our own naval authorities in the early years after the purchase of Alaska, also recognized "the Principal Chief," "the Second Chief," and so on, in various tribes, giving these individuals letters of recommendation.[9] Later, even when the limited powers of clan chiefs was beginning to be understood, the leading Raven and Wolf chiefs at Sitka were put in charge of two squads of uniformed police, made up of their respective clansmen (Beardslee 1882:43–50). This official position of "Policeman" in a way *created* chiefs.

I believe it was in the regions where Russian, British, and American influences were strongest that native chieftainship became most highly developed. So we find the great chiefs Yax̱odaqet at Yakutat, Chartrich at Klukwan and Donawak at Yandestaki, Shakes and Kadishan at Wrangell, as well as Katlyan and Annahoots at Sitka. But in aboriginal times, their predecessors had little power, and were primarily economic entrepreneurs and ceremonial leaders.

Women

In economic, political, and ceremonial matters, Tlingit women have more authority than is usually recognized,[10] perhaps even the final say. Within the household the principal wife of the house chief regulates all the domestic activity of the women, and is guardian of her husband's heirlooms. The whole Tlingit economy of subsistance and luxury wealth rests ultimately on the stores of dried salmon prepared by the women. The cutting and smoking of fish, in this wet climate, are tasks requiring far more skill and experience than catching the fish, though they are admittedly less interesting. Each housewife marks her salmon with her individual cuts, and owns her stores of preserved food, which she will bring out proudly to feed housemates and guests. Her husband shares in her shame if she cannot feast a distinguished visitor.[11] While no figures are available to compare the economic contributions of men and women in potlatching, we should note that, in addition to the female hosts who distribute property in their own names, the wives of the male hosts also contribute food, objects of their own manufacture, and wealth solicited from their brothers, as property to be distributed by the male hosts. Because a woman can demand handsome "gifts" from her brothers and clan "brothers," she plays a very important part in "underwriting" her husband's potlatch (Swanton 1908: 438; De Laguna 1972:I:495). Her brother is obliged to give her husband "anything he wanted . . . so that he would respect his wife." This relationship is exploited in dealings with the Eyak and Athabaskans, among whom the Tlingit traders take "wives." And the Tlingit wives, at home, do not object, being shrewd business women.

Since high rank is necessary for a chiefly position, a woman may become head of a house, in default of a male heir, or until the boy heir reaches his majority. But a wealthy woman may build a house and potlatch in her own right. Female shamans are reported to have as much power as the male.

Although inland trading expeditions are organized by men, usually chiefs, the Tlingit generally acknowledge the women to be the more skillful traders. And any transactions undertaken by men can be vetoed by the women. (See Beresford 1789:187–189; Wood 1882:333.)

As Vancouver (1801:IV:254–255) observed among the Stikine in 1793:

> In all the commercial transactions the women took a very principal part, and proved themselves by no means unequal to the task. Nor did it appear, that either in these or in any other respect they were inferior to the men; on the contrary, it should rather seem that they are looked up to as the superior sex, for they appeared in general to keep the men in awe, and under their subjection.

Douglas, trading with the Hoonah in 1788, reported how a business woman resorted to physical force to beat into submission a chief who interrupted her trading, while the Tlingit men present dared not interfere (Meares 1790:323-324).

Women even had their role in warfare in the 18th century, for an old woman of rank was the traditional helmsman of the large war canoe, a young male chief serving as leader in the bow (Vancouver 1801:IV:170-172, 177; V:435). Nevertheless most women were not warriors.

With this background, it is not surprising that the Tlingit women were not the lowly *squaws* or *klootchmen* expected by Americans in the 19th century (though the latter tended to treat them as such), or that the American ladies of that period found the behavior of Tlingit women to be unladylike, presumptuous, and at times unscrupulous (Scidmore 1885; Knapp and Childe 1896).

Conclusion

Weaknesses in the Tlingit sociopolitical structure are reflected in the strains of the conjugal unions upon which it is based and modeled, and show most clearly in the position of women. In time of war and feud, women are in an ambivalent position, torn between loyalty to their brothers' and their husbands' clans. Sometimes they may strive for peace, and, if bold-spoken, scold their relatives into abandoning a fight (Meares 1790:363-364). Or, they may incite their kinsmen to battle. In the Tlingit mind, women are notoriously troublesome, the causes of war, and in war untrustworthy, likely to betray their husbands for the sake of their brothers. A prudent husband may feel obliged to divorce a beloved wife and send her back to her own people in cases of trouble between their respective clans. Wars between clans in distant tribes are bloody. Male captives taken in such wars are likely to be killed on the spot, but women are more likely to dispatched by cruel, lingering torture,[12] something which suggests the tensions between the sexes in aboriginal Tlingit life.

Notes

1. The tribes are: *Southern Tlingit*: Tongass, Sanya, Stikine, Henya, Klawak, Kuyu, Kake; *Northern Tlingit*: Sumdum, Taku, Angoon, Auk, Sitka, Chilkat, Chilkoot, Hoonah; *Gulf Coast Tlingit*: Dry Bay, Yakutat, Controller Bay; *Inland Tlingit* (bands); Atlin, Teslin.

2. The anomalous position of the *Ne·x̣ʔádi*, outside of both moieties, led Boas (1916:478-487) to argue that a three-phratry, rather than a dual moiety system, may have been the original ancient type among all the peoples of the Northwest with matrilineal clans. The presence of the *Ne·x̣ʔádi* among the Sanya, with their Eagle, Halibut, Giant Clam, and Beaver crests, should rather suggest one mechanism by means of which some foreign clans and crests were adopted by the Tlingit, just as some Tsim-

Aboriginal Tlingit Sociopolitical Organization

shian traditions suggest similar increments from the Tlingit (Boas 1916:270-272). I have argued that an exogamous matrilineal system with a strong tendency to moiety organization was ancient in the Northwest (De Laguna 1975).

3. For example, a Yakutat girl was given in marriage to recover the Killerwhale Drum (De Laguna 1972:I:458-459, 489-492); Chief Donawak of Yandestaki (Chilkoot) had to marry the niece of his deceased wife, and young Shotridge had to marry his uncle's aged widow to inherit the latter's house at Klukwan (Willard 1884:98-101, 138-139, 368; Olson 1967:20-22).

4. For example, the Ahrnklin River Blanket, a crest heirloom, symbolizes not only the claims of the Yakutat Drum House Te·q^{w}e·dí to the Wolf as a crest, but also serves as the deed to their hunting lands on the Ahrnklin River (De Laguna 1972:I:252-253; III:pl. 151).

5. Swanton (1909:372-389) gives examples of funeral and potlatch oratory.

6. As an example, see the potlatch peace song about Kardeetoo, by Dry Bay Chief George, 1954, 1-1-B (De Laguna 1972:III:1244-1245, 1248-1249).

7. When the Stikine made war on the Henya, the Wolf clans of the one fought the Raven clans of the other, "so that clan and moiety brothers would not be fighting each other." Afterwards, the Henya Ravens cared for the bodies of the Stikine Wolves, and the Henya Wolves did the same for the Stikine Ravens, showing that this intertribal war was really fought on a clan basis (Olson 1967:107-108).

8. The evidence is summarized in De Laguna (1972:I:170-173).

9. Some testimonials treasured by the illiterate Indians were not, however, flattering. For examples of naval letters, see "Letters and Certificates given to Indians at the Head of Lynn Canal," Proceedings of the Alaska Boundary Tribunal, Vol. 4, pt. 3:288-290, 1903.

10. This is perhaps because most accounts of the Tlingit, even by anthropologists, have been written by men, from information given by male informants. Conscious and unconscious sex biases seem to have rubbed off on some Tlingit men. Is this why we have no adequate account of preserving fish?

11. See the story of such a situation in which a slave woman was able to produce the necessary food and was, in consequence, freed and ultimately married by her master, after he had "washed away her slavery" by distributions of wealth (Olson 1967:31).

12. See the war story recorded by Swanton (1909, Tale 29:72-79).

References Cited

Beardslee, L. A.
    1882   Reports . . . Relative to Affairs in Alaska. 47th Congress, 1st Session, Senate Exec. Document No. 71, in Vol. 4.

Beresford, William
    1789   A Series of Letters by "W. B." [George Dixon, ed. A Voyage Round the World.] 2nd ed. London: Geo. Goulding.

Boas, Franz
    1916   Tsimshian Mythology. *In* 31st Annual Report of the Bureau of American Ethnology for the Years 1909-1910, pp. 29-1037.

Coxe, William
   1803   Account of the Russian Discoveries between Asia and America. 4th ed. London: Cadell and Davies.

De Laguna, Frederica
   1952   Some Dynamic Forces in Tlingit Society. Southwestern Journal of Anthropology 8:1–12.
   1972   Under Mount Saint Elias: The History and Culture of the Yakutat Tlingit. Smithsonian Contributions to Anthropology, Vol. 7. 3 pts.
   1975   Matrilineal Kin Groups in Northwestern North America. *In* Proceedings: Northern Athapaskan Conference, 1971, A. McFadyen Clark, ed., Vol. 1, pp. 17–147. Mercury Series, Ethnology Service Paper 27. Ottawa: National Museum of Man.

Khlebnikov, Kyril Timofeëvich
   1861   First Settlement of the Russians in America. *In* Materials for the History of the Russian Settlements of the Shores of the Pacific Ocean. Supplement to Morskoi Sbornik 4(1):40–56. [Reprinted from an article in Raduga (The Rainbow), a periodical published in Revel, 1833.] Manuscript translation by Ivan Petroff in Bancroft Library, University of California, Berkeley.

Knapp, Frances, and Rheta Louis Childe
   1896   The Thlinkets of Southeastern Alaska. Chicago: Stone and Kimball.

Lisiansky, Urey
   1814   A Voyage Round the World in the Years 1803, 4, 5, and 6. London: John Booth.

McClellan, Catharine
   1954   The Interrelations of Social Structure with Northern Tlingit Ceremonialism. Southwestern Journal of Anthropology 1:75–96.

Markoff, Alexander
   1856   The Russians in the Eastern Ocean. 2nd ed. St. Petersburg. Manuscript translation by Ivan Petroff in Bancroft Library, University of California, Berkeley.

Meares, John
   1790   Voyages Made in the Years 1788 and 1798, from China to the North West Coast of America. London: Logographic Press.

Oberg, Kalervo
   1934   Crime and Punishment in Tlingit Society. American Anthropologist 36:145–156.
   1973   The Social Economy of the Tlingit Indians. Seattle: University of Washington Press.

Okun, S. B.
   1951   The Russian-American Company. B. D. Grekov, ed. Carl Ginsberg, trans. Cambridge: Harvard University Press.

Olson, Ronald L.
   1936   Some Trading Customs of the Chilkat Tlingits. *In* Essays in Anthropology Presented to A. L. Kroeber, Robert H. Lowie, ed. pp. 211–214. Berkeley: University of California Press.
   1967   Social Structure and Social Life of the Tlingit in Alaska. University of California Anthropological Records 26.

Scidmore, Eliza R.
    1885   Alaska: Its Southern Coast and the Sitkan Archipelago. Boston: D. Lothrop.

Swanton, John R.
    1908   Social Conditions, Beliefs, and Linguistic Relationships of the Tlingit Indians. *In* 26th Annual Report of the Bureau of American Ethnology for the Years 1904–1905, pp. 391–485.
    1909   Tlingit Myths and Texts. Bureau of American Ethnology Bulletin 39.

Vancouver, George
    1801   A Voyage of Discovery to the North Pacific Ocean and Round the World . . . Performed in the Years 1790, 1791, 1792, 1793, 1794, and 1795. New edition with corrections. 6 vols. London: John Stockdale.

Willard, Caroline McCoy White
    1884   Life in Alaska: Letters of Mrs. Eugene S. Willard. Eva McClintock, ed. Philadelphia: Presbyterian Board of Publication.

Wood, C. E. S.
    1882   Among the Thlinkets in Alaska. Century Magazine 5(4):323–339.

7
Ecology and Political Organization on the Northwest Coast of America

Philip Drucker

If one considers the ethnographic literature on Northwest Coast cultures in terms of volume—number of pages or feet of shelf space beginning with the massive Boas and Hunt compilations of Southern Kwakiutl data—or in terms of minuteness of detail described—Hunt's step-by-step description of Southern Kwakiutl canoe making and cuisine, or other ethnographers' voluminous descriptions—it seems most remarkable that a major domain of culture should have been sketchily reported and inadequately discussed. This unfortunately is a fact. The domain so slighted is that of political structure and function.

Older generations of Northwest Coast ethnographers, myself included, rather casually reported complex political structures for certain groups of the area: something we called the "tribe" consisting of two or more local groups said to have been organized into a fairly stable entity. I even proposed the political designation "confederacy" as a label for certain seasonal population groupings of pre-contact origin among the Northern Nootkans and similar units created in response to establishment of Hudson's Bay Company posts at Fort Rupert and Fort Simpson among some Southern Kwakiutl and Coast Tsimshian (Drucker 1951, 1965). The effect of general acquiescence to use of the terms "tribe" and "confederacy" was to characterize the Northwest Coast as an area of complex political systems. This did not seem especially remarkable in an areal culture distinguished by elaborately developed technologies, intricate and varied social structures, complicated ceremonial patterns, and sophisticated art.

But when I looked for ecological factors affecting Northwest Coast polity for this American Ethnological Society symposium, it became clear how skimpily and unsystematically the political culture of the area has been treated. What discussion exists in the literature consists of attempts to define the authority-base of "chiefs" in "tribal" systems. In ethnohistoric and ethnographic accounts authoritarian Northwest Coast chiefs are often mentioned, but the source of their power in "tribal" structure is invariably vague. Obviously to identify significant ecological factors it was essential to follow the ancient recipe and "first catch the rabbit," in this case, first define Northwest Coast basic political structure.

As I reviewed source materials I recalled that, a quarter century or so ago, two elderly Southern Kwakiutl friends, Mr. Nowell and Mr. Whonnuck, explained to me that their "tribes" and the Fort Rupert "confederacy" were not political institutions at all (Drucker and Heizer 1967). The informants were not quibbling over the definitions in political anthropology. Rather, they were explaining their people's concepts of rights and duties of chiefs. They stressed that their chiefs claimed no interest in conflict resolution on the "tribal" and "confederacy" level: there, chiefs' concern was not with political control but only with certain social affairs—marriages and associated transfer of "privileges"—and with ceremonials—potlatches and the Winter Dances. Chiefs intervened in conflict and other political situations only when they perceived potential threat to orderly procedures of the ceremonial institutions. Chiefs' only concern with non-socioceremonial affairs, that is, truly political matters, related to those of the local group nàmīmà, Boas' "numaym"), and during the informants' lifetimes, these were of diminished importance.

This explanation of chiefs' functions as seen by chiefs themselves makes clear that Southern Kwakiutl aggregations called "tribes" and the historic "confederacy" were socioceremonial entities, leaving the local group as the *only* political unit. Southern Kwakiutl polity actually consisted of a large number of independent and politically equivalent local groups, which, however, were linked by socioceremonial criteria into twenty or so internally ranked sets (the "tribes" of the older literature). The four sets who moved into the Fort Rupert trading post locality (the kwagyuɬ, qomoyue ("kwɛxa"), walas kwagyuɬ, and q!omkutis) formed themselves into the socioceremonial superset I miscalled the Fort Rupert "confederacy."

To identify areal patterns of political organization, the Nowell-Whonnuck interpretation of Southern Kwakiutl polity was converted into an area-wide hypothesis for testing:

> The basic and only political unit in native Northwest Coast culture was the local group.

To test this hypothesis a series of criteria that could be evaluated on a present-absent basis were used, taken from the characteristics of the model: the Southern Kwakiutl local group. They are as follows (see Drucker and Heizer 1967):

1. The local group was considered to be the kinship unit, descended from a mythical ancestor. (It is to be expected that the native concept of kinship was more rigidly defined among unilinear descent groups—Tlingit, Haida, Tsimshian, Xaisla—than in the ramage-like units of Nootkans, Southern Kwakiutl, Bella Bella, Bella Coola, and Xaihais.)
2. Ownership of economic resource sites was vested in local group.
3. Ownership of house sites was vested in local group.
4. Ownership of socioceremonial "privileges" was vested in local group. (These "privileges" or rights included names, "crests," dances, songs, whole ceremonials, traditions, and relative statuses. While as indicated there were larger, more complex socioceremonial units, each local group had its own stock of these incorporeal possessions and their material manifestations.)
5. Each local group had a permanently ranked set of statuses (whose occupants are usually referred to as "chiefs" and "nobles" in the literature). (The ranking within each set was immutable in theory and almost so in practice, and the status of highest rank in each set was traditionally supposed to be occupied by the most direct descendant—patrilineally among patrilineally and bilaterally reckoning groups, and matrilineally among the northern-most groups—of the mythical original ancestor.)
6. Each local group was autonomous in decisions on war and peace. (This is a powerful indicator of political autonomy, although the Southern Kwakiutl model provides fewer traditional data than the linguistically related, culturally similar Nootkan-speaking neighbors [Drucker 1951]. While alliances often were made between local groups for offense or for defense, they were always voluntarily entered into. No one group could compel its socially and ceremonially linked neighbor groups to participate in military actions. There were of course informal covert pressures that could be exerted, but overtly, participation was voluntary, indicating the seat of political authority.)

A trait distribution list using the foregoing items and all Northwest Coast adequately described divisions shows that consistently the local group had all or most of the characteristics of the model. Apparent variation in the pattern can be accounted for. Permanently ranked statuses were found only in the northern and central provinces, where the concept of ascribed status was more elaborate and rigid. A problem is created by the Coast Salish "low class villages," reported often but never explained. Some ethnographers suggest these may have been junior subdivisions that, on fission, received rights to marginal resource areas only (e.g., Collins 1974). They became impoverished, unable to give feasts and potlatches to validate such statuses as they had. But nowhere are we given facts on composition or properties real and incorporeal of such

Ecology and Political Organization · 89

units, or any other specifics. They may, for all our information on them reveals, have been historic period artifacts of White encroachment on Indian lands.

Another point that must be noted is that in northwest California and probably most of the Oregon coast the local groups were small extended families. For ecological reasons, villages often consisted of several nonetheless autonomous units.

Accepting this conclusion that the Northwest Coast local group, the areal version of the widespread western North American Indian band, was the universal political unit in the area, we can turn to the basic problem of this paper: what area-wide factors contributed to its functioning and its stability? One obvious set of factors was the time/space distribution of resources. The seasonality of the five species of salmon, of olachon, and of herring is well known. Berries, the principal vegetable food of the northern and central provinces, are seasonal resources, as are camas and acorns to the south. Among other resources of localized importance, halibut move seasonally from deeps out of reach of native tackle to moderate depths where they can be fished. Even whales, particularly the humpback and California grays, are now believed to be regularly migratory, moving northward in early summer and south to tropical waters in fall, a fact of importance not only to the few whale-hunting groups but to all who utilized blubber of whales that died and washed ashore. Even shellfish have a certain if differing periodicity, since preferred species could be collected in abundance a few days only of each lunar cycle, the days preceding and following new and full moons.

Of great importance was the spatial distribution of resources. Major resources were not distributed evenly through the water or on land. They were "clumped," that is, spottily distributed. Shellfish beds provide an excellent example of the concept of "clumping." Since most mollusks have fairly precise requirements for type of bottom, minimal depth of water, water temperature range, etc., and require current patterns that bring rather than sweep away suitable foods, shellfish beds range in extent from small to sometimes very large, and may be distant from beds of the same species. Thus whatever the rate of use of a species of shellfish, a bed or set of beds could support only a certain size group of users. In other words there were definite limits or definite maximum carrying capacities for each resource site. Salmon streams had specific limits in terms of number of species, size of cohorts entering, duration of the runs, etc., all of which variables were correlated with volume of water and length of stream bed with variation of optima according to species of salmon. In other words, accepting the assumptions that the major resources *were* abundant in season and that Northwest Coast Indians exploited them fairly efficiently with their ingenious and complex technologies, the Indians were still subject to carrying capacity constraints. Population units larger than the local groups apparently would exceed such limits and be forced to disperse frequently to exploit distant resource sites, thus disrupting any unity they might have.

On the other hand, a combination of environmental and technologic factors must have defined lower limits of efficient group size. Many fishing devices—tidal traps of stones, or the Nootkan long-winged tidal traps of lattice-work, weirs out into or across turbulent streams, the ingenious Salish reef nets, the logs festooned with hemlock boughs for herring ovipositing—all involved manipulation of large heavy component parts or of large numbers of elements. Many muscular hands and strong backs were needed to procure, transport, and install the components of many kinds of important subsistence devices. The same pattern of need for and effective utilization of large work parties recruited from the local group occurred in other cultural domains: house construction, moving of logs for memorial poles, canoe hulls, etc. Even in the early decades of this century it was difficult to get accurate figures on the size of these work parties since drastic population decline and enforced culture change had altered or eliminated many such activities. Olson (1967) cites a statement that "about 30 men" in one winter could cut and hew all the timber needed to construct a "clan house" at Kluckwan. This figure is, of course, an educated guess by a knowledgeable informant, not a precise statistic. Nevertheless, it suggests local group-derived work parties of 20 to 40 able-bodied men as reasonable sized units for accomplishing major tasks. This would suggest a minimum population size of 80 persons for the typical local group, with maximal effective size probably ranging up to nearly 200 (Weiss 1973:app. C). Such a unit, holding rights to resource sites such as summer and fall salmon streams, herring or olachon grounds, bottom-fishing banks, berry-picking and root-digging tracts, rocky islets where pinnipeds congregated, and some land game areas, was economically autonomous, an essential aspect of its political autonomy.

Let us turn back briefly to the pattern of large working parties organized to handle heavy materials for various purposes. Such tasks are best carried out under centralized direction by knowledgeable planners. It seems most reasonable that managerial roles were developed to handle these operations just as they were for food quest rituals (First Salmon rites, etc.). Filled at first by assignment on the basis of knowledge and leadership ability, these roles may easily have come to be ascribed, using primogeniture as the mechanism for hereditary transmission. It is not possible to determine whether interest in relative age, reflected in older-younger sibling terminology from Tlingit to Coast Salish (except for Tsimshian-speakers), contributed to the primogeniture pattern or if the inheritance pattern affected the kinship terms. In any case, development and eventual ascription of such managerial roles is proposed as the basic contributory process to the system of differentiated hereditary social statuses. This interpretation therefore makes the Northwest Coast concept of differentiated ascribed social statuses a second-step adaptation to ecological factors. The whole process of direction of group labor and conduct of rituals by the chief resulted in redistribution of a catch much larger than could have been obtained by unorganized efforts of individuals.

The settlement unit next larger than the local group among many Northwest Coast groups was the winter village aggregation of two or more local groups, the unit that earlier ethnographers miscalled a "tribe." These were real seasonal settlement units, not hypothetical organizations. The term "tribe," properly used, designates a political entity, and the winter village aggregations were *not* political entities. The aggregated winter village groups were ordered into socioceremonial hierarchies in which no political authority was vested. The ranking chief of the highest-ranking local group could not *order* the chief or chiefs of lower-ranked units of his winter village aggregate to fish or not to fish, to build or tear down a house, to make war or peace. For example, when the Sitka Kiksadi chiefs sought the participation of the other Sitka local matrilineage segments in a proposed massacre of American and Creole residents of Sitka in 1878 (in revenge for the hanging of Kiksadi by a U.S. court in Oregon), they regaled their fellow groups with "hoochenoo" feasts and inflammatory speeches, *inviting* their cooperation (United States Congress 1879). And a U.S. naval commander of Alaska wrote a spirited account of a shootout that assumed battle proportions between the Kagwantan and Ganaxtedi of the winter village Kluckwan (U.S. Congress 1882).

In native theory these socioceremonial, non-political winter village aggregations also were adaptive institutions. Informants of many groups used to insist that during the stormy winter season, when there were no major food sources available, access to resource localities was of course of no concern. Hence, they said, the ideal winter site was wherever there was enough soil/sand/gravel/midden to dig holes for houseposts, with shelter from storms, especially from surf, with a beach for launching canoes at any stage of tide. Such sites, they often added, are not abundant on some stretches of the coast; hence several local groups normally came to winter at the most favorable locality. Desire to participate in the exciting winter ceremonials was another oft-reported reason. It was, perhaps, as likely a result as a cause.

Some Northwest Coast divisions reportedly did not have winter village aggregations in pre-contact times. These include the Haida, Southern Heiltsuk, Bella Coola, Central Nootkans and Makah, some Coast Salish, and some southwest Oregon—northwest Californians. It should be possible to check the native interpretation of such settlements as adaptations to stormy winter seasons typical of the Northwest Coast by considering the varied environmental settings of these divisions.

Swanton (1905) was unequivocal in stating that prior to the heavy population loss of the historic period, the males of each Haida town were members of a single matrilineage, the Haida version of the local group. The multigroup villages of Swanton's ethnographic horizon, about 1850–60 (Blackman n.d.)

he believed a product of the severe population decline: survivors of decimated groups abandoned their villages to move in with others. From various descriptions of the Queen Charlotte Islands, including O'Reilly's description of the Haida reserves he set off in 1882 (quoted by Van den Brink 1974), it seems clear that on the east and north coasts of Graham Island there was little difference to be found in habitation sites, except in Masset Inlet, Naden Harbor, and Yaku on North Island. John Work (quoted by Blackman n.d.) reported large numbers of Indians at the equally exposed sites of Masset-Yan-Kayang in the late 1830's, but these assemblages were probably already historic accretions. Skidegate Inlet and the east coast of Moresby Island seem to have had, with their broken coastlines, a fair number of favorable sites with villages at Skidegate and the site on Maud Island settled by West Coast Haida and, farther south, Cumshewa, Skedans, and Tanu. The storm-lashed west coast from Parry Passage south to Ninstints appears on the map to have many sheltered bays and coves, but appearances are probably deceptive. In short, on much of Graham Island one site was little better than another; in Blackman's "Central Haida" region good sites seem abundant, while on the west coast really adequate sites must have been few. Add to this generally low site-differential incentive for the assembly of multilocal groups the smaller runs and scattered distribution of salmon streams on the Queen Charlottes, the related greater emphasis on salt water fishery, sea mammal hunting, mollusk collecting, etc., activities that kept the Haida ranging widely much of the year, and we would seem to have adequate explanations for absence of the multigroup winter village. That this socioceremonial institution was really lacking is borne out by lack of interranking of the matrilineages. An institution of "town chief," the ranking chief of the matrilineage originally owning the site of historic period multigroup communities, had developed by Swanton's time.

Lack of Southern Heiltsuk winter village aggregations can be attributed to the relative abundance of sheltered sites along the "Inside Passage" (see also Hester and Nelson 1978 and Simonsen 1973) and the divisive effect of many scattered small salmon streams in their habitat.

McIlwraith (1948) is firm in his insistence that each Bella Coola descent line/local group was independent not only economically and politically but socioceremonially. The large multigroup villages of the historic period, Kimskwit and Talio, were, he believed, completely historic developments; he found no evidence of intergroup ranking systems characteristic of the multilocal group winter village aggregations. To be sure, Bella Coola culture had suffered considerable change, even breakdown, under acculturational pressures coupled with demographic decline, but concepts of integrated relative statuses ordering winter villages aggregations survived similar impact among Southern Kwakiutl and Northern Nootka.

While for Bella Coola of the river the principle invoked for Graham Island Haida that one winter site was not much better or worse than any other would hold, this principle probably did not hold for groups on the inlets, South Bentinck Arm and Dean Channel. Nor does resource distribution resemble that of Haida and Southern Heiltsuk. The Bella Coola River is a large stream with major runs of all species of salmon as well as olachon, and the rivers at the heads of the inlets were well supplied, so that several local groups could have shared fishing rights on them. Some additional unidentified variable must have affected Bella Coola settlement patterns.

The Central Nootkan cases of lack of multiunit winter villages seem explicable in terms of the environmental factors previously discussed. There were numerous favorable winter village sites available in the region (in the case of Hesquiat Harbor all were equally bad; there was no protected site at all). Thus there were no recognizable environmental incentives for multigroup settlement.

Among Coast Salish the interplay of ecologic factors on this settlement pattern seems clear. The saltwater Salish units, more populous, with diversified possible habitation sites, some more and some less favorable for winter residence, and ample resource bases, had multilocal group winter villages; the smaller, less favorably situated upriver divisions, like the Upper Skagit, did not (Barnett 1955, Elmendorf 1974, Collins 1974).

The situation in southwestern Oregon–northwestern California differed. Coastal sites were few; the important villages were on the rivers, situated with reference to favorable salmon fishing places (Kroeber 1925). Environmental factors making some localities suitable for building weirs or setting gill nets consisted of special combinations of depth of water, current speed, type of bottom. Such places were infrequent. The number of small extended families/local groups at such places depended on possible catch at the resource site. These villages were occupied most of the year, not just in winter, because the salmon runs were of longer duration than to the north (Schalk 1977). One-family villages were situated at less favored localities.

It seems probable that the system of differentiated ascribed statuses achieved its final complexity and refinement in the northern and central provinces with the emergence of the multilocal group winter village. We have some models, based on traditional history–informant reconstruction, of how this might have been accomplished in the inter-winter village aggregate socioceremonial consolidations of the Southern Kwakiutl "festival units" (Drucker and Heizer 1967). The felt need of the Kwakiutl to order the newly combined groups for formal feasts and for potlatches must have motivated development and acceptance of more precise criteria for reckoning of relative statuses as well as proliferation of status symbols, the "privileges," and procedures for transferring them through inheritance and marriage. Those groups lacking multigroup winter villages, such as the Haida and Southern Heiltsuk, acquired the more elaborate concepts from their neighbors, for of course diffusion processes were involved also. In saying that ecological factors, such as food-getting technologies with large manpower requirements, correlate with or were favorable to the development of hereditary status, I do not mean that similar status systems burst into being independently and simultaneously in every ancestral local group in the northern and central provinces. What I do mean is that, given highly similar ecological situations in terms of natural environment and culture, and adaptation achieved in any one of the groups, being compatible with the common environment, could diffuse quite easily and rapidly to similar neighboring groups. Since the newly emerged concept, or novel "configuration," represented a solution to tensions created by preexisting configurations, its dysfunctional index should have been low, and its acceptability high. Only in this way is it possible to account for the basic uniformity of the differentiated status concept throughout the area: primogeniture as the device for hereditary transmission of status; chief as administrator of local group economic rights; chief as administrator of local group ceremonial rights; chiefly statuses in each local group arranged in fixed series from first down to N, shading into "commoner" statuses of group. Somewhat later a major change in association of hereditary status with the potlatch occurred: in the northern groups (Tlingit, Haida, Tsimshian, Xaisla), where transmission of hereditary status became linked to mortuary and memorial rites, and in the central (and to some extent in the Coast Salish–Chinook province), where formal assumption of status occurred at the heir's majority —for example, when a young Southern Kwakiutl heir-apparent gave a potlatch utilizing privileges transferred in "repayment" of his wife's "bride-price." In other words, there was a single fundamental concept of differential status on the northern Northwest Coast, and two internally consistent patterns for formal assumption of such status integrally linked to two different occasions for major potlatching.

Aggregations of groups larger than those of the multilocal group winter villages were found among the Northern Nootka, and the clustering of nine Tsimshian winter village groups of the islets along Metlakatla Passage. While different in nature, the two systems also had interesting similarities. The Nootkan assemblages created a new seasonal settlement pattern in which all or almost all the local groups of a sound or of a linked set of waterways had houses for the summer season at a single site and were thus given access to summer resources: halibut fishing and sea mammal (whale, seal, and sea otter) hunting, plus access to certain mollusk beds. The Tsimshian assemblage consisted of nine winter village aggregates situated on adjacent islets; the purpose reputedly was to enjoy the milder winters of Metlakatla Pass, milder that is compared to sites near the mouth of the Skeena River. In each of the two arrangements each local group retained its identity by having its house or houses and its political and economic autonomy. The winter village aggregates with their internal socioceremonial precedence order were themselves ordered into an all-inclusive precedence sequence in the historic period among the Tsimshian. The four Southern Kwakiutl winter village aggregations who formed a single settlement at the Fort Rupert trading post similarly worked out a precedence protocol. Actually, the Southern Kwakiutl had the beginnings of another system of ceremonial relationships that did not create new settlement patterns but that developed in the recent burgeoning of their potlatch into a pan-Southern Kwakiutl festival unit (Drucker and Heizer 1967).

In other words, there were various large aggregations of local groups among some Northwest Coast divisions. They existed. But they were not political organizations. No authority base resided in such a grouping. The chief of one local group might, if he could, persuade his fellow chiefs to join him in a military adventure. He could not order them to do so, no matter what his relative ceremonial status, just as the ranking chief of a winter village aggregate had socioceremonial status and authority in those domains but not in political ones.

It seems worth stressing that functions other than the purely political could link small sociopolitical units into formal large structures. Political acts of these large units, especially acts of aggression or of defense, occasionally occurred through special arrangements of agreement, but were not normal functions. The distinction between true political units and the larger ceremonial organizations is highly significant to an understanding of Northwest Coast political organization.

Note

Philip Drucker died while this volume was in press and did not have the opportunity to read either the final copy-edited version of his paper or proof.

References Cited

Barnett, Homer G.
  1955   The Coast Salish of British Columbia. Eugene: University of Oregon Press.
Blackman, Margaret B.
    n.d.   Haida Ethnography and Culture History. *In* Handbook of North American Indians. Vol. 7: Northwest Coast. Washington: Smithsonian Institution. In press.
Collins, June McCormick
  1974   Valley of the Spirits. Seattle: University of Washington Press.
Drucker, Philip
  1951   The Northern and Central Nooktan Tribes. Bureau of American Ethnology Bulletin 144.
  1965   Cultures of the North Pacific Coast. San Francisco: Chandler Publishing.

Drucker, Philip, and Robert F. Heizer
  1967 To Make My Name Good: A Reexamination of the Southern Kwakiutl Potlatch. Berkeley: University of California Press.
Elmendorf, William W.
  1974 Structure of Twana Culture. New York: Garland American Indian Ethnohistory Series. (Reprint of Washington State University Research Studies, No. 2.)
Hester, James J., and Sarah M. Nelson, eds.
  1978 Studies in Bella Bella Prehistory. Simon Fraser University, Department of Archaeology Publication 5.
Kroeber, A. L.
  1925 Handbook of Indians of California. Bureau of American Ethnology Bulletin 78.
McIlwraith, T. C.
  1948 The Bella Coola Indians. 2 vols. Toronto: University of Toronto Press.
Olson, Ronald L.
  1967 Social Structure and Social Life of the Tlingit in Alaska. University of California Anthropological Records 26:1–123.
Schalk, Randall
  1977 The Structure of an Anadromous Fish Resource. *In* For Theory Building in Archaeology, Lewis R. Binford, ed. pp. 207–250. New York: Academic Press.
Simonsen, Bjorn
  1973 Archaeological Investigations in the Hecate Strait-Milbanke Sound Area of British Columbia. Archaeological Survey of Canada, Paper 13.
Swanton, John R.
  1905 Contributions to the Ethnology of the Haida. American Museum of Natural History Memoir 5.
United States Congress
  1879 Report upon the Customs District . . . of Alaska by William Gouverneur Morris, Special Agent of the Treasury Department. 45th Congress, 3rd Session, Senate Exec. Document No. 59.
  1882 Reports of Captain L. A. Beardslee, U. S. Navy, Relative to Affairs in Alaska, and the Operations of the U. S. S. Jamestown under His Command, While in the Waters of that Territory. 47th Congress, 1st Session, Senate Exec. Document No. 71.
Van den Brink, J. H.
  1974 The Haida Indians. Leiden: E. J. Brill.
Weiss, Kenneth M.
  1973 Demographic Models for Anthropology. Society for American Archaeology Memoir 27.

8
Seasonal Settlements, Village Aggregations, and Political Autonomy on the Central Northwest Coast

Donald H. Mitchell

University of Victoria

The marked seasonal nature of Northwest Coast subsistence pursuits has been acknowledged enough times by enough people to have become, at least for most of us, a "given" of Northwest Coast ethnography. We all know the people moved around a lot and that they did so as a means of acquiring various resources from various places during the year.

We also know that these regular, seasonal moves were often accompanied by changes in settlement size and composition, changes that undoubtedly were intimately related to political aspects of Northwest Coast society. This paper surveys the seasonal settlement changes of groups on the central Northwest Coast (Southern Kwakiutl, Nuu-chah-nulth-aht,[1] and most of the Coast Salish north of the Strait of Juan de Fuca) and considers the nature of the largest groupings in the area. At the end I examine some reaons for variation in the political aspects of the largest settlement forms.

Settlement Types

For the purposes of this study, central Northwest Coast settlements may be classed as camps, villages, or village aggregations. Camps were small settlements consisting of one or a few houses that used permanent houseframes or were erected each season from the ground up. These are the settlements associated with what Drucker (1951:220) calls the local group; Barnett (1955:241), the house group; and, to a certain extent, Boas (1920) the *numaym*. With rare exception, those who lived in camps joined members of other camps in a village for part of the year. Villages had permanently erected houses or houseframes that usually were used only seasonally. For most groups, the principal season of village residence was winter, although village-sized settlements existed at other times of the year as well. Village aggregations were of several forms but all were composed of villages that retained their identities in the seasonal aggregation even though they were not always spatially segregated. These settlements also had permanent houseframes.

The identification of polities associated with each of these three settlement types is not an easy task. We have often been told of the relative autonomy of households or of such other sub-village units in Northwest Coast society such as the Haida, Tlingit, and Tsimshian lineages and Kwakiutl *numayma*. However, there is justification for the statement that for most of the coast (except, perhaps, for the Coast Salish) the group sharing a winter village forms the significant autonomous political unit. Everywhere the winter village group bore a name—as did the subgroupings, but not commonly the larger village aggregations. Accordingly, in this study, the units of analysis are those groups that shared a common winter village—even where their membership in a village aggregate for part of the year introduces the possibility of a higher level of political association. I can identify—that is, provide names for—123 winter village groups within the study area.

Seasonal Settlement Patterns

In this inquiry, I use the familiar four-season division of the year although a few groups may have occupied more than four seasonal settlements in the course of a year and many seem to have used fewer. I first of all describe each group according to the settlement form for each season, using a code that presents the settlement types (C=camp, V=village, A=village aggregate) in the order: spring, summer, fall, and winter. A dash indicates that no move took place in that season and a 0 represents missing data. For example, a group moving from spring village aggregation to summer camps and from there to fall camps before going to the winter village (a pattern followed by several of the Southern Kwakiutl groups) would be recorded as ACCV and a group residing from fall through the spring in a village and only dispersing in summer would be recorded as −CV−.

In theory, there are 255 possible combinations, not including the "missing data" option. In fact, the 69 groups for which information is sufficiently complete (that is, I can make at least three seasonal entries) fall into but 19 combinations, and of these, nine are solitary instances. Table 1 lists the observed combinations in decreasing frequency of occurrence.

Of the 19 distinct combinations tallied in Table 1, eight include a "missing data" entry (0) for one season. In most cases, the data are probably missing because no move took place during that season and, were the data available, the likely coding would therefore be a dash(−). However, replacing all missing data entries (0) with a dash (−) results in no reduction in the number of combi-

Seasonal Settlements and Village Aggregations

Table 1
Seasonal Settlement Combinations

S	S	F	W	No.
O	A	C	V	13
C	A	A	—	8
A	C	C	V	7
O	V	C	V	7
A	A	O	V	7
A	A	A	A	5
—	A	O	A	5
—	C	A	—	3
—	V	O	A	3
A	A	A	V	2
O	C	C	V	1
A	V	A	A	1
A	C	V	—	1
A	C	A	V	1
V	V	A	V	1
V	C	C	V	1
A	C	O	V	1
V	V	—	—	1
O	A	—	V	1
		Total		69

nations. The maximum number of category reductions, assuming "missing data" can be replaced with any settlement type (C, V, or A) is three, leaving us with a minimum of 16 discrete combinations. We have to conclude that although the seasonal settlement arrangements were far from random in occurrence, still no single pattern dominated the central Northwest Coast and there is considerable variety in the seasonal sequence of concentration and dispersal.

Village Aggregations

Of the 123 winter villages identified, there is sufficient information on 101 to say with reasonable certainty whether or not the winter village group joined an aggregation at some time during the year. (Our "N" grows in this case because we can now tolerate two seasons of missing data.) For 35 groups, the village was the largest gathering, while the remaining 66 winter village units spent at least part of the year in an aggregation—some of them, as we shall see, joining different groups at different times of the year.

In all, I can document the existence of 20 distinct village aggregations

(Figure 1) and suspect the presence of several more. They occurred at all seasons. There were four restricted to the spring, eight to the summer, two to the fall, and three to the winter. In addition, one spanned fall and winter, one winter and spring, and one fall, winter, and spring. So the village aggregations are clearly not a phenomenon restricted to any particular season—as we might well expect, given the variety seen in the seasonal patterns of concentration and dispersal.

Village Aggregations in Spring

In the spring there were gatherings of larger-than-winter-village size at five locations.

Tsawatti. Tsawatti was situated at the head of Knight Inlet, where nine of the Southern Kwakiutl winter village groups and a few families from one *numaym* of the Nimpkish assembled to collect and process eulachon in the Klinaklini River (Curtis 1915:23; Boas 1934:map 22). The Southern Kwakiutl winter village groups involved were the Kwagiutl, Walas Kwagiutl, Kweha, Komkiutis, Mamalillikulla, Tlawitsis, Matilpi, Awaitlala, and Tenaktuk.

Quaee. Quaee was located at the head of Kingcome Inlet, where a comparable assemblage of five other Southern Kwakiutl groups (including the bulk of the Nimpkish) met to harvest the Kingcome River eulachon (Curtis

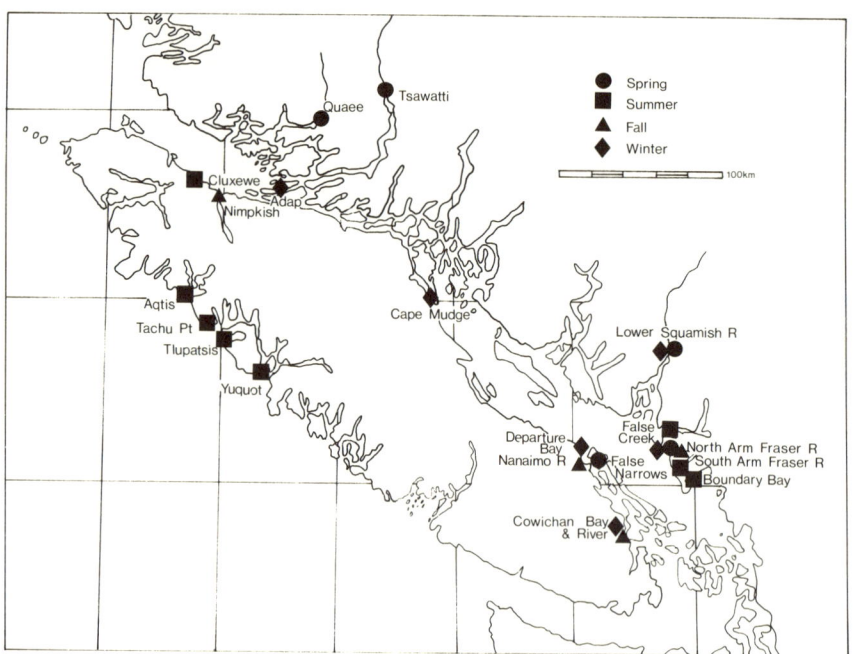

Figure 1. Seasonal village aggregations of the central Northwest Coast.

Seasonal Settlements and Village Aggregations 101

1915:22). In addition to the Nimpkish, groups assembling at Quaee included the Tsawataineuk, Kwiksutaineuk, Hahuamis, and Kwawwawaineuk. The Tlitliket were also probably a part of this village aggregation.

Lower Squamish River. According to Barnett (1955:31), the Lower Squamish River at the head of Howe Sound was "the common resort of all the Squamish in the spring when the eulachon were running." "All the Squamish" taken literally would mean the inhabitants of some 15 independent winter villages—eight of whom also resided during winter at this eulachon fishery.

False Narrows. Four of the five Nanaimo village groups traveled to Gabriola Island in the Gulf Islands for "clamming, egging, and other gathering activities" (Barnett 1955:22). "Most of the people," Barnett notes, "stayed together, with the exception of the salαxαl . . . [who] for some reason . . . held aloof from the other four villages." The groups staying together included occupants of the winter villages of αnwinic, yicαxɛn, tèwαxαn, and q!αlsiowαL.

North Arm of the Fraser River. Most of the Musqueam people remained in residence at their principal villages (LeLt, winialts, and male) from fall to spring. Some villagers seem also to have stayed there through summer.

Village Aggregations in Summer

Summer aggregations included the assembly of members from 12 Northern Nuu-chah-nulth-aht winter village groups in four settlements on the open coast. The best known of these was Yuquot at Nootka Sound, where people from two Moachat winter villages congregated. But the three Nuchatlet winter groups, the three Ehetisat, and the four Kyuquot also gathered at substantial summer villages (Drucker 1951) to fish halibut and to hunt whales. With one exception, the other summer assemblages (one Kwakiutl and three Salish) were at salmon fisheries.

Aqtis. Located on an island at the entrance to Kyuquot Sound, Aqtis was the summer village of the Kyuquot "confederacy" at which Tlaath, Chawispath, Qanopittakamtlath, and Qwixquath assembled.

Tachu Point. The Ehetisat groups gathered here at Tachu Point the entrance to Esperanza Inlet. These included the Ehetisat proper, Chinexnitath, and Tatchuath.

Tlupatsis. At Tlupatsis, at the entrance to Nuchatlitz Inlet, was the "confederacy" village of the Nuchatlet groups—the Okhats, Chachachinik, and Apaqtoo.

Yuquot. During the summer, the constituent winter village groups of the Moachat—the Koopti and Tlupana—resided at Yuquot at Nootka Sound.

Cluxewe River. All four of the Fort Rupert Kwakiutl groups (Kwagiutl, Walas Kwagiutl, Kweha, and Komkiutis) met at the Cluxewe River on northeastern Vancouver Island to fish for salmon.

Boundary Bay. Two Saanich groups (the tcαLαp and saigwαm) and probably some Lummis gathered at Boundary Bay on the southern edge of the Fraser Delta in what Barnett (1955:20) described as a single village "to fish for sockeye, humpback, and sturgeon."

South Arm of the Fraser River. The south arm of the Fraser River was the gathering place of an unknown number of the Cowichan and Nanaimo winter village groups along with the Penelekut, some Tsawassan and Musqueam, and possibly members of other groups, where they had access to one of the great salmon fisheries of the coast. Some of the Nanaimo seem also to have gone to the Nanaimo River to fish at this time.

False Creek. The one exception to these salmon-oriented summer pursuits was a concentration of Squamish in Burrard Inlet around the entrance to False Creek, where four winter village groups (the tcαmai, tcaktcαkts, yιLi:-ukL, and hukyaiαkιn) settled, according to Barnett (1955:31) to collect "berries, clams, and sturgeon."

There may have been other Squamish aggregations in Burrard Inlet. Barnett exempts only one of the 15 named village groups from the summer move to this inlet and, apart from the four already referred to, some of the remaining ten may well have been in close proximity. It is also possible they were joined by Musqueam at this time (Barnett 1955:34).

Village Aggregations in Fall

The four fall aggregations were all at productive salmon-fishing locales.

Nimpkish River. At the Nimpkish River, on northeastern Vancouver Island, the four Fort Rupert Kwakiutl groups and the Tlawitsis joined with the Nimpkish.

Nanaimo River. On the lower reaches of the Nanaimo River were villages of all five Nanaimo groups. According to Barnett (1955:22) it was here that "their salmon fishing was done . . . from August until December."

Cowichan Bay and River. The eight Cowichan groups settled close to one another at Cowichan Bay and River for fall salmon fishing and then to spend the winter (Barnett 1955:22).

North Arm of the Fraser River. The three Musqueam groups congregated at the north arm of the Fraser River from fall through spring.

Village Aggregations in Winter

The winter aggregations mostly involved Coast Salish but even prior to the move to Fort Rupert two Southern Kwakiutl groups seem to have shared a single winter settlement.

Adap. The Walas Kwagiutl and some Komkiutis spent the winters at Adap on the south shore of Turnour Island in the archipelago south of the entrance to Knight Inlet (Boas 1966:46).

Cape Mudge. Five of the ten Comox groups clustered at Cape Mudge at the southern entrance to Seymour Narrows. These groups included the säsitla, yayaqwiLtah, saLαLt, kαtkαduL, and komokwe (Barnett 1955:25). There was possibly an aggregation of other Comox groups nearby at the mouth of the Campbell River (Barnett 1955:25).

Departure Bay. Four of the Nanaimo village groups (the same four that gathered in spring at False Narrows) settled at Departure Bay from December to March (Barnett 1955:23).

Cowichan Bay and River. As already noted, the eight Cowichan groups spent the fall and winter at Cowichan Bay and River.

North Arm of the Fraser River. The Musqueam continued in residence at their three villages.

Lower Squamish River. Eight of the Squamish villages seem to have been situated close enough to one another to be considered an aggregation. They spent the winter on the Lower Squamish River and were joined in the spring, as already described, by the other seven groups for the eulachon fishery.

Village Aggregations as Polities

From the preceding survey it is obvious that most winter village groups on the central Northwest Coast spent at least part of the year—and sometimes substantial parts of the year—in the company of other winter village groups. So many authorities emphasize the autonomy of the winter village units that the question of how villages interacted when aggregated becomes of some interest. In the main, our sources have little to say about the political dimension of the largest seasonal gatherings. For the Salish, Barnett (1955:18) emphasizes the independence of the villages that comprised such winter concentrations as those of the Cowichan, Nanaimo, and Squamish. He does note that "particularly among those congregating at one locality in winter an attempt was made to preserve peaceful relationships" (Barnett 1955:267) and that "the several winter villages on Cowichan Bay achieved a somewhat superior unity because of their nearness to each other," and "the Squamish villages along the Squamish River appear to have maintained friendly relations" (Barnett 1955:267).

Although harmony was sought at these Salish winter aggregations, there was no formal supra-village political order, and, as if to underscore the absence of a polity, Barnett (1955:18–34) labeled those that joined these winter assemblies "ethnic divisions." Drucker (1951), on the other hand, describes those who joined the Nuu-chah-nulth-aht summer assemblages as "confederacies"—an explicitly political concept—and he notes that the status hierarchy provided what organization there was for the big summer villages.

> The confederacy was cemented by ties of the same nature as those uniting a number of local groups into a tribe: a common village site—in this case a summer one—to which all, or most of the people repaired for sea fishing

and hunting; seriation of their chiefs, expressed in the order of seating on ceremonial occasions, and a name. . . . There was a very real feeling of solidarity within these confederations. They were units for war as well as ceremonials. Intraconfederacy wars were rare, almost unknown, in fact, except for one or two remote traditions. [Drucker 1951:220–221]

On the nature of the other aggregations, our sources are silent. In fact, there is probably not much to say. One would not expect a high order of political organization to accompany any of the village aggregations. After all, what was needed was simply peaceful coexistence at some unusually productive resource locus or particularly desirable wintering location. No great feats of organization were necessary for employment of the technology, for gaining access to the resources, for dividing up the resultant harvest, or for simply waiting out the winter. The constituent village units of an aggregation merely did, side by side, what other village units on the coast were doing in isolation. The only difference was the proximity of a neighboring village.

In this context, the case of the Nuu-chah-nulth-aht confederacies is all the more intriguing. The summer whale-hunting and halibut-fishing assembly was based on access to resources that in some respects were no more demanding of organization than were the Kwakiutl or Salish eulachon or salmon fisheries. But there are some characteristics of the whale hunt and of whales that made this animal a different sort of resource. First, whales are large creatures, and as such they present unusual problems of butchering and preservation. At the eulachon or salmon fisheries it was possible to adjust the daily take to an amount the fisherman's group could process without great spoilage. This could not be done with whales. You cannot go out and get just so much whale and, furthermore, when you have caught one you have a lot of whale. The answer, of course, is to distribute your surplus; and to avoid the preservation problem the distribution must be done at the butchering stage. Hence the people are assembled near at hand.

There were two ways of acquiring whales and at least two modes of distribution. Whales might be hunted and killed with a harpoon or a beached one might be discovered. Neither means can be considered very productive, but however improbable it may seem at first, I think there may be a reason to consider that strandings were the more rewarding source.

Hunting seems to have been primarily a "chiefly" pursuit (Drucker 1951: 49–50) engaged in by very few from each village. And hunters, even famous ones, killed relatively few animals over the years. Drucker (1951:50) summarizes the body count recorded by Jewitt as follows:

During the one partial and two complete whaling seasons that Jewitt reports on (1803, 1804, and 1805), the chief devoted himself energetically

Seasonal Settlements and Village Aggregations 105

to the hunt, but the box score is not impressive. It reads: Days hunted, 53; struck and lost, 8; killed, 1. Four more whales were killed by Moachat chiefs during the same time, presumably after the investment of a similar amount of time and effort.

As Drucker (1951:50) comments, "clearly the economic reward in proportion to the expenditure of time and energy was slight."

But maybe all that energy that Maquinna and the other Moachat "chiefs" devoted to the hunt paid off anyway. Look again at the box score: 8 struck and lost, 1 killed. If that same ratio applied as well to the efforts of the other Moachat hunters, that is 40 wounded whales.

Curtis reported that a harpooner would aim for the lungs or heart in an attempt to kill the animal on the first thrust, and, in fact, the last two whales killed by the whaler whose activities he described "did not even take out all the line" (Curtis 1916:35). One can imagine, then, that given what the hunters were trying to do, many of those whales that got away would be more than superficially wounded and some of these, crippled or dead, would eventually drift to shore. We do not know what proportion suffered this fate, but it would not take many to exceed the direct take from hunting.

Harpooned and drift whales could be distributed in different ways. Set portions of an harpooned and caught whale were divided among the crew and those who assisted in the arduous tow, and the balance was distributed by the hunter to ranking members of his winter village group, or "tribe" as Drucker (1951:55) calls this social unit. But at least some drift whales were distributed more widely.

When drift whales came ashore, and no one could really predict where that would be, they might become the property, not of the discoverer, but of the "chief" or chiefs who owned the beach on which they stranded—if they washed up on an owned segment of beach. The distribution then would follow much the same pattern as for the harpooned animal: the ranking members of the winter village group were the usual recipients. If, however, the drift whale landed on a section of beach not claimed by an individual chief, it was treated as a bonanza for the members of the confederacy. Drucker (1951:255) describes what happens to a whale that beached in "unowned" Kyuquot territory: "The first chief of the confederacy owned both sides of the head . . . ; the tiláth chief owned the lower jaw. The qa'ō'qáth chief had the right and the cawisáth chief the left sides of a strip from the blowhole to the "saddle" in width, from back to belly in length. The tacīsáth chief owned the right side of the "saddle," and so on to describe the allotment of eight more portions to ranking individuals in the confederacy.

Here we may have a reason why the political arrangements associated with the seasonal assembly of several Northern Nuu-chah-nulth-aht groups differed from those obtaining at other central Northwest Coast village aggregations. In forming a "confederacy" and tolerating what amounted to a seasonal loss of autonomy, winter village groups could assure themselves of a share of some drift whales recovered each year—even if their hunters came home empty-handed and the sea gave up none to their own beaches.

This interpretation leaves some questions unanswered. Why distribute harpooned whales only to the tribe and drift whales to the confederacy? And why a confederacy at all, instead of simply giving the stuff away to reinforce the prestige hierarchy as Kwakiutl might have handled it?

I really have no answer to the first question, unless it is that maybe there just were more drift than harpooned whales. And for the second, I do not suggest that the confederacies were formed solely to divide up the drift whale harvest however much they may have facilitated that task. They were, in addition and ultimately perhaps more importantly, an advantage in making war and keeping peace, and they may even have encouraged a pooling of other important resources as well. But these are, at best, more speculations.

My concern in this paper has simply been to indicate that although most winter village groups on the central Northwest Coast spent at least part of the year in assembly with others, they did so with no significant reduction in their independence. The gatherings were merely ones of settlements in proximity. Some Northern Nuu-chah-nulth-aht winter village groups, however, perhaps in part because of the nature of the resource exploited, associated as members of a larger political unit and they must as a consequence have given up some of their autonomy.

Note

1. The name Nuu-chah-nulth-aht is that adopted by the West Coast Tribal Council in 1978 for the peoples known in the literature as Nootka or West Coast Indians. The orthography used is that employed by the Tribal Council.

References Cited

Barnett, Homer G.
   1955   The Coast Salish of British Columbia. Eugene: University of Oregon Press.
Boas, Franz
   1920   The Social Organization of the Kwakiutl. American Anthropologist 22: 111–126.
   1934   Geographical Names of the Kwakiutl Indians. Columbia University Contributions to Anthropology, No. 20.
   1966   Kwakiutl Ethnography. Helen Codere, ed. Chicago: University of Chicago Press.

Curtis, Edward S.
   1915   The North American Indian. Vol. 10: The Kwakiutl. Seattle: E. S. Curtis.
   1916   The North American Indian. Vol. 11: The Nootka. Seattle: E. S. Curtis.
Drucker, Philip
   1951   The Northern and Central Nootkan Tribes. Bureau of American Ethnology Bulletin 144.

9
Was Nuu-chah-nulth-aht (Nootka) Society Based on Slave Labor?

Leland Donald

University of Victoria

This paper[1] argues that at the time of earliest European contact (circa 1780) the institution of slavery and thence slave labor was fundamental to the mode of production and social formation of the peoples known as Nootka, sometimes as West Coast Indians, and most recently as Nuu-chah-nulth-aht[2] living on the west coast of Vancouver Island. "Fundamental" here means that without slavery Nuu-chah-nulth-aht society and culture would have been very different in most aspects, but does not imply that Nuu-chah-nulth-aht social life or culture was a simple reflection of the fact of a productive system based on slave labor.

Although the analysis and argument are applied to Nuu-chah-nulth-aht materials, work on other Northwest Coast groups suggests that for many of them a similar case can be made. Indeed, given the place of the Southern Kwakiutl in the Northwest Coast ethnographic literature and their relative fame outside Northwest Coast circles, I would prefer to ask my title question about the Kwakiutl. But, as with many other topics, the Kwakiutl ethnographic and historic material on slavery is too thin for independent treatment. There will, however, be a few comparative references to the Kwakiutl.

The paper consists of four parts: first, a brief reconstruction of "aboriginal" Nuu-chah-nulth-aht society; then, a description of the Nuu-chah-nulth-aht mode of production and the place of slaves in it; next, a consideration of the role of slavery in other aspects of Nuu-chah-nulth-aht life; and, finally, a few comparisons with other slave societies.

"Aboriginal" Nuu-chah-nulth-aht Society[3]

Nuu-chah-nulth-aht subsistence was based primarily on fishing, hunting and gathering of marine resources, and hunting and gathering of land resources.

Relative dependence on particular resources varied from area to area. This extractive subsistence technology led to a seasonal round that produced a concentration of people in winter (and, in some areas, the summer also) and dispersal of people in the spring and fall.

There were three major levels of territorial unit—the non-unilineal descent group, the local group, and the federation.[4] The Nuu-chah-nulth-aht non-unilineal descent group seems to have been of the type sometimes called the "patrilineal stem lineage" (see Sahlins 1957 for a description of this type of descent group). In patrilineal stem lineages leadership of the group is vested in a formal office (the Nuu-chah-nulth-aht "lineage chief") that is inherited patrilineally. Outside the chiefly line individuals validate claims to unit membership through non-unilineal genealogical ties. Thus, any Nuu-chah-nulth-aht was potentially a member of several patrilineal stem lineages. A person (usually male, as post-marital residence was normally virilocal) activated membership in a unit by residing with other members of that unit. Patrilineal stem lineages were localized and members had access to resources in territories "owned" by the unit's head. Thus the descent group was the minimal resource controlling unit in Nuu-chah-nulth-aht society.

The local group consisted of two or more non-unilineal descent groups who shared a common winter village. In addition, the leading members of each descent group were united in a ranked local group hierarchy and there was generally cooperation for common defense. These local groups were usually named, the names often ending in *aht,* which means "people of." In winter, descent units of a local group resided alongside each other in houses built at the joint village site. In the fall and spring, the component descent groups and households were normally dispersed, with the major place of residence being the descent group's fishing station.

For most Nuu-chah-nulth-aht, in common with other Northwest Coast peoples, the polity was the local group focused on the winter village. But some local groups joined together to form larger political units. These are commonly termed confederations (following Drucker 1951), but I will call them federations. The connotations of the word confederacy do not fit the Nuu-chah-nulth-aht case very well. The Nuu-chah-nulth-aht federation bears little resemblance to such anthropologically better-known confederations as the League of the Iroquois. Nowhere on the Northwest Coast was there regular political unification above the local community level and even the Nuu-chah-nulth-aht federation was no exception to this. Federations were groups of winter village communities that resided together in the summer. Federations were, in effect, summer versions of the winter village community, whose building blocks were local groups rather than the descent groups of the winter village communities. The constituent groups of a federation shared a common village, their leaders were ranked in a common hierarchy, and so on. Like the more common winter village-based local groups, federations were primarily ceremonial and war units (these are probably the same thing on the Northwest

Coast). Because of the lack of intrafederation fighting and the integration of the component descent and local groups through the hierarchy of ceremonial places, I feel that the label "federation" has more appropriate connotations than the looser organization implied by the term "confederacy."

Why some local groups federated and others did not is not entirely clear. One variable involved was the character of the resource base. Research on the salmon resources of Nuu-chah-nulth-aht territorial units shows that local groups attached to federations generally had poorer salmon streams than did unattached local groups (Morgan 1981:39). It is possible to reconstruct the territories of twenty independent Nuu-chah-nulth-aht polities for the period 1800 to 1830 (six federations and fourteen independent local groups). In the period just before this there were certainly two or three and perhaps as many as a dozen additional local groups whose territories cannot now be reconstructed.

Nuu-chah-nulth-aht society was stratified. Each descent group (and hence each local group and federation) contained members of two strata: "title-holders" (*ha'wit*) and "commoners" (*mdstcum*). Membership in these strata was determined by birth and the strata tended toward endogamy. Some members of the third stratum, "slaves" (*kōt*), were attached as property to each descent group. Slave status was also hereditary, although most slaves were war captives (obtained either through capture or through trade).

Title-holders validated their positions in the hierarchy of titles at feasts[5] given for fellow title-holders. At these feasts varying amounts of prestige and economic goods were distributed. When he participated in such feasts, a title-holder commanded the material assistance of his descent group's commoners and slaves.

Both commoners and slaves are best regarded as types of dependent labor. Commoners obtained access to resources only through a title-holder, but, at least in theory, commoners could change their descent group affiliation by activating another descent group tie. Slaves could not, of course, change their owners, so that, although members of both strata were dependent, the degree and kind of dependency were quite different.

Nuu-chah-nulth-aht "Mode of Production" and the Place of Slaves in It

Nuu-chah-nulth-aht food production was based on the exploitation of food resource loci, access to which was controlled by descent groups heads. The evidence is poor, but the production unit seems to have been either the household, a set of households, or the entire descent group depending on the loci being exploited. From the point of view of amount and reliability, the most important loci seem to have been salmon-fishing stations, herring-fishing stations, and halibut-fishing stations. From the Nuu-chah-nulth-aht perspective

Was Nuu-chah-nulth-aht Society Based on Slave Labor? 111

the most "interesting" resource was the whale, normally taken in the open sea by title-holders.

As anadromous fish, salmon could be exploited only as they approached and made their spawning run up their natal stream. Herring were also available at only one season of the year, the spring. Halibut were available year round, but weather conditions confined intensive halibut exploitation to certain seasons of the year. Thus major Nuu-chah-nulth-aht food production activities were seasonal and not continuous.

Such resource seasonality meant that preservation for future use was often more important than production for current consumption. Two kinds of work had to be organized: production and preservation. This distinction is important, especially because the productive potential of particular resource loci (a good salmon stream, for example) was often great enough to mean that the problem was not sufficient labor power or skill to *produce* satisfactory amounts of salmon or herring, but sufficient labor power to *preserve* what was produced. The sexual division of labor meant that the heavy labor inputs required for preservation fell almost entirely on women. Work on Kwakiutl as well as on Nuu-chah-nulth-aht resource exploitation suggests that over much of the Northwest Coast this was the crucial area for labor power—amassing enough female hands to enable adequate stores of foodstuffs to be preserved. This means that, when we try to determine the relationship between the resource base and other aspects of society and culture on the Northwest Coast, the interaction of the characteristics of the resource base, the size and composition of the labor force, and such culturally defined phenomena as appropriate work for each sex must all be taken into account.

All productive activity was organized by and was under the control of the "owners" of the various resource loci, i.e., the appropriate title-holders. How did title-holders solve their labor problems? Title-holders did relatively little of the drudgery associated with subsistence. The first source of labor power was the commoners of a title-holder's descent group—men procured fish, women preserved them. But the part played by slaves seems to me to have been crucial. A quote from Sproat illustrates this point nicely:

> When the canoes return to shore from fishing the men fill the baskets with the fish and place them on the women's shoulders. The latter, *assisted by slaves,* immediately cut off the heads, open, and wash the fish, press out the water, and afterwards hang them up to dry. [Sproat 1868:53–54; emphasis mine]

To assess fully the value of this observation it is important to note that Sproat was a long-time resident of the central part of the west coast of Vancouver Island, had a reasonably good acquaintance with the Nuu-chah-nulth-aht of the area, and did not confuse commoners and slaves. (Such a confusion reduces the value of many of the earliest accounts of the Nuu-chah-nulth-aht, such as Mozino's [1970].) Sproat's observation suggests that slave labor offers a solution to any shortages of female labor power due to a rigid division of labor by sex. Slaves are human and can be made to do the work of humans, but they are also property. They cannot choose the role they are asked to fill in any particular situation. In this particular context they are not "men" or "women" but "slaves"—undifferentiated labor power. It is not inappropriate to demand that a male slave do "women's work," because a male slave is not a "man" in the fullest cultural sense. So slaves can be used as needed without the kind of consideration for the appropriateness of the demands made upon them that are necessary with followers (commoners of one's descent group).

The importance of female labor power also fits in with the preference for female slaves, although there are clearly additional reasons for preferring female slaves—their greater docility, for example, and the smaller likelihood that they will try to escape.

The value of slaves in situations where there is a shortage of a particular kind of labor is now obvious. But are there *enough* slaves to make much difference? Is there enough assignable labor power available to have a real impact on a Nuu-chah-nulth-aht descent group's capacity to preserve and store food? Unfortunately the demographic data available for the Nuu-chah-nulth-aht are among the poorest for any Northwest Coast people. Sproat's (1868:117) is the only estimate of the proportion of slaves in a typical Nuu-chah-nulth-aht local group: about one-fourth title-holder, one-half commoner, and one-fourth slave. Although he implies a range of variation around these proportions he does not indicate what it was. A few other figures are available that give some indirect support to Sproat's estimate that slaves formed a fairly high proportion of the Nuu-chah-nulth-aht population. In the early 1790's Spanish voyagers had no difficulty in quickly obtaining twenty or more slaves along a short stretch of the west coast of Vancouver Island (Wagner 1933). Jewitt (1974:65) says that around 1803–5, Maquinna (the head of the Moachat federation) had fifty slaves, while no other title-holder had more than twelve. And even in the mid-19th century the Moachat took thirteen slaves in a single attack (Sproat 1868:188–96, Jacobson 1977:66–69). If 25% is a reasonable approximation of the proportion of slaves—and I think that it is—then clearly there was enough slave labor available to make a real difference to Nuu-chah-nulth-aht production.

Most slaves were war captives—either captured by their owners or acquired by them in trade. Warfare on the Northwest Coast has often been argued to be non-economic in character—the Nuu-chah-nulth-aht always recognized as an exception since Swadesh (1948) showed that Nuu-chah-nulth-aht local groups often fought over resources. Slaves were a normal consequence of success in war (among all Northwest Coast peoples as far as I can tell). Therefore, wherever slaves had economic value (as among the Nuu-chah-nulth-aht this gave war an economic component. It should be further noted that even for a Northwest Coast people for whom slaves were not important for their labor (if there were such groups) the lively intergroup slave trade networks made slaves economically important. In addition, the economic (and other social) consequences of losing community members to slavers should not be overlooked.

Slavery in Other Aspects of
Nuu-chah-nulth-aht Cultural Life

The argument and data just presented support the idea that the most important aspect of slavery among the Nuu-chah-nulth-aht was the economic contribution made by slave labor, but slavery also touched other aspects of Nuu-chah-nulth-aht culture in important ways.

Slaves played a significant role in the internal politics of the Nuu-chah-nulth-aht local group. As has been noted, the local group was a union of descent groups. It was also made up of three classes whose membership crosscut descent group membership. All three classes—title-holders, commoners, and slaves—played their role in local group politics. Title-holders commanded, decided, and aggrandized. Commoners supported their title-holders, but they could also withdraw support from unpopular, inept, or too overbearing leaders. They could do this by using the same mechanism that ties them to their old leader—they activated another line of descent and joined a different descent group. This freedom of movement was counterbalanced by the dangers inherent in switching groups, especially given the state of war or near war that seems to have been a constant feature of Nuu-chah-nulth-aht life in traditional times. An alternative to changing allegiances was to withhold support from a title-holder, especially in preparations for feasts. A title-holder who demanded too much of too many numbers of his followers undoubtedly had to face the threat of loss of support.

Title-holders had the hereditary right to lead and dominate commoners. But they had to enforce these rights. When faced with the problem of maintaining order and discipline within the group the Nuu-chah-nulth-aht leader had the classic problem of social control within a kinship-based society—how to get consanguines, or even affines, to act against kinsmen. In this area slaves played an active role in local group politics. They were the property and agents of title-holders and having no kin ties in a local group, they had no scruples (or choice) about acting for a title-holder against a commoner. Several sources make it clear that within the local group slaves were used extensively as agents of a title-holder and that they did carry out his orders against commoners (e.g., Curtis 1916; Jewitt 1974; Sproat 1868). Another quote from Sproat shows this role of slaves and also makes clear the important distinction between intra- and inter-local group affairs: "The chief has no officers, except his slaves, who could enforce obedience in his own tribe [local group]; but there are proper tribal officers through whom he communicates all resolutions of his own people to other tribes" (Sproat 1868:114). Local group could (and often did) act against local group and in such encounters title-holders and commoners usually stood together, united in their opposition to outsiders. But internally, title-holders could (and at times probably had to) use their slaves as a force against their commoners, so that while hierarchy and mutual need united the local group, class divided it and sometimes the top used the bottom to control the commoner majority.

The slave role in food production has already been described in the context of the division of labor. Slaves also undertook a wide range of productive and domestic activities that contributed to both the economic well being and the way of life of their masters. The tasks of slaves mentioned in the sources include: "all menial offices," bringing water, cutting wood, making canoes, assisting in building and repairing houses, supplying masters with fish, manufacturing cloth, cooking, collecting berries, waiting on family and guests (then taking their own meal afterwards), and paddling canoes (Drucker 1951; Jewitt 1974; Sapir and Swadesh 1955; Sproat 1868). There are also numerous mentions in the sources of high-ranking children (especially girls) having slave attendants (e.g., Curtis 1916; Drucker 1951). Slaves also seem to have frequently accompanied title-holders when they went into ritual seclusion, or on journeys. All in all, slaves clearly were a normal part of the economic and domestic life of title-holders.

As noted previously, slaves were bought and sold in intergroup trade. But slaves changed hands in other transactions too. Slaves were sometimes a part of marriage arrangements between title-holders of different local groups. There are two clear recorded examples of such exchanges in the sources (Drucker 1951:273; Sapir and Swadesh 1955:176–177) and one general statement that slaves commonly changed hands at marriage (Curtis 1916:64), but the Nuu-chah-nulth-aht record does not suggest that slaves were as important a part of title-holder marriage exchanges as does the record for the Kwakiutl (see especially the family histories in Boas 1921). Slaves sometimes changed hands at ceremonies, although this seems not to have been too common.

Slaves had other places in Nuu-chah-nulth-aht ritual life. One major role of slaves was that of victim. We do not know how frequently slaves were killed as a part of ceremonies, but references to slave killing appear in the historical record from the late 1780s until the 1880s. It is obvious that slaves were not killed at every ceremony or even on every important ceremonial occasion, but some slave deaths almost certainly occurred. Others, perhaps more numerous, were probably acted out, even though no one was actually killed. At least three kinds of occasion could lead to the death of a slave: the so-called Wolf Ceremony, the killing of a whale, and mourning (especially that over the death of a principal title-holder) (Brabant 1900:21; Curtis 1916:70; Drucker 1951:33–34, 440–441; Howay 1941:77–78, 288–289; Jacobson 1977:64; Sproat 1868:155–156; Wagner 1933:160–161). These are all key events in Nuu-chah-nulth-aht cultural life. Drucker (1951:386) describes the "Wolf Ceremony" or "Shamans' Dance" as "the most spectacular and most important ceremonial in Nootkan culture." Whaling was a title-holder's activity and symbolic of the greatness of title-holders. All available data suggest that actual whale kills were relatively rare, so that a successful hunt must have been an important religious as well as economic occasion.

What did the deaths of these slaves mean? We do not know nearly enough about aboriginal Nuu-chah-nulth-aht religion to answer this question. In particular, we lack texts dealing with the ideology of both head taking and the ritual killing of slaves. The value of human life or the meaning of taking it (whether it is that of an active enemy—head taking—or that of a defeated enemy—ritual slave killing) are unclear. But the taking of heads in war and the killing of slaves during religious ceremonies are both such prominent events that it is certain the destruction of life played a major part in Nuu-chah-nulth-aht religious observances.

On various parts of the Northwest Coast the ritual killing of slaves (when it is accepted as having happened) is frequently cited as evidence that slaves had little economic value, since who would destroy something (or someone) of productive value? Two points are relevant: (1) lack of economic rationality is not a useful argument against the occurrence of a cultural practice in *any* society; (2) from various parts of the coast fragmentary data suggest that when slaves were killed ceremonially they were either old and/or worn out or were rebellious and thus poor slaves.[6] For example, Drucker (1951:383) describes an instance of competitive gift giving where a slave given away was chosen because he had been trying to escape.

Was Nuu-chah-nulth-aht Society a "Slave" Society?

In this brief conclusion the title question is posed in a form that leads to comparison: to what extent is it justifiable to call Nuu-chah-nulth-aht society a "slave" society?

"Slave society" is often accepted as an appropriate label for two historically disparate blocks of societies: ancient Greece and Rome, and the New World plantation societies of the 18th and 19th centuries. There is more disagreement over whether or not certain 18th and 19th century West African societies were slave societies properly speaking, or by-products of the trans-Atlantic Slave trade.

Do the Nuu-chah-nulth-aht (and certain other Northwest Coast societies) belong within this grouping? The obvious answer might seem to be a clear no. But the Nuu-chah-nulth-aht share two of the most important characteristics that distinguish the slave societies from their neighbors: slaves were numerically important[7] and production was heavily dependent on slave labor.

The clear and obvious difference between the Nuu-chah-nulth-aht and

Athens in the 4th century B.C. or the southern United States in the 18th century is that the Nuu-chah-nulth-aht were not organized into a state and the others were. (Although, to my knowledge, the problem of when in their political evolution the Greek polities became slave societies has not been pursued.) The state is a cultural and social watershed of tremendous importance and obviously care must be taken when comparing features of non-states with similar-appearing features of states. But, in addition to the points previously mentioned, other common themes emerge when Greece and the Northwest Coast are compared. In Greek society slavery was an ever-present fact—Plato and Aristotle, for example, accept it as natural. But slavery was also an ever-present danger—anyone, no matter how high, could become a slave literally overnight if the fortunes of war shifted, as they often did throughout the turbulent history of Greece.[8]

The same danger existed for the Nuu-chah-nulth-aht. War was common and everyone was continually exposed to the consequences of failure in war: death or slavery. And among the Nuu-chah-nulth-aht repatriation (when it occurred) could never completely remove the fact of previous enslavement. There was a permanent social scar. Even as late as the 1880s the historic literature contains convincing references to Nuu-chah-nulth-aht traveling away from their homes with reluctance and in great fear of being captured and enslaved (Brabant 1900:12; Moser 1926:171).

In a slave society everyone is affected (infected) by slavery: slave, master, and ordinary citizen. The Greek literature makes this clear (although the Greeks were not self-conscious about slavery). The literature on the Nuu-chah-nulth-aht is much less rich on the subject, but nothing I have read contradicts this view and the violence so common in the early accounts of Nuu-chah-nulth-aht life is certainly appropriate to a slave society.

If we accept that traditional Nuu-chah-nulth-aht society was a slave society, there are a number of implications for our ideas about social evolution including the suggestion that one important type of class society, the slave society, may be not only either capitalist or pre-capitalist (southern United States versus Greece), but also either state or pre-state (Greece versus Nuu-chah-nulth-aht) as well. These implications are best worked out in the context of a full-scale analysis of slavery and warfare among all Northwest Coast societies. Therefore, rather than end on a general note, I will make a brief suggestion about Northwest Coast ethnography. That the Northwest Coast is a very distinct culture area in the North American context is well established. Nowhere else in North America do we find slavery important either numerically or productively. I suspect that many of the other distinctive features of the culture area are associated with the fact that many of the Northwest Coast societies were, like the Nuu-chah-nulth-aht, based on slave labor.

Notes

Acknowledgments. This paper reports one aspect of research that Donald H. Mitchell and I have been doing since 1976 on Northwest Coast slavery and warfare. The financial assistance of the University of Victoria Faculty Research and Travel Committee, the Province of British Columbia Youth Employment Programme, the Canada Council, and the Social Sciences and Humanities Research Council of Canada is gratefully acknowledged. I would like to thank Chris Morgan for his research assistance and Donald H. Mitchell, Kathleen Mooney, Chris Morgan, and David Moyer for their helpful comments on earlier versions of this paper.

1. Those interested in slavery will recognize that I owe more than the title to Moses Finley's (1973) work on Greek slavery.

2. The name Nuu-chah-nulth-aht is that adopted by the West Coast Tribal Council in 1978 for the peoples known in the literature as Nootka or West Coast Indians. The orthography used is that adopted by the Tribal Council.

3. The major source for Nuu-chah-nulth-aht ethnography (especially social organization) is Drucker (1951). Other important sources include Curtis (1916); Jewitt (1974); Sapir and Swadesh (1939, 1955); and Sproat (1868).

4. In the earlier literature the Nuu-chah-nulth-aht non-unilineal descent group has been called the "sept" (Sapir 1915), the "lineage" (Drucker 1951), and the "local group" (Rosman and Rubel 1971); the local group has been called the "tribe" (Sapir 1921; Drucker 1951; Rosman and Rubel 1971); and the federation has been called the "confederation" (Drucker 1951; Rosman and Rubel 1971).

5. Nuu-chah-nulth-aht versions of the so-called potlatch.

6. Other economically valuable items were also occasionally destroyed. These included coppers, eulachon oil, and canoes. Canoes, like slaves, were a part of productive capital.

7. Hopkins (1978:99) suggests a minimum of 20% slave to classify a society as "slave," but goes on to argue that even a minimum of 15% or even 10% would not augment the number of slave societies, since very few societies approach even 10% slave. Even allowing for error in our estimate of the number of slaves, the Nuu-chah-nulth-aht easily exceeded this figure.

8. In additon to Finley (1973) on Greek slavery, Hopkins (1978) on Roman slavery offers much for the comparatively inclined to think about. The more I read about the Greeks the more they seem to illuminate, by both similarity and contrasts, features of various Northwest Coast societies. A sociologically informed treatment of the Greeks is Gouldner (1965). Although his analysis is marred by its functionalist cast, the book contains many useful insights and comments and will repay careful reading.

References Cited

Boas, Franz
    1921   Ethnology of the Kwakiutl. *In* 35th Annual Report of the Bureau of American Ethnology, pp;. 43–1481.

Brabant, A. J.
   1900   Vancouver Island and Its Missions, 1874–1900. New York: Messenger of the Sacred Heart Press.:
Curtis, Edward S.
   1916   The North American Indian. Vol. 11: The Nootka. Seattle: E. S. Curtis.
Drucker, Philip
   1951   The Northern and Central Nootka Tribes. Bureau of American Ethnology Bulletin 144.
Finley, M. I.
   1973   Was Greek Civilization Based on Slave Labor? *In* The Slave Economies, Eugene D. Genovese, ed. vol. 1, pp. 19–45. New York: John Wiley and Sons.
Gouldner, Alvin W.
   1965   Enter Plato, New York: Basic Books.
Hopkins, Keith
   1978   Conquerors and Slaves. Cambridge: Cambridge University Press.
Howay, Frederick W., ed.
   1941   Voyages of the "Columbia" to the Northwest Coast, 1787–1790 and 1970–1793. Boston: Massachusetts Historical Society.
Jacobson, Johan Adrian
   1977   Alaskan Voyage, 1881–1883. Erna Gunther, transl. from the German text of Adrian Woldt. Chicago: University of Chicgo Press.
Jewitt, John R.
   1974   [1824] The Adventures and Sufferings of John R. Jewitt, Captive among the Nootka, 1803–1805. D. G. Smith, ed. Toronto: McClelland and Stewart.
Morgan, R. Christopher
   1981   The Economic Basis of Nootka Politics. Canberra Anthropology 4:29–44.
Moser, Charles
   1926   Reminiscences of the West Coast of Vancouver Island. Victoria: Acme Press.
Mozino, J. M.
   1970   [1804] Noticias de Nutka. I.H. Wilson, transl. Seattle: University of Washington Press.
Rosman, Abraham, and Paula Rubel
   1971   Feasting with Mine Enemy. New York: Columbia University Press.
Sahlins, Marshall
   1957   Differentiation by Adaptation in Polynesian Societies. Journal of the Polynesian Society 66:291–300.
Sapir, Edward
   1915   The Social Organization of the West Coast Tribes. Proceedings and Transactions of the Royal Society of Canada Series 3, Vol.9, Part 2, pp. 355–374.
   1921   The Life of a Nootka Indian. Queen's Quarterly 28:232–243, 351–367.
Sapir, Edward, and Morris Swadesh
   1939   Nootka Texts: Tales and Ethnological Narratives. Philadelphia: Linguistic Society of America.
   1955   Native Accounts of Nootka Ethnography. Indiana University Research Center in Anthropology, Folklore, and Linguistics Publications, No. 1.
Sproat, Gilbert Malcolm
   1868   Scenes and Studies of Savage Life. London: Smith, Elder and Co.

Swadesh, Morris
   1948   Motivations in Nootka Warfare. Southwestern Journal of Anthropology 4:76–93.

Wagner, H. R.
   1933   Spanish Explorations of the Straits of Juan de Fuca. Santa Ana, CA: Fine Arts Press.

10
Pre-contact Political Organization and Slavery in Aleut Societies

Joan B. Townsend
University of Manitoba

Slavery and stratification traditionally have been associated with agrarian societies. Marine-oriented hunting, fishing, and gathering societies are generally thought to be more egalitarian, perhaps with forceful leaders rising from time to time. Although the Northwest Coast often is singled out as an exception, a debate has raged as to whether true slavery existed and whether "real" stratification actually occurred in the area (e.g., Ruyle 1973). There is even greater reluctance to accept these features as characteristic of societies further north along the Alaskan Pacific Rim. Reports of "slaves" and "classes" in early descriptions are generally assumed to be in error, to be explained by "diffusion" from more complex societies of the Northwest Coast, or a result of contact with the European mercantile fur trade.

But I contend that rather complex structures do appear to have developed in fairly small-scale societies and, further, a mixture of forms occurred—for example, slavery within a familial rather than a full class system (Townsend 1980). It is my hypothesis that these developments were indigenous and not in response to the fur trade.

The Aleuts are a case in point. Complex patterns existed throughout the Alaskan Pacific Rim among the Aleuts, Koniag and Chugach Eskimos, Tanaina, Eyak, and Ahtna (Townsend 1980), but because of the complexity of the southern Alaskan area, the Aleuts, particularly of the Fox Islands, eastern Aleutians, and secondarily the Koniags of Kodiak Island will be the focus of this discussion. These societies possessed the most complex systems and were in the most intensive contact with the Russian mercantilists during the earliest period of contact in the late 18th century.

The initial discussion is devoted to an elaboration of the evolution of political organization among the Aleuts in what I consider was the late pre-contact period, and relation of slavery to it. The focus will then be directed to the nature of the mercantile fur venture instituted by the Russians and to the kinds of Russian-Aleut and Russian-Koniag contacts that preclude the possibility that the complex structures described resulted from European contact.

Traditional Social Organization and Evolution

The Aleutians and Kodiak

Although land-based resources were negligible or absent in the Aleutians and Kodiak, marine and littoral resources were especially rich. Seals, sea lions, whales, sea otter, fish, invertebrates, and seaweeds were important in subsistence. The region supported a comparatively large population, minimally 8,000 on Kodiak and 16,000 in the Aleutians with the greatest densities in the Fox Islands and Kodiak. Village populations ranged from about 100 up to perhaps 1,000.

Each island, or in some cases a cluster of islands, constituted an autonomous society (Levy 1966:20–21 n.10) composed of several villages. The village consisted of one or more local descent groups. Both Koniag and Aleut societies appear to have been unilineal. The Koniag situation is unclear, but there are strong indications that the Aleuts were matrilineal with an emphasis on avunculocal residence (e.g., Lantis 1970:227–235; Jochelson 1933:71–72; Sarychev 1807:77).

The societies shared similar sociopolitical and economic structures creating the foundation upon which the entire system of regional interaction, including trade, warfare, and intermarriage, rested (Townsend 1979, 1980). Broadly, these societies can be characterized as ranked ones (cf. Fried 1967) with a richman at the apex of the system. From the time of first European contacts, descriptions clearly suggest a well-developed rank system. Trade systems were highly developed (Townsend 1979, 1980).

The *institution* of slavery rather than an incidental retention of captives as human chattels existed throughout the Alaskan Pacific Rim during the 18th and 19th centuries, and the Aleuts and Koniags maintained slaves until their subjugation by the Russians in the last two decades of the 18th century. Slavery is used here in its broad but fundamental definition as a condition in which a person is the property of another and forced to work for him. It is the totality of the slave's powerlessness in principle and the idea of the slave as a piece of property that is significant (Nieboer 1910:5; Finley 1972:4). If, as I will maintain, slavery was a pre-contact phenomenon, then the existence within these societies of a non-free group of slaves de facto established a minimal stratification into the free and the non-free.

Slaves were clearly disenfranchised individuals and cannot be written off simply as "captives." Slaves, either male or female, prisoner or orphan, were the property of their masters, and could be punished or killed, traded for other goods or slaves, or given as presents or as a part of bride price. They could be freed or, frequently, sacrificed at the death of the master. Slaves could not own property; anything they acquired became their masters'. They were, themselves, extremely valuable commodities. Many slaves were well treated and prestige accrued to a kind master, but kindness or cruelty was entirely up to the master (e.g., Black 1977:84, 85, 87; Davydov 1977:163; Lisianski 1814:200; Merck 1980:80, 108-109, 174, 177, 201, 206; Sarychev 1807:76–77; Sauer 1802:175, 177, 181; Veniaminov 1840:II:165–166; III:10). They were expected to accompany and protect their master. Apparently slaves could marry, but their children remained slaves. However, the offspring of a female slave and her master were free (Veniaminov 1840:II:77, 165, 239 n.; Masterson and Brower 1948:91).

At any particular time, these societies varied in degree of ranking and incipient stratification within the free class. The Near Islands were the least complex, the Fox Islands and Kodiak the most. Essential resources were normally available to all in the free class, but non-essential goods of high value, such as amber, dentalium, and slaves were used in part as a means of validating rank distinctions.

Rank was based on two related factors: wealth and inheritance. A person inherited the right to a position, and he also inherited wealth. Together, these created the potential for the development of a leader—or richman—who demonstrated his worthiness through generosity, bravery, and support for the ideals of the society. A large following of relatives was paramount to attaining and maintaining the position of richman (Coxe 1787:181; Masterson and Brower 1948:59–60).[1] Without relatives a man could not achieve high rank (Townsend 1980).

Although some wealth was inherited, most had to be acquired. This was accomplished by: (1) the application of human energy to the creating of wealth (location of amber deposits, preparation of food stuffs and other goods for trading, etc.); (2) aggression to obtain booty and slaves; and (3) trade for goods and slaves (Townsend 1978, 1980). Success in all these endeavors depended on the number of helpers. Relatives were essential, but slaves also contributed to the production of wealth to be used in one way or another in redistribution and ostentatious display through which prestige accrued as well as to subsistence activities (e.g., Black 1977:85; Veniaminov 1840:II:165 ff.).

The Fox Islands Case[2]

The Fox Islands were larger than islands to the west and strategically located in an area of particularly rich subsistence resources. They were also at the crossroads of trading networks to the continent and therefore had access not only to island resources but, through raiding and trade, to those of mainland Alaska as well. This advantageous location provided opportunities for acquisition of wealth and so for an elaborate rank system beyond that possible in the western Aleutians. It also made possible a population growth that by the 18th century had escalated to the point where every suitable place on every island was settled (Veniaminov 1840:II:176–177).

With increase in population pressure and the importance of resources to enhance position, villages established exclusive rights to resources within their immediate territories. It was a serious offence to hunt in another village's territory (Veniaminov 1840:II:166, 279–290). The result was a volatile situation in which raiding was encouraged not only by a desire for booty but also by population pressure when desirable locations were no longer available for expansion. Within this context, Fox Islands societies maximized ranking in the free class and verged on stratification, but the destructive effects of the escalation in aggression and the appearance of the Russians in the 1760s disrupted the evolution.

Richmen with large local kin groups were able to gain access to sources of wealth by several means unavailable to lower-ranked people. A policy of intermarriage between high-ranked individuals of different descent groups and occasionally different societies (Veniaminov 1840:II:76–77) provided links through which advantageous trade could be conducted. Such alliances gave the richman access to a wide range of affines in a number of locales who could be called on in case of need. His position became more secure from attack as his relatives—affines and consanguines—expanded.

Although throughout the Aleutians and Kodiak a village normally had one or two richmen who were essentially wealthy heads of large descent groups, in the Fox Islands in the late pre-contact period apparently a single "chief" gained authority over all the villages of an island. Each "chief" was descended in a direct line from the founder of the island settlement (Veniaminov 1840:II:167) and presumably could muster a major portion of the population as relatives. A richman had rights only to a share of the resources, such as whales or wood, cast up on the beach adjacent to his own village; the island chief received a part of such resources cast up *anywhere* on the island and, consequently, was the wealthiest (Veniaminov 1840:II:167–168).

Another and extremely important prerogative of the high-ranked individuals and the island chief that was crucial in maintaining their positions was the exclusive right to initiate and carry out raids in which wealth, captives, and prestige for valor could be obtained. But, before richmen could embark on raiding enterprises, the island chief had to grant permission (Veniaminov 1840:II:167). Such special rights made it possible for the island chief to control and manipulate the degree of affluence lesser richmen could attain (Townsend 1980).

Raiding was a kin-based affair, and the major benefits accrued to the high-ranked kin. Although low-ranked people who participated in the raid received part of the booty, only richmen could keep certain kinds of spoils including slaves (Veniaminov 1840:II:103–104, 165). Raiding had a positive feedback aspect but was, by and large, a closed system within the allied high-ranked groups. A successful raid brought the richman prestige for valor and wealth goods. A reputation for valor and successful raids was necessary in order to gain a following and to be permitted to initiate raids from which more valor and wealth could be won. Food and goods were redistributed throughout the groups of kinsmen or society, but distribution was in accord with position.

One product of raiding was prisoners, who were either killed or enslaved. It was probably early in the evolution of ranking that the obvious advantages of keeping captives as slaves to trade for other goods, or for work and display as valued goods, were realized. With abundant but not regularly distributed resources and large populations, rank, raiding, wealth, and slavery emerged together as mutually reinforcing elements contributing to social evolution.

The slave contingent was enhanced further by those widows and orphans not in the richman's descent group who were converted to slavery (e.g., Coxe 1787:218). The use of orphans, that is, those without kin, for virtual serf-like labor in exchange for the bare necessities of life was fairly common in Alaska among some interior Athapaskans and North Alaskan Eskimos (e.g., Burch 1975: Townsend 1960–73), so a pattern of intrasocietal servitude for unfortunates was present in many Alaskan areas. Then, with the exacerbation of raiding in the Aleutians and Kodiak in pre-Russian times, many small descent groups were almost wiped out, leaving a few orphans and widows as survivors. These went to the richman for his care and apparently were merged into the existing slavery system, where they were worked or traded.

For a prospective richman, the crux of the problem of rising in rank was to retain more followers than another aspirant. Followers were essential to the undertaking of raids and for protection against reprisals. They also produced necessary goods and food for the kin group and for local redistribution as well as valued goods for display or trade. Relatives were the most reliable source, but their number was finite, and they had to be courted to retain their support. If an aspiring individual could augment his group with non-relatives who, because of their slave status, could make no demands on the aspirant or his resources, he could further enhance his wealth and position.

One of the most important uses of slaves, then, was to provide labor. Subsistence activities were one set of time-consuming tasks and these required frequent and, in some cases, daily work (e.g., Turner 1976:27). Free men did marine hunting and fishing. Free women were responsible for cleaning and preparing the fish and animals. Women, children, and disabled or elderly men collected wood along the beaches and scoured the shorelines for sea urchins, mussels, and other invertebrates and seaweed (Veniaminov 1840:II:73; Turner 1976:27–28; Laughlin 1963:637–638). It is probable that when they were available, slaves carried a major portion of the gathering burden. Slaves were also responsible for housekeeping and similar menial tasks such as carrying water and wood (Andreyev 1952:33; Veniaminov 1840:II:73). A typical richman owned three or four slaves, but those who were very wealthy had between 5 and 20 (Masterson and Brower 1948:91; Veniaminov 1840:II:239) so that the addition to the productive workforce could be considerable.

By performing menial but necessary tasks, slaves freed others for more prestigeful activities that also required considerable time. According to early sources, free women did very fine sewing, but the work went slowly. It required two months to make a *kamleika* (a rain shirt made of sea mammal intestines) and all winter to plait a grass mat (Merck 1980:71). A year was required for a craftsman to complete a *baidarka* (a one- or two-hole kayak) for the work necessitated collecting considerable driftwood as well as the actual construction (Sarychev 1807:73). The covering lasted less than a year but a well-made frame might be good for several years if repairs were made (Veniaminov 1840:II:244). Although the labor time quoted may be somewhat excessive, the point remains that these activities were highly time-consuming. The goods produced had very important practical uses and were valuable exchange items and symbols of prestige. Some, such as *baidarkas*, were also critical for subsistence.

Being freed from low-valued activities was in itself a mark of prestige. The degree of stratification in the free sector may have been related in part to the number of slaves owned by a richman because the more slaves a richman had for drudge labor, the more relatives could be encouraged to join and assist him. Extra workers, free and slave, provided greater access to strategic and wealth resources. As the richman's position grew and greater numbers of relatives were attracted, his kin group might begin to crowd out less advantaged groups and usurp resources.

Within the relative increase in size and power of some kin groups over others, the exclusive rights of a village's members to resources in their territory and the responsibility of the richman to enforce these exceeded the usual limits: "Weaker and poorer families were excluded more and more from the means of sustenance and thus were compelled to leave their territory and seek the means of existence in other localities" (Veniaminov 1840:II:94–95).

But attempts at resource usurpation caused an escalation of feuds. Not only did people of each island attack others, but often those living on the same island refused to come to each other's aid, and attacked each other when possible (Veniaminov 1840:II:185–186). Chiefs and richmen lost necessary followers when numbers were killed. Their authority diminished (Veniaminov 1840:II:170), and the system reverted back to a ranked one—a case of aborted stratification.

In summary, within what would be considered small-scale societies, complex structures appeared that were compatible with the simpler ones.

Within a single society, there were two systems of social relations working—two ways of accomplishing necessary work. One was ranked familial and one was slave. Since slaves did contribute to some degree, both in work and in inherent value, to the ranked position of the richman, the slave system pressured the familial system toward a ruling class/commoner class system. However, factors within the ranked familial system, such as need for kin support and the potential for kin to strike out on their own if not kept pacified with appropriate gifts, as well as the ability of the displaced to retaliate, worked against completion of this shift (Townsend 1978, 1980).

Also acting against this shift to a more stratified system was the availabilty of frontier territory. Many of the Fox Islands were crowded, but unlike Fried's (1957:22) stratification scenario in which there is no frontier territory, displaced Aleuts sometimes might find some unoccupied areas in island groups to the east or they might find areas where they could displace others. After gaining strength they might return to attack their old homeland (Veniaminov 1840:II:94–95). The lack of a frontier may be one of the most crucial factors in any successful independent development of social stratification. With a frontier, the potential oppressed could move in order to escape oppression. Only when a portion of the population *must* remain, for whatever reason, in their situation and submit to unequal rights is the development of stratification a possibility.

Historic Perspective

The history of European contact along the Northwest Coast, the Aleutians, and Kodiak, and the nature of Russian-Aleut and Russian-Koniag relationships preclude the kinds of developments in social and political organization just discussed simply in response to European mercantile activities. It is to this evidence that I now turn.

Northwest Coast

The first recorded European contact along the Northwest Coast was Juan Josef Perez Hernandez's with the Haida of the Queen Charlotte Islands in 1774 (e.g., Gunther 1972), 15 years *after* slavery was reported by the Russians in the Fox Islands of the Aleutians over 1,500 miles away. Perez traded trifles for fish; the fur trade had not yet started. Although they do not disprove the suggestion that slavery diffused from the Northwest Coast, these data establish that European contact on the Northwest Coast and the fur trade were *not* the impetus.

Diffusion, however, seems a simplistic answer for the occurrence of slavery in the Aleutians and Kodiak. More preferable is the view that slavery developed throughout the North Pacific Rim as all these societies became involved in rank, wealth, trade, and war.

Aleutians and Kodiak[3]

In 1745, the Russians began their slow eastward encroachment along the Aleutian chain in quest of sea otters. They came in tiny 45-foot boats, sewn together because of shortages of iron, that carried less than 20 tons and had crews of around 40. As they were poorly provisioned, they had to hunt and prepare their own food as well as hunt for furs. Trade goods carried were minimal—usually beads, tobacco and snuff, and occasionally a few pieces of iron. It was not until after 1760 that larger boats, about 60 feet long with crews of about 60, began to make the trip to the Aleutians. The Russian fur hunters did not come with the intention of inducing natives to hunt furs for them; until at least the 1770s, the Russians did most of their fur hunting themselves.

In the western Aleutians, clashes with the Aleuts did occur but overall the relations were comparatively amicable. That the Russians entered into contact with Aleuts at all was, first, for the purpose of ensuring their own safety by gift-giving and requesting hostages and, second, that of inducing Aleuts to pay tribute.

Aleuts were interested in trade and were sophisticated traders. Usually the Russian fur hunters' leader and an Aleutian richman struck a partnership, which was maintained throughout the Russians' year or two stay. The richman's relatives then hunted a bit for furs to trade to the Russians. Some of the furs they brought in were earmarked as tribute, but it is likely the Aleuts simply considered this tribute as one aspect of the over-all trade relationship because the Russians gave "gifts" in exchange. The furs brought by the Aleuts, however, never approached the quantity obtained by the Russian hunters (e.g., Berkh 1974:100–103), nor were they as important to the Russian hunters since they were designated for the crown, not for the crew's profit. True fur *trade*, then, was minimal.

Ethnographic information for the very early contact years is scarce or lacking, but by the early 1760s reports document slaves everywhere. The earliest report of slavery dates from the discovery of the Fox Islands in the eastern Aleutians in 1759 (Andreyev 1952:20). These islands were the most remote from initial Russian contracts, the most populous, most socially complex of all the Aleutians, and the area where the most extensive and elaborate use of slaves is reported. In 1759, captives were reported as being slaves and in reports soon after, in 1762 and 1768, widows and orphans were said to be made slaves and traded to others (Coxe 1787:181, 218; Makarova 1975:83; Masterson and Brower 1948:59). When Kodiak was discovered in 1763, slaves were documented as being there (Coxe 1787:125–126).

During the first 14 years of contact (1745–59), the level of direct trade between Russians and western Aleuts was low; at this time, of course, it was non-existent in the Fox Islands and Kodiak. It seems unlikely that the small amount of Russian trade goods put into the system and the minor incentives the Russians gave the western Aleuts to hunt furs in this period would have created the stimulation necessary to initiate slavery, perhaps escalate warfare, and induce stratification in the Fox Islands, over 125 miles from the nearest western Aleutian island and in Kodiak Island, 900 miles away.

The subsequent history of Russian relations on the Fox Islands and Kodiak lends further support to the hypothesis that slavery was not an artifact of the fur trade. Although the initial relations with Fox Islands Aleuts in 1759–62 were generally friendly, this changed abruptly. When four Russian ships arrived in 1763, the Aleuts killed all but six of the 175 men aboard. Russians arriving the following year discovered the killings and set out to extract revenge, almost wiping out or subjugating most of the Fox Islands Aleuts.

Fights and attrocities continued into the 1770s and 1780s. Russian ships with larger crews arrived more frequently than they had in earlier years, and continued the oppression. Aleuts were forced to hunt sea otter in large *baidarka* flotillas for the Russians as well as to help maintain them by preparing equipment and foodstuffs. By the 1790s only about a third of the approximately 10,000 Fox Islands Aleuts remained (Sarychev 1807:72). Not only fighting with the Russians but also food shortages resulting from disruptions in subsistence activities, Russian demands for difficult and dangerous work, and diseases caused the Aleut deaths.

Although Kodiak was discovered in 1763, it was not until 1784, after subduing or killing many hostile Koniags, that the Russian entrepreneur, Shelikhov gained a foothold. During the fighting, many of the Koniags' slaves escaped to the Russians in hope of better treatment.

After the Fox Islanders' and Koniags' defeat, some slavery continued in Aleut and Koniag areas not under Russian domination, but many of the old practices connected with slavery quickly died out. For example, by 1777 in the Aleutians slaves rarely were sacrificed at the death of their owners (Masterson and Brower 1948:91). By about 1800, slavery itself had virtually ceased. Where the Russians were in heavy force, they commandeered all slaves as *Kaiurs*, a kind of indentured servant. When these *Kaiurs* died, they were replaced by some free natives who had been sentenced to this lifetime position for minor or imagined offences (Black 1977:86; Davydov 1977:190–191; Okun 1951:205–206; Sarafian 1970:173–174). In essence, Russians took over the slaves of the natives for their own use, and then converted many of the natives themselves to a virtual slavery for minor breaches of Russian law.

Following Russian contact in the Fox Islands and Kodiak, traditional richmen and chiefs lost their authority and privilege. They were compelled to work alongside other Aleuts for the Russians. Poverty prevailed. Some of the Aleuts and Koniags were so burdened with obligations for corvee work for the Russians that they had difficulty providing sustenance for themselves and their families.

By the beginning of the 19th century, Aleuts and Koniags ceased to exist in independent societies. Their traditional rank/incipient stratification system had collapsed, and they were incorporated into the Russian class system in a category similar to state peasants in Russia.

Summary

Slavery and at least a degree of ranking were in existence in the Fox Islands by the time the Russians arrived there in 1759. For the Fox Islanders to have originated and developed slavery and intensified ranking and evolved a system of incipient stratification in response to stimuli from Russian contact far to the west seems highly improbable.

Between 1745 and 1758, there were 12 Russian voyages to the western Aleutians—a total of perhaps 500 men who were poorly provisioned, carried few trade goods, and acquired most furs by their own efforts. In order to derive Fox Islands slavery from Russian contact, we must hypothesize that the activities of these few hunters created such a level of trading and fur activity among western Aleuts that people as far away as the Fox Islands and Kodiak were stimulated to begin to convert captives, widows, and orphans to slave status to be used as wealth objects, in trade, and for labor within a maximum of 13 years (1745-58). If this were the case, then slavery and perhaps ranking and incipient stratification could have existed a maximum of only 55 years (1745-ca. 1800); during 32 of those 55 years in the Fox Islands (1768-1800), and 16 on Kodiak (1784-1800), the natives were subject to severe, often oppresive Russian domination, and many richmen lost their high-ranked positons.

It seems more feasable to postulate that slavery, together with rank and incipient stratification, were pre-contact phenomena. The system was already under stress from escalated raiding prior to Russian arrival; the Russians simply completed the destruction of the system that had already begun. Indigenous conflicts, in fact, seem a major factor in the speed of the Russians' successful subjugation of the people.

The Aleut case indicates that true slavery and political evolution to the point of stratification can occur within a familial type of system having a hunting, fishing, and gathering base. Where ranking is important and a means of achieving rank is through items of value, some of which are redistributed to gain followers, slavery can be a compatible institution, and it may contribute to the evolution of more complex systems.

Notes

Acknowledgments. I wish to acknowledge with appreciation the advice and assistance of Edwin O. Anderson, and the support of The Canada Council and the Northern Studies Committee of the University of Manitoba. I also want to thank

Louise E. Sweet and Jean-Luc Chodkiewicz for their very valuable comments on an earlier version of this manuscript.

1. The Coxe reference is a portion of Soloviev's notes that dates approximately 1764; the Masterson and Brower source contains a translation of the records of the voyage of Captain Krenitsin and Lieutenant Levashev in 1768.

2. Sources are derived from early Russian *promishlenniki* (fur hunter) accounts of societies at or shortly after contact. Additional ethnographic data were obtained from Russian priests' writings: Iosaf, who was on Kodiak in 1794–99, 10 to 15 years after the Russians established a post on the island in 1784, and Gedeon (Gideon) at Kodiak between 1804 and 1807. The most extensive "ethnographic present" account of the Fox Islands Aleuts was by Veniaminov, who was priest there in 1824–34. Although more than 68 years had elapsed since the Russian conquest of the islands, Veniaminov made careful attempts to describe Aleut society just before the advent of the Russians and to point out changes that had occurred subsequent to the takeover. I have found an over-all consistency between the sources and believe they deserve a high degree of confidence. I make the assumption that descriptions written shortly after contact, such as those of the Russian *promishlenniki* and Kodiak priests, are valid pictures of the societies as they were just prior to contact, due to the nature of the Russian contacts and the short time that had elapsed since contact.

3. Much of this summary is taken from my monograph in preparation: *Russian Mercantilism and Alaskan Native Social Change*. Sources for historic materials include Berkh (1974), Cox (1787), Fedorova (1973), Makarova (1975), and Okun (1951).

References Cited

Andreyev, A. I.
    1952   Russian Discoveries in the Pacific and in North America in the Eighteenth and Nineteenth Centuries. Carl Ginsburg, transl. Ann Arbor: J. W. Edwards.

Berkh, Vasilii Nikolaevich
    1974 [1823]   A Chronological History of the Discovery of the Aleutian Islands or the Exploits of Russian Merchants. Dmitri Krenov, transl. Richard A. Pierce, ed. Materials for the study of Alaska History, No. 5. Kingston, Ont.: Limestone Press.

Black, Lydia T., ed.
    1977   The Koniag (The Inhabitants of the Island of Kodiak) by Iosaf [Bolotov] (1794–1799) and by Gideon (1804–1807). Artic Anthropology 14(2):79–108.

Burch, Ernest S., Jr.
    1975   Eskimo Kinsmen: Changing Family Relationships in Northwest Alaska. American Ethnological Society Monograph 59. St. Paul: West Publishing.

Coxe, William
    1787   Account of the Russian Discoveries between Asia and America. 3rd ed. London: J. Nichols for T. Cadell. (Reprinted: Augustus M. Kelley, New York, 1970.)

Davydov, Gavriil Ivanovich
    1977 [1810–12]   Two Voyages to Russian America, 1802–1807. Colin Bearne,

transl. Richard A. Pierce, ed. Materials for the Study of Alaska History, No. 10. Kingston, Ont.: Limestone Press.

Fedorova, Svetlana G.
1973 The Russian Population in Alaska and California: Late 18th Century–1867. Richard A. Pierce and Alton S. Donnelly, transls. and eds. Materials for the Study of Alaska History, No. 4. Kingston, Ont.: Limestone Press.

Finley, M. I.
1972 The Extent of Slavery. *In* Slavery: A Comparative Perspective, Robert W. Winks, ed. pp. 3–15. New York: New York University Press.

Fried, Morton H.
1957 The Classification of Corporate Unilineal Descent Groups. Journal of the Royal Anthropological Institute of Great Britain and Ireland 87:1–29.
1967 The Evolution of Political Society, An Essay in Political Anthropology. New York: Random House.

Gunther, Erna
1972 Indian Life on the Northwest Coast of North America as Seen by the Early Explorers and Fur Traders during the Last Decades of the Eighteenth Century. Chicago: University of Chicago Press.

Jochelson, Waldemar
1933 History, Ethnology and Anthropology of the Aleut. Carnegie Institution of Washington Publication 432.

Lantis, Margaret
1970 The Aleut Social System, 1750 to 1810, from Early Historical Sources. *In* Ethnohistory in Southwestern Alaska and the Southern Yukon: Method and Content, Margaret Lantis, ed. pp. 139–301. Lexington: University Press of Kentucky.

Laughlin, William S.
1963 Eskimos and Aleuts: Their Origins and Evolution. Science 142:633–645.

Levy, Marion J.
1966 Modernization and the Structure of Societies: A Setting for International Affairs. 2 vols. Princeton: Princeton University Press.

Lisianski, Urey
1814 A Voyage Round the World in the Years 1803, 4, 5, and 6. London: John Booth.

Makarova, Raisa V.
1975 Russians on the Pacific, 1743–1799. Richard A. Pierce and Alton S. Donnelly, transls. and eds. Materials for the Study of Alaska History, No. 6. Kingston, Ont.: Limestone Press.

Masterson, James R., and Helen Brower
1948 Bering's Successors, 1745–1780: Contributions of Peter Simon Pallas to the History of Russian Exploration toward Alaska. Seattle: University of Washington Press.

Merck, Carl Heinrich
1980 Siberia and Northwestern America, 1788–1792. Fritz Jaensch, transl. Richard A. Pierce, ed. Materials for the Study of Alaska History, No. 17. Kingston, Ont.: Limestone Press.

Nieboer, H. J.
   1910   Slavery as an Industrial System. 2nd ed. The Hague: M. Nijhoff. (Reprinted: Burt Franklin, New York, 1971. Research and Source Work Series No. 770.)
Okun, S. B.
   1951   The Russian-American Company. Carl Ginsburg, transl. Cambridge: Harvard University Press.
Ruyle, Eugene E.
   1973   Slavery, Surplus, and Stratification on the Northwest Coast: The Ethnoenergetics of an Incipient Stratification System. Current Anthropology 14:603–631.
Sarafian, Winston Lee
   1970   Russian-American Company Employee Policies and Practices, 1799–1867. Ph.D. dissertation. History Department, University of California, Los Angeles.
Sarychev, Gawrila (Sarytschew)
   1807   Account of a Voyage of Discovery to the North-east of Siberia, the Frozen Ocean, and the North-east Sea. Vol. 2. London: Richard Phillips.
Sauer, Martin
   1802   An Account of a Geographical and Astronomical Expedition to the Northern Parts of Russia. London: T. Cadell, Jun. and W. Davies.
Townsend, Joan B.
   1960–73   Field Notes, Tanaina Region, Southern Alaska. Manuscript in files of author.
   1978   Human Chattels in Southern Alaska. Paper presented at the American anthropological Association meetings, Los Angeles, California.
   1979   Indian or Eskimo? Interaction and Identity in Southern Alaska. Artic Anthropology 16(2):160–182.
   1980   Ranked Societies of the Alaskan Pacific Rim. In Alaska Native Culture and History, Senri Ethnological Studies, No. 4, pp. 123–156. Osaka: National Museum of Ethnology.
Turner, Christy G., II
   1976   The Aleuts of Akun Island. The Alaska Journal 6(1): 25–31.
Veniaminov, Ivan Evsieevich Popov [Innokentii, Metropolitan of Moscow]
   1840   Zapiski ob ostrovakh Unalaskhkinskago otdela [Notes on the Islands of the Unalaska District]. 3 vols. St. Petersburg: Russian-American Company. (Transl. by B. Keen and A. Kardenelowska of Vol. 2 and part of Vol. 3 in Human Relations Area Files, New Haven, n.d.)

11
Warfare and Redistributive Exchange on the Northwest Coast

Brian Ferguson
Columbia University

War on the Northwest Coast affected many areas of social life. The purpose of this paper is to investigate its relation to the pattern of redistribution of food and property. My thesis is that war made redistributive exchange between neighboring groups necessary; such exchange was a means of preventing attacks and building alliances in an atmosphere charged with potential violence. In a final section, I will show how this perspective relates to several established views of the potlatch.

Northwest Coast warfare was no game. As I discuss in detail elsewhere (Ferguson in press), war was deadly serious struggle. Sneak attacks, pitched battles, ambushes, prolonged attritional campaigns, treacherous massacres, sporadic raiding—these were facts of life from before contact to "pacification" in the 1860s. Casualties and captives, at least in some historic periods, occurred at rates certainly equal to any reported for non-state-level warfare.

Warfare was, in large part, a contest over control of valuable resources. Before depopulation, wars were fought over prime subsistence areas. Upstream, inland, or coastal groups tried to conquer rich estuarine territories. Groups owning no salmon streams sought to take them by force. Peoples from coasts exposed to the full brunt of Pacific storms tried to push their way into more sheltered locales.

Control of trade was another source of conflict. Before and after contact, middlemen interceded in long distance trade, commonly amassing considerable fortunes. Middleman positions involved geographic control of maritime trade routes, passes to the interior, or, after contact, western posts. In some cases, middleman activity was beneficial for all involved. But in most, the intrusion was unnecessary and resented by other parties. Aggressors in trade wars were attempting to establish themselves as middlemen or to avoid giving a cut to another group.

Many raids aimed at capturing food, property, or slaves. Other commonly expressed goals were to obtain revenge or a fearsome reputation. In some cases these goals must be accepted at face value. In others, they apparently were part of a strategy of warding off future attacks or were rationalizations of more mundane interests. Wars fought solely to capture ceremonial titles or crests seem to have been rare, despite the prominence given to this motive in ethnographies.

The clear picture emerging from available data is that, up to the 1860s, peoples of the Northwest Coast were living in a constant "state of war." Endemic warfare can have a profound effect on other areas of social life. It may be the greatest single hazard faced by a people, a challenge that must be met. As one of Gunther's (1927:182) Klallum informants put it, "all they [his ancestors] wanted was enough to eat and to be ready for war." Throughout the Northwest Coast, preparations were taken against the threat of war.

Villages were located in or near defensible positions, with sophisticated defensive structures incorporated in their redoubts (Drucker 1951:67; Gunther 1972:75; Gormly 1971:158, 163; MacDonald 1980:12, 20; Niblack 1970:303; Vancouver 1967:I:324–333). The first explorers found an elaborate war armor and weaponry, including blades of precious iron (Drucker 1963:96–98; Gunther 1972:42–45; MacDonald 1978:16–29). After contact, a major portion of the wealth obtained in the fur trade was expended on weapons (Wike 1951:41–44). In some areas at least, specialized training and conditioning of warriors was highly developed (Boas 1966:106; De Laguna 1972:583; Drucker 1951:345–347). The strategic and tactical planning observed in the war accounts reveals an astonishing sophistication. The posture assumed at meetings with strangers displayed a tense mixture of peaceful overtures and demonstrations of military preparedness (Beaglehole 1967:298; Bolton 1971:323, 342; Dixon 1968: 206; Jewitt 1896:199; Smith 1940:153; Sproat 1868:57). In some extreme cases, the threat of external attack gave war leaders a great deal of power over daily life (Collins 1950:339; McIlwraith 1948:I:175; II:364–369). Another response to this threat was a pattern of redistribution enmeshing neighbors in networks of mutually beneficial alliances.

Food and property were accumulated and redistributed in a wide variety of quantities and contexts. In the following discussion, I will adhere to traditional usage by distinguishing "feasts" (redistributions of food) from "potlatches" (redistributions of property). It must be noted, however, that these two handy categories simplify a more complex reality, a continuum of redistributions ranging from simple sharing of food with kin to elaborate ceremonials involving the destruction of property (see Blackman 1976; Goldman 1975).

To understand feasting as a response to war, we must first understand an important feature of the regional subsistence base. Food resources were subject to unpredictable local fluctuations. Local variations in the quantity and arrival times of salmon have been ample documented (Blackman 1976; Donald and Mitchell 1975; Langdon 1979; Neave 1958; New York Times 1979; Schalk 1977; Sneed 1972; Suttles 1960). Although some questions remain on the applicability of these figures to pre-commercial fishing times, the studies strongly implicate natural conditions as a major cause of the variation. Some of the more perceptive early explorers report fluctuations comparable to those of modern times (Brabant 1900:54; Jewitt 1931; Sproat 1868: 216). Other resources also varied according to localized environmental perturbations (Blackman 1976; Drucker and Heizer 1967:139; Suttles 1974).

These temporary inequalities among neighbors could be equalized by feasts. Feasts were common affairs in early times, given whenever anyone had a surplus of food (Drucker 1951:368–371; Drucker and Heizer 1967:35; Jewitt 1896:151, 172, 179; Oberg 1973:96; Sproat 1868;59). Jewitt (1931:9–12), for instance, recorded nine feasts among local Nootka in one month (June) alone. As Suttles (1960) and others have observed, redistributive sharing of food in an environment of localized resource fluctuations would have long-term advantages for all involved. But in the near-term, families or local groups might be tempted to retain surpluses for personal use. Consideration of warfare explains why they would share with their fellows even when, as is recorded (Jewitt 1931), a threat of imminent food shortage was perceptible. Hoarding food when your neighbors are hungry is a very dangerous thing to do. By redistributing food surpluses, potential enemies were neutralized. There is no need to take forcibly that which is freely and regularly given.

That accumulated food stores could invite a raid is not in dispute. After studying hundreds of pages of unpublished war texts, MacDonald (1980:24), concluded that the "first and foremost" reason for early wars among the Tsimshian, Tlingit, and Haida was to capture accumulated food. McIlwraith (1948:II:339) ascribes the same motivation to later Kwakiutl raiders of the Bella Coola further south. The idea that food redistributions occurred under the implicit threat of violence is supported by other observations. Drucker (1951:372–374) reports an instance when the takers of an early salmon run were prompted to give a feast by the grumblings of hungry neighbors. (Perhaps such grumblings contributed to the development of the regional pattern of ceremonial communal consumption of the first salmon catch of a season—see Drucker 1963:156). Oberg (1934:150) notes that, while the Tlingit considered trespass on resource territory a crime punishable by death, *powerful* intruders would instead be invited to feast. Drift whales provided critical food supplies to Nootka and Haida at times when other resources were at their lowest ebb. Whale flesh was a major feast food at these times (Jewitt 1931). But this feasting occurred in a context of competing claims to the whales—a competition that was often marked by quarrels and fights (Brabant 1900:59; Collison 1915:172; Sapir and Swadesh 1955:346–349, 383).

More than eliminating neighbors as potential enemies, feasting bound them as allies. Neighbors had a vested interest in aiding people who regularly contributed to their sustenance. They often provided critical information, support, or refuge in wars over territory, trade, or slaves. Given the general militarist approach to resolving conflicts over resources, and the pervasive threat of attack from the outside, a strategy of local self-sufficiency in food production would be self-destructive.

Redistributions of property involved similar considerations. Accumulations of property far above the local norm could invite a raid. Such raids did occur (Boas 1969:93; Curtis 1915:114, 143; Piddocke 1960; also see Boas 1935:61). Two contrasting incidents involving windfalls of property illustrate the dangers of accumulation. When the Yakutat Tlingit overran a Russian post during the early fur trade, word spread of the wealth they had acquired and kept to themselves. Other Tlingit finally decided to "take it away from them." Most of the Yakutat were killed in the subsequent raids (De Laguna 1972:261–263). But when the Moachat Nootka plundered the trade ship *Boston* and other Nootka "from no less than twenty tribes" arrived within days, the wily chief Maquina avoided violence by giving away great quantities of goods in a potlatch (Jewitt 1896:76–82).

The complex web of debts and expectations of returns that linked potlatching groups worked against open hostilities. It made little sense to wipe out people who owed you something, or to watch passively while someone else did (see Adams 1973:114). A negative illustration of this is provided by McIlwraith (1948:I:230; II:376), who describes a war caused by the failure of one group to repay debts incurred in potlatching. Such a failure to repay was very unusual, and this is the only case I found of a regular potlatch relationship degenerating into open warfare. The affinal links upon which potlatch relations were built (Rosman and Rubel 1971) also inhibited warfare between linked groups. Ties of sentiment were considered in planning military actions, and the presence of relatives in the settlements of intended victims made it difficult to preserve the vital element of surprise (De Laguna 1972:583; Drucker 151:357–363; Garfield 1939:268; McIlwraith 1948:II:371; Sapir and Swadesh 1955:363).

The discussion so far has been concerned with exchanges between neighboring groups. Most potlatches involved neighbors (Donald and Mitchell 1975:325; Drucker and Heizer 1967:79, 142, 145; Garfield 1939:193). This redistribution-as-military-alliance perspective can, however, be applied to relations between more distant groups that had mutual interests in trade or war. Potlatching and marriage between such groups became more common during the height of the western trade than they had been (Drucker and Heizer 1967:42–44; Garfield 1966:37; Goldman 1940:340–353; McIlwraith 1948:II: 357–359; Sproat 1868:99). But the military alliance aspect of potlatching was sometimes eclipsed in the historic period, when a few local groups became so wealthy and powerful that they were immune to attack (Fisher 1977:46; MacDonald 1980:20; McIlwraith 1948:II:339; Wike 1951:99).

Warfare and Redistributive Exchange

Several lines of evidence support the argument that redistributive exchange was used to forestall aggression and build alliances. Gifts of food, property, and women were used to prevent attacks (Boas 1935:61; Haeberlin and Gunther 1930:51; Oberg 1973:99); to bring wars to an end (Boas 1970:378; Collison 1915:104, 221; Curtis 1913:34; Drucker 1951:357, 364; McIlwraith 1948:II:357–359; Swadesh 1948:80); to recruit allies in war (De Laguna 1972:581; Duff 1959:30; Garfield 1939:193, 268; Haeberlin and Gunther 1930:13; Swadesh 1948:80); and to maintain alliances in warfare situations (Boas 1966:41; Grant 1857:296; Haeberlin and Gunther 1930:51; Mayne 1969:258; Murdock 1935:40). Within the circle of potlatching exchange, groups generally did not make war on each other, and often acted together in war (Donald and Mitchell 1975:325; Drucker and Heizer 1967:39, 75, 142–145; Mayne 1969:263; McIlwraith 1948:I:22; Piddocke 1960:46; 1965:150 n.; Sanger 1959; Smith 1940:151). The similarity of peace-making ceremonies and potlatches has been noted (De Laguna 1972:147; McClellan 1954:96), as has the extensive warfare imagery in potlatch ceremonies (Codere 1950:119–123; Haeberlin and Gunther 1930:14; McClellan 1954:86; Smith 1940:108; Snyder 1975:153). Some accounts suggest that the frequency of potlatching increased in proportion to the intensity of regional hostilities (Brown 1896:17; Murdock 1935:240). Meares' (1790:267–268) observation in 1788 is particularly interesting:

> the Nootka nations are not only in frequent hostilities with more distant tribes, but even among themselves . . . they can never be said to be in a state of peace: They must live in constant expectation of an enemy, and never relax from that continual preparation against those hostilities and incursions which doom the captives to slavery or to death. The chiefs of this country have a custom which . . . appears to be derived from the wars of the different states with each other. . . . This custom consists in yielding up their wives to, or interchanging them with, each other. . . . [A] woman is sometimes found necessary to sooth a conquerer, or to purchase a favorable article in a treaty.

Given the pattern of potlatching to one's affines (Rosman and Rubel 1971), it seems likely that these intermarriages were accompanied by regular redistributive exchange.

I have argued that war made redistribution necessary for survival. The tactical manipulation of exchanges for military advantage shows that the participants were clearly aware of their value in this context. As one Salish informant described this aspect of redistribution: "Potlatch is like shaking hands in a material way" (Snyder 1975:151). But if any local group failed to build alliances in this manner, war provided a mechanism for selectively eliminating such groups. Thus it can be seen why Northwest Coast peoples universally emphasized redistribution in spite of their diverse cultural backgrounds. It can also be inferred that the emphasis on redistribution is as old as the pattern of military competition over resources. MacDonald (1979, and personal communication) has archaeological evidence for a developed war complex dating to ca. 1000 B.C. So the redistributive pattern is probably at least 3,000 years old, and perhaps much older.

If war can explain the necessity of redistribution in Northwest Coast economies, it cannot by itself "explain the potlatch." The ceremonial events we call "potlatch" were more than just redistribution. Anthropological speculation on the custom has often focused on aspects far removed from subsistence and survival. Anthropologists have studied the relation of potlatching to social structure, political economy, and cosmology, providing answers to questions not directly related to the issues discussed here.[1] But other explanations do overlap sufficiently to warrant reconsideration in light of that of war. These are discussed next.

From an ecological perspective, Suttles (1960), Vayda (1968), and Piddocke (1965) explain the potlatch as part of a self-regulating system involving exchanges of food, wealth, and prestige. Prestige was enhanced, they argue, by giving to the needy, so the system functioned to equalize local fluctuations in resources by transferring food from "haves" to "have-nots." Consideration of war preserves this last and basic point. In fact, it is strengthened. If redistributions were means to non-aggression/mutual defense alliances, their function in equalizing resources can be explained while avoiding objections to the current ecological model.

Critics (Drucker and Heizer 1967; Orans 1975; Ruyle 1973) have attacked this ecological model on several points. They dispute the aboriginal existence of the food-for-wealth accounting system posited by the ecologists, and assert that there is no evidence that redistributions raised carrying capacity by preventing actual starvation. The explanation of redistribution as a defensive tactic suggests neither point, but simply that a group with food or property in temporay abundance would be obliged to share with less fortunate neighbors.

By explaining redistribution as motivated by rational calculation of material self-interest, three other objections to the Suttles-Vayda-Piddocke formulation can be neutralized. First, in shifting the motivation of redistributors away from the pursuit of prestige, which ecologists have emphasized, this view avoids what Ruyle (1973:605) has called "an inherently mystical interpretation of the role of mentalistic phenomena [prestige-seeking] in a population's adjustment to its environment." Second, the redistribution-as-military-alliance explanation is not cast in functionalist form (see Orans 1975). It is based on the principle of self-interest, not system maintenance. Third, the distant origins of redistribution can be attributed to conscious strategy rather than to some vaguely defined process of random variation and selective retention (see Suttles 1960:304; 1973:622).

Warfare and Redistributive Exchange

A variation of the ecological approach states that displays of wealth at potlatches resulted in the long-term reapportioning of popuation to available resources (Adams 1973; Harris 1980; Hazard 1960). The productivity of a local group's territory could be judged by the scale of their potlatches. Individuals would then, over time, shift residence from areas of scarcity to surplus. The factor of war can help explain why it was that nobles in rich but relatively underpopulated areas would want to attract more people. More men meant increased military strength.

Barnett (1938), Drucker (1939), Drucker and Heizer (1967), and Garfield (1939) have offered a "social validation" explanation of the potlatch. Their writings vary considerably in specifics, but they share the central thesis that the potlatch was a mechanism for obtaining social recognition or validation of a noble's claim to hereditary titles. The guests at a potlatch were, in effect, paid to witness the rite of accession. These titles included ceremonial and status prerogatives, but more importantly (for this review) they included titles of ownersip to productive resource territories and trade positions (Netting 1971:11–12).

All productive areas of the Northwest Coast were claimed by individual groups (Beaglehole 1967:306; Garfield 1966:14; Linton, in Drucker 1939:141; Service 1963:216; Blackman 1976). At potlatches a noble, as the representative of his group, obtained the recognition of others of his right to control these resource areas. By considering the factors of competition over resources and warfare, why the people went to such trouble to obtain recognition of their claims can be understood.

It is one thing to share a surplus by redistribution. It is quite another to have outsiders move into your territory whenever they feel like it. Most reports indicate that outsiders would be granted permission if they asked to use a group's territory, usually with some restrictions on the amount taken or requirements of payment of part of the take (Beaglehole 1967:306; De Laguna 1972:361; Krause 1970:16; Service 1963:216). But that tension existed over these restrictions is demonstrated by the common reports of violence related to unauthorized usage (Boas 1966:35, 110; Collison 1915:307–309; Duff 1959:30–36; Haeberlin and Gunther 1930:12; Oberg 1934:149).

Ethologists have observed that many species, when in situations of competition over resources, employ behaviors that clearly demarcate territories. These displays are adaptations that result in the avoidance of open, costly conflict (Eibl-Eibesfeldt 1979). I am *not* suggesting that Northwest Coast validation procedures resulted from a similar genetic adaptation, but by analogy that the validation aspect of the potlatch resulted in widespread recognition (and "sacralization"?—Rappaport 1979) of clearly demarcated claims to specific resources. This would certainly reduce the bloodshed that would otherwise result from encroachments on vaguely defined or disputed territories.

Mauss (1967), Levi-Strauss (1969), and Sahlins (1972) have emphasized the multifaceted nature of the potlatch. They see it as a "total social fact" (Levi-Strauss 1969:58) involving the exchange of economic valuables and, more importantly, the complex manipulation of power, influence, and status. Through the potlatch, Northwest Coast peoples effected the transcendance of a state of "warre" (Sahlins 1972:173) between isolated, autonomous social groups. Their perspective would be enhanced by the conclusions developed here. The reality of the other manipulations they stress is not denied, but the economic significance of redistribution is deemed more important than they imply. And the antagonisms that are being transcended are not an abstract, Hobbesian "warre," but real, deadly warfare.

Codere (1950; 1961) has described the potlatch as a temporal replacement of war. She portrays war as primarily a quest for prestige, which was abandoned when the potlatch system floresced in the mid-1800s. Elsewhere (Ferguson in press) I have disputed both her characterization of Kwakiutl warfare and her claim that it ended with the take-off of potlatching. Potlatch and warfare were co-existing parts of one system. Codere's is the only theory of the potlatch in direct contradiction to the view presented in this paper, although this view might not have been developed had it not been for Codere's pioneering insight on the linkage of war and potlatch.

Finally, Ruyle (1973) explains the potlatch as part of a larger "incipient stratification system." It was, he believes, a mechanism by which nobles extracted "ethnoenergy" or surplus value from commoners and slaves. Ruyle bases this explanation on the fact that commoners contributed to the amassing of goods for a chief's potlatch. He (Ruyle 1973:615) then argues that at potlatches "less was distributed [by chiefs to commoners] than was obtained (a logical concomitant of the . . . fact that chiefs were wealthier and worked less than commoners)." But this logic is based on a questionable implicit assumption—that the wealth of the local group was internally produced. Ruyle would have done better to place more emphasis on the distinction he (Ruyle 1973:614) makes between internal and external exploitation.

The primary sources of wealth for the wealthiest groups of the historic period up to the 1860s were raiding and, more importantly, the control of trade (Ferguson in press; and see MacDonald 1980). At times this trade control seems to have operated through forced unequal exchange at potlatches, in which cases the potlatch ceased to be a mutually beneficial exchange between military equals and became instead a means of exploiting military inferiors. Success in raiding and trade control required the support of a sizable, loyal force of men-at-arms. Many authors, including Ruyle (1973:615), have noted that nobles were intensely interested in attracting and holding followers (Adams 1973:116; Jewitt 1896:216; Oberg 1973:60; Rosman and Rubel 1971:78; Vayda 1968:175). It would seem to be not only a logical possibility but also a practical probability that nobles seeking to maximize their own wealth adopted a strategy of sharing part of the wealth they extracted from outsiders within their own group. Commoners then would have received more wealth than they directly contributed to the nobles, although less than what the nobles gained from outsiders. These observations would not apply to the condition of slaves. The primary sources leave little doubt about the accuracy of Ruyle's portrayal of slaves as being consistently exploited.

Ruyle's argument cannot be treated quite so simply, however. The potlatch changed with the times.[2] Under a certain combination of circumstances related to war, trade, and Western contact, his description of the potlatch as a mechanism of intragroup exploitation in an incipient stratification system appears to be more accurate. I (Ferguson in press) have been able to document this combination of circumstances and the apparent development of an unstable stratified system only for the Clayoquot and Moachat Nootka of ca. 1785–1802. (Much of the data supporting Ruyle's argument pertains to these two groups.) While similar developments probably occurred in other instances, it is clear that they were definitely a result of contact, and atypical even in the post-contact period. So Ruyle's analysis may be accurate for some cases, but not of general applicability. As with the other theories reviewed above, consideration of war and related factors can put his explanation in proper context.

Throughout this paper, I have followed the lead of Swadesh (1948:76), who wrote of the Nootka: "the entire social structure of band and tribe, kinship and caste, as well as economy and social philosophy, are illuminated against the war background." My central point has been that the emphasis on redistribution in Northwest Coast economies can be explained as a response to a social environment of intense warfare. Exchanges of food, property, and women between neighbors were means of defusing potential conflicts over resources, and simultaneously building alliances needed in conflicts with more distant groups. The redistributive pattern is seen primarily as a result of conscious strategizing, but war is identified as a selective mechanism capable of eliminating groups that did not redistribute surpluses.

Notes

Acknowledgments. An earlier version of this paper was read and discussed at the Columbia University seminar on warfare. I wish to thank the following participants for their constructive criticism: Bill Balee, Jane Bennett Ross, Tom Biolsi, Jeff Bonner, Nick Flanders, Ashraf Ghani, Neil Goldberg, Dave Nugent, Barbara Price, and William Salgado. I also wish to thank Leslie Farragher-Ferguson, Morton Fried, Marvin Harris, Robert Murphy, and Paula Rubel for encouragement and/or readings of earlier drafts and Andrew Vayda for giving me access to papers from his 1960 seminar on the Northwest Coast.

1. To be precise, I include here the explanations of: Benedict (1932; 1934), Bishop (Chapter 12; this volume), Boas (1897), Dundes (1979), Fleisher (1981), Gold-

man (1975), Herskovits (1952), Murdock (1936), Rosman and Rubel (1971; 1972), Snyder (1975), and Weinberg (1965). See Irvin (1977) for a review.

2. Space limitations prohibit discussion here of potlatching after the end of warfare in the 1860s. In a future study, I hope to show that the perpetuation and fantastic escalation of potlatching in the late 19th century was a result of nobles' attempting to protect their positions against an onslaught of social mobility in a changed social and economic environment.

References Cited

Adams, John
    1973   The Gitksan Potlatch: Population Flux, Resource Ownership, and Reciprocity. Montreal: Holt, Rinehart and Winston of Canada.
Barnett, H. G.
    1938   The Nature of the Potlatch. American Anthropologist 40:349–357.
Beaglehole, J. C., ed.
    1967   The Voyage of the Resolution and Discovery, 1776–1780. Cambridge: Cambridge University Press.
Benedict, Ruth
    1932   Configurations of Culture in North America. American Anthropologist 34:1–27.
    1934   Patterns of Culture. Boston: Houghton Mifflin.
Blackman, Margaret
    1976   Northern Haida Ecology: A Preliminary Discussion. Paper prepared for the Northwest Coast Studies Conference, May 12–16, 1976, Vancouver, B.C.
Boas, Franz
    1897   The Social Organization and Secret Societies of the Kwakiutl Indians. Report of the U.S. National Museum for 1895, pp. 311–738.
    1935   Kwakiutl Culture as Reflected in Mythology. American Folklore Society Memoir 28.
    1966   Kwakiutl Ethnography. Helen Codere, ed. Chicago: University of Chicago Press.
    1969   Kwakiutl Tales. New York: AMS Press.
    1970   Tsimshian Mythology. New York: Johnson Reprint.
Bolton, H. E.
    1971   Fray Juan Crespi: Missionary Explorer on the Pacific Coast, 1769–1774. New York: AMS Press.
Brabant, A. J.
    1900   Vancouver and Its Missions, 1874–1900. Hesquiat, B.C.: Apostleship of Prayer.
Brown, Robert
    1896   Introduction to the Adventures of John Jewitt. London: Clement Wilson.
Codere, Helen
    1950   Fighting with Property: A Study of Kwakiutl Potlatching and Warfare, 1792–1930. Seattle: University of Washington Press.

1961 Kwakiutl. *In* Perspectives in American Indian Culture Change, Edward H. Spicer, ed. pp. 431–516. Chicago: University of Chicago Press.
Collins, June
 1950 Growth of Class Distinctions and Political Authority among the Skagit Indians During the Contact Period. American Anthropologist 52:331–342.
Collison, W. H.
 1915 In the Wake of the War Canoe. London: Seeley, Service.
Curtis, Edward S.
 1913 The North American Indian. Vol. 9: The Salish. Seattle: E. S. Curtis.
 1915 The North American Indian. Vol. 10: The Kwakiutl. Seattle: E. S. Curtis.
De Laguna, Frederica
 1972 Under Mount Saint Elias: The History and Culture of the Yakutat Tlingit. Smithsonian Contributions to Anthropology Vol. 7. 3 pts.
Dixon, George
 1968 A Voyage Round the World. New York: DaCapo Press.
Donald, Leland, and Donald Mitchell
 1975 Some Correlates of Local Group Rank among the Southern Kwakiutl. Ethnology 14:325–346.
Drucker, Philip
 1939 Rank, Wealth, and Kinship in Northwest Coast Society. American Anthropologist 41:55–64.
 1951 The Northern and Central Nootkan Tribes. Bureau of American Ethnology Bulletin 144.
 1963 Indians of the Northwest Coast. Garden City: Natural History Press.
Drucker, Philip, and Robert Heizer
 1967 To Make My Name Good: A Reexamination of the Southern Kwakiutl Potlatch. Berkeley: University of California Press.
Duff, Wilson
 1959 Histories, Territories, and Laws of the Kitwancool. Victoria: British Columbia Provincial Museum.
Dundes, Alan
 1979 Heads or Tails: A Psychoanalytic Study of the Potlatch. Journal of Psychological Anthropology 2:395–424.
Eibl-Eibesfeldt, Irenaeus.
 1979 The Biology of Peace and War. New York: Viking.
Ferguson, Brian
 In press A Re-examination of the Causes Northwest Coast Warfare. *In* Cultures at War: Essays on the Ecology and Economy of Warfare. Brian Ferguson, ed. New York: Academic Press.
Fisher, Robin
 1977 Contact and Conflict: Indian-European Relations in British Columbia, 1774–1890. Vancouver: University of British Columbia Press.
Fleisher, Mark
 1981 The Potlatch: A Symbolic and Psychoanalytic View. Current Anthropology 22:69–71.

Garfield, Viola E.
  1939 Tsimshian Clan and Society. University of Washington Publications in Anthropology, Vol. 7, No. 3.
  1966 The Tsimshian and Their Neighbors. In The Tsimshian Indians and Their Arts. Viola Garfield and Paul Wingert, eds. pp. 5-17. Seattle: University of Washington Press.
Goldman, Irving
  1940 The Alkatcho Carrier of British Columbia. In Acculturation in Seven American Indian Tribes, Ralph Linton, ed. pp. 333-389. New York: Appleton--Century.
  1975 The Mouth of Heaven: An Introduction to Kwakiutl Religious Thought. New York: John Wiley and Sons.
Gormly, Mary
  1971 Tlingits of Bucareli Bay Alaska (1774-1792). Northwest Anthropological Research Notes 5:157-180.
Grant, W. Colquhoun
  1857 Description of Vancouver Island. Journal of the Royal Geographical Society 27:268-320.
Gunther, Erna
  1927 Klallam Ethnography. University of Washington Publications in Anthropology, Vol. 1, No. 5.
  1972 Indian Life on the Northwest Coast of North America. Chicago: University of Chicago Press.
Haeberlin, Hermann, and Erna Gunther
  1930 The Indians of Puget Sound. Seattle: University of Washington Press.
Harris, Marvin
  1980 Culture, People, Nature. 3rd ed. New York: Harper and Row.
Hazard, Thomas
  1960 On the Nature of the Numaym and Its Counterparts Elsewhere on the Northwest Coast. Paper presented at the 127th Annual Meeting of the American Association for the Advancement of Science, Denver.
Herskovits, Melville
  1952 Economic Anthropology. New York: Knopf.
Irvin, Terry
  1977 The Northwest Coast Potlatch since Boas, 1897-1972. Anthropology 1:65-77.
Jewitt, John
  1896 The Adventures of John Jewitt. London: Clement Wilson.
  1931 A Journal Kept at Nootka Sound. Boston: C. E. Goodspeed.
Krause, Aurel
  1970 The Tlingit Indians. Seattle: University of Washington Press.
Landgon, Steve
  1979 Comparative Tlingit and Haida Adaptation to the West Coast of the Prince of Wales Archipelago. Ethnology 18:101-119.
Levi-Strauss, Claude
  1969 Elementary Structures of Kinship. Boston: Beacon Press.

Mauss, Marcel
   1967   The Gift. New York: Norton.
Mayne, R. C.
   1969   Four Years in British Columbia and Vancouver Island. New York: Johnson Reprint.
McClellan, Catharine
   1954   The Interrelations of Social Structure with Northern Tlingit Ceremonialism. Southwestern Journal of Anthropology 10:75–96.
MacDonald, George F.
   1979   Kitwanga Fort National Historic Site, Skeena River, British Columbia: Historical Research and Analysis of Structural Remains. Ottawa: National Museum of Man.
   1980   The Epic of Nekt: The Archaeology of Metaphor. Banquet Address to the 13th Annual Meeting of the Canadian Archaeological Association, Saskatoon, April 24-27, 1980.
McIlwraith, T. F.
   1948   The Bella Coola Indians. 2 vols. Toronto: University of Toronto Press.
Meares, John
   1970   Voyages Made in the Years 1788 and 1789 from China to the North West Coast of America. London.
Murdock, George Peter
   1935   Our Primitive Contemporaries. New York: Macmillan.
   1936   Rank and Potlatch among the Haida. Yale University Publications in Anthropology, No. 13.
Neave, Ferris
   1958   Stream Ecology and Production of Anadromous Fish. *In* The Investigation of Fish-Power Problems, P. A. Larkin, ed. pp. 43–51. Vancouver: Institute of Fisheries, University of British Columbia.
Netting, Robert McC.
   1971   The Ecological Approach in Cultural Study. Reading, Mass.: Addison-Wesley Publishing.
New York Times
   1979   Salmon Almost Wiped Out by 1977 Drought in Idaho. May 27, p. 26.
Niblack, Albert
   1970   The Coast Indians of Southern Alaska and Northern British Columbia. New York: Johnson Reprint.
Oberg, Kalvervo
   1934   Crime and Punishment in Tlingit Society. American Anthropologist 36:145–156.
   1973   The Social Economy of the Tlingit Indians. Seattle: University of Washington Press.
Orans, Martin
   1975   Domesticating the Functional Dragon: An Analysis of Piddocke's Potlatch. American Anthropologist 77:312–328.
Piddocke, Stuart
   1960   The Social Order of the Southern Kwakiutl. Unpublished paper.

1965 The Potlatch System of the Southern Kwakiutl: A New Perspective. *In* Environment and Cultural Behavior, Andrew Vayda, ed. pp. 130–156. Garden City: Natural History Press.

Rappaport, Roy
1979 Ecology, Meaning, and Religion. Richmond, CA: North Atlantic Books.

Rosman, Abraham, and Paula Rubel
1971 Feasting with Mine Enemy: Rank and Exchange among Northwest Coast Societies. New York: Columbia University Press.
1972 The Potlatch: A Structural Analysis. American Anthropologist 74:658–671.

Ruyle, Eugene
1973 Slavery, Surplus, and Stratification on the Northwest Coast: The Ethnoenergetics of an Incipient Stratification System. Current Anthropology 14:603–631.

Sahlins, Marshall
1972 Stone Age Economics. Chicago: Aldine.

Sanger, David
1959 Warfare amongst the Tlingit and Haida. Unpublished paper.

Sapir, Edward, and Morris Swadesh
1955 Native Accounts of Nootka Ethnography. Indiana University Research Center in Anthropology, Folklore, and Linguistics Publication 1.

Schalk, R. F.
1977 The Structure of an Anadromous Fish Resource. *In* For Theory Building in Archaeology, Lewis Binford, ed. pp. 207–249. New York: Academic Press.

Service, Elman
1963 Profiles in Ethnography. New York: Random House.

Smith, Marian
1940 The Puyallup-Nisqually. New York: Columbia University Press.

Sneed, P. G.
1972 Of Salmon and Men: An Investigation of Ecological Determinants and Aboriginal Man in the Canadian Plateau. *In* Aboriginal Man and Environments on the Plateau of Northwest America, A. Stryd and R. Smith, eds., pp. 229–238. Calgary: University of Alberta Press.

Snyder, Sally
1975 Quest for the Sacred in Northern Puget Sound: An Interpretation of Potlatch. Ethnology 14:149–161.

Sproat, Gilbert
1868 Scenes and Studies of Savage Life. London: Smith, Elder.

Suttles, Wayne
1960 Affinal Ties, Subsistence, and Prestige among the Coast Salish. American Anthropologist 62:296–305.
1973 Comment on "Slavery, Surplus, and Stratification on the Northwest Coast" by Eugene Ruyle. Current Anthropology 14:622.
1974 Variation in Habitat and Culture on the Northwest Coast. *In* Man in Adaptation: The Cultural Present, 2nd ed., Yehudi Cohen, ed. pp. 128–141. Chicago: Aldine.

Swadesh, Morris
1948 Motivations in Nootka Warfare. Southwestern Journal of Anthropology 4:76–93.

Vancouver, George
  1967 Voyage of Discovery to the North Pacific Ocean and Round the World. 3 vols. New York: DaCapo Press.
Vayda, Andrew
  1968 Economic Systems in Ecological Perspective: The Case of the Northwest Coast. *In* Readings in Anthropology, Vol. 2, Morton H. Fried, ed. pp. 173–178. New York: Thomas Crowell.
Weinberg, Daniela
  1965 Models of Southern Kwakiutl Social Organization. General Systems 10:169–181.
Wike, Joyce
  1951 The Effect of the Maritime Fur Trade on Northwest Coast Indian Society. Ph.D. dissertation. Anthropology Department, Columbia University.

12
Limiting Access to Limited Goods: The Origins of Stratification in Interior British Columbia

Charles A. Bishop
State University of New York at Oswego

How egalitarian societies are transformed into ranked ones recently has become a subject of some interest. Fried, who defined a ranked society as "one in which positions of valued status are somehow limited so that not all of those of sufficient talent to occupy such statuses actually achieve them" (Fried 1967:109), attributes the emergence of such societies to the availability of abundant foods and to redistribution mediated by a leader who attains his status by the act (Fried 1967:110–118, 182–184). Likewise, Service (1975:74–79) argues that environmental diversity favors the practice of intercommunity exchange and localized specialization, which give rise to hereditary offices filled by leaders who coordinate these activities. Embryonic chiefdoms with achieved leadership (a "big man" system), he suggests, mature into full chiefdoms as the tendency for the leader's achieved position to be transmitted to his eldest son is strengthened by the extension and formalization of redistribution practices.

However, not all have concurred with Fried's and Service's interpretations, particularly in respect to the role they attribute to redistribution in the development of ranked societies and chiefdoms. For example, on the basis of their analysis of data from the Mississippian Moundville site, Peebles and Kus (1977) reject redistribution as a necessary correlate of ranked societies. Somewhat similarly, Earle (1977:227) concludes from his examination of Hawaiian chiefdoms that communities there were self-sufficient and that "environmental diversity among districts was largely resolved by different options in the subsistence economy and not by extensive exchange." Nevertheless, in Hawaii, some evidence suggests "that the paramount chief occupied the central node of a redistributive network that received and allocated *sumptuary* items" (Peebles and Kus 1977:425).

These studies have implications for understanding the evolution and functioning of ranked societies on the Northwest Coast. There, social recognition of hereditary rank required public validation through the redistribution of property by a potlatch, but the purpose of the potlatch has been the subject of much debate. Some stressing resource abundance explain the potlatch in terms of sociological factors such as status validation, social integration, and dramatization of cultural values (Codere 1950:62-64; Drucker 1965:55-61; Drucker and Heizer 1967:8, 133-154). Others, noting regional and temporal variation in subsistence resources (Suttles 1960) and even scarcity (Piddocke 1965), see the redistributive potlatch as guaranteeing to different groups equal access to basic resources. But although Drucker and Heizer (1967:142-143) state that ecological variation cannot explain the potlatch since there were no "rigorously formalized food-for-wealth" exchanges, Donald and Mitchell (1975:343) show that among the Kwakiutl high rank, resource abundance, and demographic factors are correlated—a correlation that suggests ecological variables were operative although not necessarily that potlatches provisioned members of the society.

But whatever the purposes of the potlatch in relatively recent times—the potlatch was obviously multifunctional and there were regional and temporal variations in emphasis (Netting 1977:38-39)—these purposes are not necessarily the reasons behind the development of the potlatch. Factors explaining the persistence and/or elaboration of the potlatch among societies that are already ranked cannot automatically be projected backwards in time to account for origins. In order to distinguish causes for emergence from those for persistence, it is necessary to examine a society in the process of becoming ranked.

The Argument

The thesis suggested here is that hereditary rank first developed through inter- and intra-societal exchanges in luxury commodities and/or ritual objects. As groups in one area came to exchange on a regular basis certain non-essential, but not necessarily non-utilitarian, commodities with groups residing in different habitats, certain persons emerged as traders. These traders would have required the support of their kinsmen, from whom they acquired materials for exchange. Thus, as a quid pro quo, upon returning to the community, they would ceremonially redistribute the goods obtained elsewhere to those who had supported them. Such validation rituals for the maintenance of a privileged trade position was, it is conjectured, the source of the potlatch. This suggests why potlatches usually involved groups closely linked by kin ties (Drucker and Heizer 1967:39-40).

Initially, those who potlatched would have been more akin to "big men" than to "chiefs" (Sahlins 1963). If this was the case, the first step in the process of converting achieved positions derived from trade to hereditary offices would have involved maintaining control over exchange alliances over time. Irregular trade would produce only "occasional leaders," individuals who were important only when and only as long as they functioned in the exchange system. But regular trade would have required continual access to luxury goods and consequently continual kin support to produce the items needed for exchange. Thus, in time, intercommunity trading links, privileges, and the associated prestige could have been consolidated into offices with rights that were passed on at death in accordance with kinship practice.[1] The mortuary potlatch, it is suggested, became the means whereby this was accomplished.

Regional variation in resources was critical to the emergence of the rank system even though these resources were not essential to survival. The relative abundance of certain raw materials in localized areas permitted specific groups to control access to them and through their trader-chiefs to exchange them for non-local items. Such goods as dentalium shells, oulachan oil, Chilkat blankets, horn, and furs, all of which were traded during the historic period (Drucker 1965:110, 117, 168–174), may have been exchanged. At certain times, intertribal conflict over access to exchange networks may have severed some relationships. However, once established as a widespread pattern, potlatching to validate claims that had become hereditary could have persisted and accrued additonal functions.

Subsistence resource abundance alone would have been insufficient to generate hereditary positions; hunter-gatherers generally produce no more than is required for local needs, and there are many horticultural societies that lack hereditary offices that either produce or are capable of producing food surpluses. This is not to deny that there is a relationship between high rank, resource abundance and variety, and population size among societies that are already ranked (Sahlins 1958; Donald and Mitchell 1975).[2] The requirements of those of rank to be generous will result in an increase in productive efforts. The holders of rank (Fried 1967:114–115, 131) and / or the kinsmen who support them will produce more to be exchanged at intercommunity feasts and at potlatches among groups linked by kin ties (Drucker and Heizer 1967:46, 39–40). In turn, increased productivity will select for a larger population within the limits of resource availability and the extent to which the principle of least effort is overruled in order to increase the status of the community and its high-ranking representatives. Thus, in locales where subsistence resources are more abundant, the type of correlation noted by Donald and Mitchell (1975) would be expected.

Given that Northwest Coast ranking predates White contact, an examination of a society in the process of developing the system provides evidence in support of the trade-in-luxury-goods hypothesis. Historical evidence pertaining to the Carrier Indians, inhabitants of the region immediately inland from the coast, provides such information. Although the Carrier adopted the rank system from coastal groups (Morice 1892; Goldman 1940, 1941; Jenness

1943; Steward 1960), thus giving it secondary status (Fried 1967;198, 203), the processes of development although greatly accelerated among the Carrier, it is argued, paralleled those among coastal societies at an earlier period.

The Genesis of Carrier Ranking

The Prehistoric Carrier Habitat: The Ecological Base

The prehistoric Carrier occupied an extensive tract of land from about 52° 30' on the Fraser River to 55° 30' on the Babine River, and from the mountains east of the Fraser to the Coast Range in the west. On the north, their territory bordered upon that of the Sekani, and on the south that of the Chilcotin. To the west, from north to south respectively, lived the Tsimshian, Kwakiutl, and Bella Coola.

The main source of food in what was then called New Caledonia was salmon. Salmon runs, however, were variable from year to year, and Indians unable to acquire salmon locally would visit fishing stations elsewhere, trade for salmon from other villages, or pursue "starvation" foods. In the fall, whitefish and trout were obtained, while sturgeon were taken in a few locations in the spring. The most important vegetable food was berries. Caribou, although not numerous, were killed as were bear when they came to eat salmon. Beaver flesh was especially relished. Nevertheless, said the Hudson's Bay Company trader, John Stuart, "so scarce are animals that excepting at the public feasts given in honour of the dead nine tenths of the Natives do not taste meat perhaps not once in ten years" (Hudson's Bay Company 1823–34:B.188/e/1 [1822–23]). While this may be an exaggeration, it does suggest that hunting was at best an occasional practice and/or that feasts of beaver and other land mammal meat were relatively infrequent events.

Although resources were variable from area to area, and from year to year, as well as less abundant than on the coast, periods of extreme scarcity for any specific village were rare. Alternate food resources and/or intervillage trade provided the means of preventing death by starvation. However, there is no evidence that resource variability itself led to the rank system out of redistributive necessity. In fact, feasts were held during times of general abundance, not during ones of scarcity. Most frequently these occurred during the early summer following beaver hunts, or in the late fall after salmon had been taken. Further, if the Carrier adopted hereditary rank positions during the protohistoric period as most scholars believe, and if the subsistence resources of the prehistoric and early historic periods remained unchanged, then these basic resources cannot be used to explain the development of the rank system.

Early Contact Carrier Social Organization

When first contacted by Whites, the Carrier occupied some twenty semipermanent villages varying in size and proximity to each other in accordance with resource (i.e., salmon) availability and abundance.³ The largest villages numbered several hundred persons, and the densest populations were near Babine Lake and along the Bulkley River in western Carrier territory. The five villages near Stuart Lake affiliated with the Fort St. James Hudson's Bay Company trading post in 1823 ranged in size from about 40 persons to 108 persons (Hudson's Bay Company 1823–34:B.188/e/1 [1822–23]). Those nearer Fort Alexandria to the south on the Fraser River and about Babine Lake (Ogden 1853:90) were considerably larger; both areas produced larger quantities of salmon.

Among the 270 Indians in the five villages near Stuart Lake in 1824, there were five chiefs and seven "men of note" (presumably high-ranking individuals) (Hudson's Bay Company 1820–41:B.188/a/2 [James McDougall, Summer Report, 1824]). These data and additonal evidence in the Hudson's Bay Company Archives indicate that a rank system was then present. However, it appears to have been of recent origin. Chiefly positions do not seem to have been firmly consolidated during the early 19th century. According to Daniel Harmon, our earliest detailed source and one dating to the 1810s, Carrier chiefs called "Mi-u-ties" (Lamb 1957:249; see also Morice 1892:118; Goldman 1940:355) "have not much authority or influence over the rest of the community. Any one is dubbed a Mi-u-ty, who is able and willing, occasionally, to provide a feast, for the people of his village." There is nothing in Harmon's journal or elsewhere at this time to indicate that materials other than food were distributed at these feasts. The important foods allocated were beaver or bear meat. When food scarcities occurred, salmon were traded; they were not ceremonially redistributed as were such gourmet foods as beaver. Feasts were held for social reasons and/or to honor the dead.

Early 19th-century Carrier communities appear to have lacked centralized leadership and regularized intercommunity exchanges of materials, two features often associated with rank societies. Community autonomy is further reflected by village dialect differences, wrote Harmon (Lamb 1957:243), "to such an extent, that they often give different names to the most common utensils." In this context, the data giving evidence for a small nobility during the early 1820s suggests the recency of the rank system.

The adoption of rank positions seems to have been producing other social changes. Dyen and Aberle (1974:416), in contrast to other Carrier ethnologists (Morice 1892; Goldman 1940, 1941; Steward 1960; Grossman 1965), favor the view that the prehistoric Carrier were "matrilineal, organized, with bilateral cross-cousin marriage and Iroquois cousin terms." Prehistoric postmarital residence may have been matrilocal (Morice 1906–10:I:248).⁴ However, to consolidate a rank position it would have been expedient for a prospective title-holder to marry his mother's brother's daughter, since he would inherit rank prerogatives from her father. Thus, during the late 19th century Morice (1892:112) states that marriage with female Ego's father's sister's son "was quite common and in some cases, almost obligatory." If matrilateral cross-cousin marriage and avunculocality (Morice 1890:142) developed from a generalized matrilineal base, it would seem that these shifts were causally linked to the emergence of the rank system as hereditary titles became associated with matrilineages (Dyen and Aberle 1974:417).

The evidence at present appears to be too meager to make any positive statements about prehistoric social organization. However, persons who had achieved a degree of prestige by virtue of their management of subsistence production and distribution within the village might also have been those who gained control over other aspects of the economy during protohistoric times. Such control, it is suggested, provided the basis whereby achieved status was converted to hereditary office. The mechanism whereby this came about was trade with coastal chiefdoms.

The Significance of Trade

Most scholars argue that the Carrier obtained the rank system from the Northwest Coast as the European fur trade stimulated trade and contact. While there must have been some prehistoric trade between the coast and the interior, the fur trade altered the nature of exchange relationships and led to an increase in the volume and regularity (Steward 1960:735). As early as 1793, Alexander Mackenzie saw trade items among the Sekani, who had received them from the coast through Carrier middlemen; and in 1806 Simon Fraser reported that the Carrier were then acquiring iron works and ornaments from the coast (Lamb 1960:170). Six years later, Daniel Harmon was shown "Guns, Cloth, Blankets, Axes and cast Iron Pots" (Lamb 1957:150) acquired by the Carrier from the coast. They also obtained shell beads from the coast in exchange for furs. Harmon (Lamb 1957:244) remarked that, "in their dealings with each other, they constitute a kind of circulating medium, like the money of civilized countries. Twenty of these beads, they consider as equal in value to a beaver's skin."

Although early 19th-century Carrier communities nearer the seacoast engaged in trade more frequently and on a grander scale than their inland counterparts, most Carrier villages appear to have practiced it. By the 1820s, trade with the coast was increasing. In exchange for furs, the Carrier received European goods from the Tsimshian, who themselves got them from Russian and American ships. For example, in 1823, William Brown wrote from Babine Lake in western Carrier country that the Indians there had no furs,

> having carried all they had to the Atnah [Tsimshian] Village at the Forks, where they were met by the Inhabitants of the Sea Coast, who traded the whole of them at a high price—So that numbers of the Indians talk of going there with their hunts [the] ensuing Summer—If this Traffic is not put a Stop to, I must doubt the whole of the upper Establishments in New

Caledonia will suffer by it. [Hudson's Bay Company 1821–28:B.188/b/2 (Jan. 17, 1823)].

Over the years which followed, attempts to curtail trade between the Carrier, Babines, and coastal groups met with only partial success. Western Indians continued to trade many of their furs with coastal tribes so long as the price remained lower than that given by the Hudson's Bay Company. These annual trade fairs provided the context within which nobility titles were obtained by the Carrier.[5] As certain members of lineages within villages established direct links with coastal trading partners, they adopted the totemic crests of the Tsimshian (Jenness 1943:482–495). This would have elevated the status of the Carrier traders by equating them with their Tsimshian partners. Later, the totem emblem (but not the rank and title) appear to have been extended to other members of the matrilineage, thus facilitating travel and trade (Morice 1892:112). The Babines were likely the first to acquire the rank system from the neighboring Tsimshian, perhaps during the last half of the 18th century. By the mid-1820s, most Carrier communities had a small core of nobles.

The significance of rank titles within the community required that they be socially recognized and accepted as legitimate. While chiefs had very little authority, the early documents indicate that they were maneuvering to acquire more goods to distribute. Whether to obtain trade goods from coastal Indians or from local trading posts depended on price and geographical proximity: Indians further inland came to trade most of their furs at trading posts.

Territoriality and Production

Since maintaining rank positions over time required gaining permanent control over the fur resources, we can speculate that changes in the land tenure system were also occurring during the early 19th century. Whatever the nature of the aboriginal land tenure system, it would appear that during the early 19th century leaders belonging to particular matrilineages in each village were in control of tracts of land where beaver could be found. This is suggested by William Connolly's 1825 statement that "the Country is shared amongst a certain number of Families who will not permit others to work upon the Lots which respectively belong to them" (Hudson's Bay Company 1823–34: B.188/e/3)[1824–25]. In theory, a noble's sister's sons would inherit the rights to these beaver tracts. Post-marital avunculocality and matrilateral cross-cousin marriage would have facilitated consolidation of land tenure rights. In some cases, it would seem that several matrilineally related males (often siblings) controlled access to fur tracts. A noble's sons had no rights to their father's lands (Hudson's Bay Company 1820–41:B.188/a/19[Peter Ogden, April 13, 1841]). In practice, however, the system was unstable since the efforts of nobles to control a labor source sometimes resulted in further structural changes. For example, Chief Kwah of Stuart Lake managed to keep his sons in his village even after they were married and received debt at the trading post for them, "they being Under his *Immediate Influence,* Pay Just what he *pleases to allow them* to do" (Hudson's Bay Company 1820–41:B.188/a/1 [George McDougall, April 17, 1821]). After Kwah's death in 1840, the sons were able to usurp control over their father's beaver lands and thereby permanently change the land tenure system to one involving patrilineally inherited family tracts (Steward 1960:741).[6]

Attempts to consolidate and maintain newly acquired titles led to a rise in productive efforts. The quantities of furs and fish taken increased significantly by the 1820s. The small nobility regulated the production of both items. Since 36,450 salmon were required by traders from Indians to conduct the annual business of the district (Hudson's Bay Company 1823–34:B.188/e/1 [William Connolly, 1825]), the traders, to maintain the good will of chiefs, treated them "with some distinction to avoid any mischief" (Hudson's Bay Company 1820–41:B.188/a/5[William Connolly, 1826]). This would have reinforced their influence among the other villagers.

Nevertheless, the atomizing effect of the fur trade—traders encouraged Indians to deal with the trading post as individuals and most hunters could acquire furs other than beaver—made it difficult for nobles to accrue much power. While Kwah was unquestionably the most important chief among the Upper Carrier, a prominence that had grown by the 1830s despite his advanced age and that was reflected in his ability to host feasts for several villages (Morice 1904:193), his power remained limited. Upon his death, Peter Ogden remarked that from the Company's point of view the institution of chiefly offices was practically useless. "Such men," he stated, "give more trouble than help; they reign without governing" (Morice 1904:195). Most traders seem never to have fully comprehended why chiefs who considered themselves to be so important could not or would not force their fellow villagers to perform certain tasks desired by the Company. However, as the value of trade items to Indian economy increased, the fur traders because they were in control of the distribution of wealth were increasingly able to manipulate the behavior of Indians.

Discussion and Conclusions

Given Carrier dependence on salmon fishing, it would have been expedient in prehistoric times for some person or persons to have acted as coordinator for such activities. Likely, such positions would have been open to whoever demonstrated the most competence. It is also possible that leaders gave feasts to further enhance their prestige. An incipient ranking system based upon achievement, then, may have existed even in the absence of direct or regular contact with the Northwest Coast since prestige could be gained by coordinating the construction of the salmon weirs and by giving periodic feasts of beaver and bear.

But although the prehistoric Carrier had a surplus of foods that combined with techniques for storage permitted them a relatively sedentary existence, they seemed to have lacked or had an insufficient quantity of certain resources desired by coastal peoples that would have permitted them to engage in regular and large-scale trade, and hence lacked the motivating force for the validation of titles through potlatches. Thus, it was only when furs for trade with Europeans on the coast became sufficiently important that a hereditary rank system could have been adopted.

Once the fur trade began, hereditary titles, the crest-clan system, and potlatching (as distinct from feasting) spread very rapidly to all Carrier groups (Goldman 1940:339; 1941:400). The attributes of rank appear to have first been obtained through trade contacts by leading members of particular Carrier lineages with the Tsimshian near the Bulkley River during the late 18th century. Some of the more easterly Carrier along the Fraser River may have attained titles indirectly through intermarriage with noble families further west at a later date. The Fraser River and its western tributaries became major thoroughfares for Indians and traders alike after the 1820s, thus increasing contacts and the likelihood of intermarriage among Indians.

The significance of the Carrier case for understanding how a rank system develops is that the factor of subsistence environment can be viewed as a constant. It is not that ecological factors were unimportant or that the Carrier habitat was in any sense uniform. The geographical location of villages and their demographic composition make this apparent. Further, the relatively small number of nobles and the attenuated power of these persons is a reflection of the limited capacity of the habitat to generate wider political and economic integration. However, since the prehistoric Carrier apparently lacked ranking, or at least a hereditary title system validated through the potlatch, the absence of the system cannot be explained with reference to subsistence factors alone. The Carrier, then, provide a unique opportunity of isolating the factors that transformed their society.

The fact that virtually every scholar of Carrier sociology has attributed the rank system to contacts with the coast involving trade in what were originally luxury items should not lead us to reject this case for the broader theoretical implications because of its secondary status (Fried 1967:198). Unless one assumes that the early inhabitants of the Northwest Coast potlatched because of ecological necessity (Piddocke 1965), or wished to produce enormous surpluses for redistribution to validate status, an egalitarian heresy, neither scarcity nor abundance can account for the potlatch as a vehicle for validating rank. There is, however, considerable variation in habitat along the coast and this variation could have provided the context within which intertribal and intercommunity trade became established and routinized. Once established, trade networks might have come to have been controlled within certain families so that the privileges of trade became hereditary rights, which also were extended to control over resources for trade, and the potlatch a means of publicly validating these rights among kinsmen whose assistance had made possible the wider exchange relationships.

A major difficulty with many evolutionary theories that attempt to account for the emergence of ranking is that they argue that changes in subsistence practices underlie political change. Despite lip service to the view that hunters approximated the "Original Affluent Society," it, nevertheless, has been assumed that non-food producers, except under "unusual" circumstances such as on the Northwest Coast, were incapable of generating more complex institutional structures. This may be due to the marginal existence of many recent hunters. However, many good cases have been ignored, perhaps because they have not conformed to preconceived views. For example, evidence clearly indicates that Australians in the Arnhem Land area were ranked (Berndt and Berndt 1964:117). Thus, if it is assumed that hunters value leisure and are capable of satisfying their gastric needs with relatively little difficulty, one is forced to look beyond the food resources for an explanation for the development of ranking. On the Northwest Coast, the complexity of social life and the rich resource base appear to have obscured cause and effect relationships and led to theoretical impasses. The flowering of the arts and the embellishment of social and ceremonial life in this region, however, should not blind us to the original and underlying motivating force behind the potlatch. If the somewhat simpler Carrier can provide an explanation, it is that regularized trade in non-essential commodities monopolized by a few, the precursors of the nobility, was the prime mover generating the rank system on the Northwest Coast, and perhaps elsewhere.

Notes

Acknowledgments. I wish to thank the governor and committee of the Hudson's Bay Company for their permission to view the microfilm materials in the Public Archives of Canada, Ottawa, pertaining to the New Caledonia region. I also wish to express my gratitude to my wife, M. Estellie Smith, for many helpful suggestions.

1. The manner in which this may have occurred is suggested by the Oceanic data. Among the Trobriand Islanders, Uberoi (1962:107) has demonstrated how the exchange partners of a deceased member assemble for a distribution in which the "proceedings serve, in effect, to pull together *kula* links of the dead man for the last time in his own name, and establish them afresh for his successor." According to Gluckman (1965:119), in Melanesia the struggle for power among individuals involved in such ceremonial trade was so intense that they refused to let the positions elapse upon death: "They occupy such key positions, that neither their own groups, nor their trading-partners, can afford to let the particular network of exchanges drawn together in the positions collapse." Brunton's (1975) elaboration on this theme and his explanation for why the Trobrianders have chiefs parallels that presented here.

2. Nor does it mean that the exchange of consumer goods did not accompany luxury trade. Even ancient Polynesia did not "ignore commerce; it subordinated commerce—utilitarian exchage—to a greater interest in ritual circulation of goods" (Goldman 1974:477).

3. The 1823 Hudson's Bay Company District Report for Fort St. James, the New Caledonia headquarters, compiled by John Stuart, provides a demographic survey of the Carrier as far as it was then known. The five villages near Stuart Lake whose Indians traded at Fort St. James numbered about 285 persons. Along the Fraser River near Fort Alexandria were two villages numbering some 539 persons. There were several villages further to the west, including the remnants of these later studied by Goldman (1940, 1941). Near Fort George were 113 Indians, while near Fraser Lake were at least 400 more. About 50 more Carrier lived or traded at Fort McLeod. The Indian population along the Bulkley River and near Babine Lake to the west was quite dense, there being perhaps 2,000 persons in this area. In all, I estimate that there were perhaps 3,700 Carrier during the early 1820s. This, however, was a decline from prehistoric times resulting from European diseases. Mooney's estimate of 5,000 Carrier in 1780 just prior to direct contact seems to be an accurate estimate, while Morice's (1932:xv) figure of "nine or ten thousand souls" would appear to be much too high.

4. The only specific case for post-marital residence predating the 1820s applies to chief Kwah of the village next to the Fort St. James post. Kwah resided in his father-in-law's community, which was not Kwah's own natal village (Morice 1904:20–23). An alternative possibility for the aboriginal condition might have been a situation where Carrier villages were matrilocal, exogamous, and non-unilineal but linked by bilateral cross-cousin marriage. This reconstruction would avoid the problems associated with the isolated monolineage community (Dyen and Aberle 1974:379–380). As Kloos (1963:855) has noted, "where leadership is completely an achieved status, not influenced by descent, matrilocal and intercommunity marriage provide few difficulties." Given the structural implications of these arguments, it is possible that matrilineages were absent at some point in the past. Regardless, if Kloos' argument can be generalized, leadership positions would have been achieved among the prehistoric Carrier especially if some of the rather small villages were monolineages.

5. It would appear that members of the same matrilineage and from the same village or from adjacent villages formed the core of each trading group. For example, in 1820, James McDougall stated that "Qua [Kwah], Hoolson–Malle de Gorge, CaSsienne & several followers left this on their way to the Babines [to trade]" (Hudson's Bay Company 1820–41:B.188/a/1[Dec. 10, 1820]). Kwah, Hoolson, and Malle de Gorge were three brothers. Also, Carrier villages were named after fishing sites and these names appear to have had nothing to do with totemic crest designations (Hudson's Bay Company 1820–41:B.188/a/5[William Connolly, 1826] Lamb 1957:243). This could be interpreted to signify the absence of crest totems for villages unless villages were not monolineages (Dyen and Aberle 1974:379–380).

6. Steward (1960) believed that the pre-fur trade Carrier formed patrilineal territorial bands in line with his earlier theoretical work. There is no evidence for this. The distinction between village chief and a nobility title that he (Steward 1960:735–736) notes at Stuart Lake reflects the way in which Kwah's son, Prince, set himself up as

community head. Even though Prince could not claim his father's nobility title, he was able to gain control over his hunting lands, which were partitioned among his brothers and sons.

References Cited

Berndt, Ronald M., and Catherine H. Berndt
    1964   The World of the First Australians: An Introduction to the Traditional Life of the Australian Aborigines. Chicago: University of Chicago Press.
Brunton, Ron
    1975   Why Do the Trobriands Have Chiefs? Man 10:544–558.
Codere, Helen S.
    1950   Fighting with Property: A Study of Kwakiutl Potlatching and Warfare, 1792–1930. American Ethnological Society Monograph 18. Seattle: University of Washington Press.
Donald, Leland, and Donald H. Mitchell
    1975   Some Correlates of Local Group Rank among the Southern Kwakiutl. Ethnology 14:325–346.
Drucker, Philip
    1965   Cultures of the North Pacific Coast. San Francisco: Chandler Publishing.
Drucker, Philip, and Robert F. Heizer
    1967   To Make My Name Good: A Reexamination of the Southern Kwakiutl Potlatch. Berkeley: University of California Press.
Dyen, Isidore, and David R. Aberle
    1974   Lexical Reconstruction: The Case of the Proto-Athapaskan Kinship System. New York: Cambridge University Press.
Earle, Timothy K.
    1977   A Reappraisal of Redistribution: Complex Hawaiian Chiefdoms. In Exchange Systems in Prehistory, Timothy K. Earle and Jonathon E. Ericson, eds. pp. 213–229. New York: Academic Press.
Fried, Morton H.
    1967   The Evolution of Political Society: An Essay in Political Anthropology. New York: Random House.
Gluckman, Max
    1965   Politics, Law and Ritual in Tribal Society. Chicago: Aldine.
Goldman, Irving
    1940   The Alkatcho Carrier of British Columbia. In Acculturation in Seven American Indian Tribes, Ralph Linton, ed. pp. 333–389. New York: D. Appleton-Century.
    1941   The Alkatcho Carrier: Historical Background of Crest Prerogatives. American Anthropologist 43:396–418.
    1974   Ancient Polynesian Society. Chicago: University of Chicago Press.
Grossman, Daniel
    1965   The Nature of Descent Groups of Some Tribes in the Interior of Northwestern North America. Anthropologica 7:249–262.

Hudson's Bay Company
  1820–41   Fort St. James Post Journals. Manuscript B.188/a/1–19 in Hudson's Bay Company Archives. Public Archives of Canada, Ottawa.
  1821–28   Fort St. James Account Books. Manuscript B.188/b/1–6 in Hudson's Bay Company Archives. Public Archives of Canada, Ottawa.
  1823–34   Fort St. James District Reports. Manuscript B.188/e/1–5 in Hudson's Bay Company Archives. Public Archives of Canada, Ottawa.
Jenness, Diamond
  1943   The Carrier Indians of the Bulkley River: Their Social and Religious Life. Bureau of American Ethnology Bulletin 133:469–586.
Kloos, Peter
  1963   Matrilocal Residence and Local Endogamy: Environmental Knowledge or Leadership. American Anthropologist 65:854–862.
Lamb, W. Kaye, ed.
  1957   Sixteen Years in the Indian Country: The Journal of Daniel Williams Harmon. Toronto: Macmillan Company of Canada.
  1960   Simon Fraser's Letters and Journals, 1806–1808. Toronto: Macmillan Company of Canada.
Morice, A. G.
  1890   The Western Denes, Their Manners and Customs. Proceedings of the Canadian Institute 1888–89, 3rd ser., Vol. 7, pp. 109–174.
  1892   Are the Carrier Sociology and Mythology Indigenous or Exotic? Royal Society of Canada Proceedings and Transactions for the Year 1892, Vol. 10, Section 11, pp. 109–126.
  1904   The History of the Northern Interior of British Colubia Formerly New Caledonia 1660 to 1880. Toronto: William Briggs.
  1906–10   The Great Dene Race. Anthropos 1:229–277, 483–508, 695–730; 2:1–34, 181–196; 4:582–606; 5:113–142, 419–443, 643–653, 969–990.
  1932   The Carrier Language (Déné Family): A Grammar and Dictionary Combined. 2 vols. St. Gabriel-Mödling, Austria: Verlag der Internationalen Zeitschrift "Anthropos."
Netting, Robert McC.
  1977   Cultural Ecology. Menlo Park, CA: Cummings Publishing.
Ogden, Peter Skene
  1853   Traits of American-Indian Life and Character by a Fur Trader. London: Smith, Elder.
Peebles, Christopher S., and Susan M. Kus
  1977   Some Archaeological Correlates of Ranked Societies. American Antiquity 42:421–448.
Piddocke, Stuart
  1965   The Potlatch System of the Southern Kwakiutl. Southwestern Journal of Anthropology 21:244–264.
Sahlins, Marshall D.
  1958   Social Stratification in Polynesia. American Ethnological Society Monograph 29. Seattle: University of Washington Press.
  1963   Poor Man, Rich Man, Big Man, Chief: Political Types in Melanesia and Polynesia. Comparative Studies in Society and History 5:285–303.

Service, Elman R.
   1975   Origins of the State and Civilization: The Process of Cultural Evolution. New York: W. W. Norton.
Steward, Julian
   1960   Carrier Acculturation: The Direct Historical Approach. *In* Culture in History: Essays in Honor of Paul Radin, Stanley Diamond, ed. pp. 732–744. New York: Columbia University Press.
Suttles, Wayne
   1960   Affinal Ties, Subsistence, and Prestige among the Coast Salish. American Anthropologist 62:296–305.
Uberoi, J. P. Singh
   1962   Politics of the Kula Ring: An Analysis of the Findings of B. Malinowski. Manchester: Manchester University Press.

III

13
The Recognition of Leadership in Egalitarian Societies of the Northeast

Nan A. Rothschild
Barnard College

Those societies described alternately as exhibiting band (Sahlins 1961; Service 1962; Steward 1955) or egalitarian social systems (Fried 1967) are usually assumed to subsist by collecting food and to have a characteristic nonsedentary settlement pattern marked by seasonal movements and changes in aggregate group size (Damas 1972; Helm 1972; Leacock 1969; Lee and DeVore 1968; Steward 1955). Such societies are also said to have minimal institutionalized political structures (Sahlins 1961). Political behavior, however, is found in all societies, even if it is difficult to separate this behavior from the matrix of "total social phenomena" (Mauss 1967) in some cultures.

This paper will use a type of archaeological data—mortuary data—to examine an aspect of political organization—leadership—in two egalitarian societies of the northeastern United States and Canada. My examination will focus on the manifestations of leadership and on how positions of relatively high rank were distributed to males and females in these two societies. I also will suggest that these two societies differed in their need and potential for leaders because of differences in their respective adaptations. Specifically, the deer hunting practiced in one of these societies required a somewhat different group organization than did the caribou and marine mammal hunting of the other. Also, the presence of resources such as salmon, marine mammals, and shellfish in the latter society allowed for year-round settlements, sedentism unlike that usually assumed to be characteristic of egalitarian societies.

General Considerations

The ethnographic evidence indicates that although decision making in egalitarian societies is, in large part, a communal process, some individuals have more active roles in arriving at such decisions than others, and these individuals are, ipso facto, leaders. And while leadership may often be ephemeral, there will be, I suggest, some situations in which it will persist long enough to leave reflections accessible to the archaeologist.

Leaders in egalitarian societies can be recognized in two major complementary ways. One is by their responsibilities, or by the group's actions in which they play a dominant decision-making role, such as initiating a group movement. The other is by their access to and control of information (Flannery 1972; Johnson 1978). Information is a necessary prerequisite to decision making and it is to the entire social unit's benefit that individuals in decision-making roles be as knowledgeable as possible. One can thus view these two means of recognizing leaders as two parts of a system analogous to a redistributive model (Polanyi et al. 1957; Flannery 1972), a system in which information flows in to the "leader" or responsible individual, who then plays a dominant role in making decisions affecting the whole group.

There are several means of acquiring information, three of which can readily be identified. One is simply through life experience; people in leadership positions are rarely young. A second is via the supernatural; leaders are often shamans. Finally, information may come from others, so that the wider an individual's network, the better informed are his or her decisions. And since by definition leadership is not institutionalized in egalitarian societies, a leader retains his or her position as long as the decisions made are seen as advantageous to the group. A positive feedback model will apply so that the volume of information flowing from one of the information sources, namely "others' experience," to a leader will directly reflect the perceived efficacy of his or her leadership.

All societies including egalitarian ones have a greater need for leaders in some situations than others, a need that is correlated with a number of environmental and subsistence factors. For example, the exploitation of certain resources makes increased social coordination adaptive, and the need for leaders more acute (Wright 1978). If resources of this type are being exploited, we may expect to see greater evidence of leadership.

A broader environmental factor influencing the development of leadership is the nature of the adaptations. Because of the stability and richness of the resource base, certain kinds of adaptations, specifically those emphasizing coastal resources, have been seen ethnographically as permitting a greater degree of sedentism and cultural elaboration than others (Moseley 1975; Watanabe 1972). We would expect to find an increased development of leadership among people living in such settings.

The recognition of leadership in prehistoric societies is more elusive than in living societies. The most obvious means for recognizing individuals of unique status is in their mortuary treatment. It may be argued that people in unique status positions need not be leaders, but egalitarian societies, as a rule, have few special statuses, and the weight of ethnographic evidence suggests that these statuses, for the most part, could be described as leadership ones. There may be some individuals who are leaders (or have other special status) and whose position is not reflected in burial, but if some individuals are set apart by their mortuary treatment, these people, I would argue, are most likely to be leaders.[1]

It must be recognized that status distinctions in egalitarian societies are quite different from those in more complex social systems. In egalitarian societies, most distinctions apply to broad categories related to factors of age and sex (Binford 1971), and so are not evidence of leadership. Within age-sex groups, other status distinctions exist but are open to all in a given group, based on achieved rather than ascribed attributes (Fried 1967), and may therefore be difficult to recognize. They may, in fact, be reflected by clinal differences rather than discontinuities in any characteristic considered.

In trying to distinguish individuals who may have held leadership positions, I will follow Binford's reasoning (1971). The death of a leader may be expected to be recognized by more individuals (i.e., a larger social unit) than the death of a non-leader, factors of personality, success in leadership, and the like being equal. This is analogous in our society to measuring the status of individuals by the number of people attending a funeral (e.g., John and Robert Kennedy, Pope John), visiting the grave, and so on. The recognition of the death of a leader may well have material correlates, either in mode of burial or grave good inclusions. One cannot know, a priori, which mode of burial will be significant in a given society, but importance, which I am equating with leadership, might be apparent in grave good distribution in at least one of two ways: a greater quantity or a greater variety of objects included in a grave. Greater variety may not reflect the various particular statuses of an individual's composite status, or *persona* (Binford 1971; Saxe 1970); it is possible that any given status can be manifested by a variety of objects. It is also possible that importance may be indicated by evidence of a greater than normal effort put into grave construction, although there are few examples of such recorded for sites of the type I will discuss.[2]

Data and Analysis

Data from two sizeable Archaic period cemeteries are here considered. The first is Frontenac Island, located on an island in Cayuga Lake, Cayuga County, New York, excavated by William Ritchie (1945) in 1939–40. The dates for the site range from 4930 ± 260 to 3673 ± 250 B.P. The site, which contains 159 burials from two phases as well as a few later ones not included in this analysis, was defined by Ritchie as the type site of the Frontenac focus of the Archaic, having traits from both Lamoka and Brewerton phases.

The second site is Port au Choix (Tuck 1976), located on the Strait of

Belle Isle on the west coast of Newfoundland, excavated by James Tuck in 1967–69. It is one of the important components used in defining the Maritime Archaic (Tuck 1971). The dates for this site are very similar to those from Frontenac Island, ranging from 4290±110 to 3410±100 B.P. (Tuck 1976:162). One hundred and one burials were excavated, 89 of them at one locus.

These sites were chosen for several reasons. First, because they are Archaic period sites, both can be postulated as probable remains of egalitarian societies. While not all Archaic cultures (Rothschild 1979; Winters 1968, 1974) are identical in their social organization, none yet known represents ranked or stratified systems. Second, the sites are similar in size, extent of excavation, and the unusual conditions of preservation (both have soil pH's of 8, a significant factor when comparing burials from different sites and facing problems of sampling error). Third, they are located in different environments. Although both artifactual assemblages suggest a broadly similar reliance on a diverse set of collected resources, in some critical specific resources available the two areas differ. At Frontenac Island, the major animal eaten was deer; black bear and elk are also significant sources of meat. Fish (especially pike and bullhead) were also important, as were wild fowl. Hickory, butternuts, and acorn were all significant in the diet, but no other wild plant foods are noted by Ritchie. In contrast, at Port au Choix, the major animal food was provided by caribou. Bear, fox, and other fur-bearing animals were also taken, and moose, elk, and deer may have been present. Both fresh and salt-water fish species were important, notably salmon and cod, and shellfish and many types of birds, both migratory fowl and seabirds, were utilized. Various sea mammals, several species of seal in particular, were also present and significant in the diet.

It is possible to make certain predictions about the burial programs at Port au Choix and Frontenac Island as the remains of egalitarian societies. If the societies were egalitarian, we would expect that variation along any specific variable or dimension will be clinal in nature and that variation between sexes or age classes will be greater than within each sex or age group. If the reverse situation obtains, the society in question no longer fits the classical egalitarian model.

Predictions as to which specific age-sex distinctions will be socially recognized are sometimes difficult to formulate. Some of my own earlier research suggests that sex is not always an axis of variation in Archaic societies, but that age tends to be more consistently relevant (Rothschild 1975). Regarding age, Binford (1971:21) has said that children are excluded from expressions of status in societies in which status is achieved; I think that infants are often treated differently from other children, and often more closely reflect the status of their parents than older children do. Braun (1979:68) has recently renewed Saxe's (1970) point that children may be found with indicators of wealth in societies in which such wealth has been achieved by the child's family.

Other expected differences in mortuary practices pertain to environmental differences between the sites and the degree to which the exploitation of resources might call for social coordination. As has been noted, certain resources may be exploited more successfully with a degree of social coordination. One expected difference in mortuary practice relates to the relative richness, diversity, and stability of resources in the two environments. All available evidence suggests that a coastal environment, such as the setting for Port au Choix, and especially one in which sea mammals are present, is a rich and diverse one (Binford 1968; Moseley 1975), and one in which the resources are unusually stable. These environmental factors may allow the development of an increasingly sedentary and dense population, but leadership may be critical in developing a rational schedule for resource exploitation.[3]

Caribou hunting may be another situation in which strong leadership is adaptive (Rogers 1969:40). Caribou can, of course, be hunted by small groups, but there are many descriptions in the historical literature of large seasonal drives involving large temporary aggregations, and these aggregations might well have required increased organization in the same way that the Plains buffalo hunt did. The presence of caribou at Port au Choix suggests that this leadership requirement may have existed there, not only for hunting but also for the butchering and storage of the hundreds of carcasses killed (Reynolds 1978:102). Deer hunting, on the other hand, which provided the bulk of meat at Frontenac Island, is not likely to have favored the same group size or organization because of the smaller size of deer herds. Therefore, we would expect less of a need for leadership at Frontenac Island.

In summary, this consideration of environmental factors suggests that the peoples inhabiting the two sites may not have been identical in their organization and in their need for leaders. Those differences that exist can be expected to express more organization, cohesion, and leadership at Port au Choix than Frontenac Island, leading us to expect more variation within age and sex groups at the former site than the latter.

Since there is no way of knowing what particular mortuary variables expressed what specific aspect of status, all characteristics that varied were examined. These attributes were then cross-tabulated against each other and against age and sex in order to assess differences among age and sex classes. If the societies were egalitarian, we would expect to find status distinctions based largely on these two biological attributes. A second level of analysis investigated variation *within* categories delineated by age and sex. Because each variable cannot be assumed to have a single meaning, in this study I will focus on individuals or groups distinguished by more than one variable. As Braun (1979) notes, archaeologists depend on redundancy (or repetitive signals) in mortuary programs in order to isolate dimensions of status.

Aspects of variation in mortuary behavior investigated were: access to the mortuary site; burial position and orientation; presence, quantity, and diversity of grave goods; and intra-site spatial variation.

Access to the Mortuary Site

At both sites, access to the cemetery was open to some individuals from all age groups and both sexes. Although burials from neither site can be compared in a life table or mortality curve because of the missing adult age identifications, it can be noted that while the number of children and adolescents at both sites is typical of many other populations, Port au Choix (Figure 1) has an abnormally large number of infants represented, while Frontenac Island has an abnormally small number. The large number of infants at Port au Choix can be interpreted in one of two ways. Either infants were preferentially included in the cemetery at a higher rate than adults, or there was both a high birth rate and a high infant mortality rate.

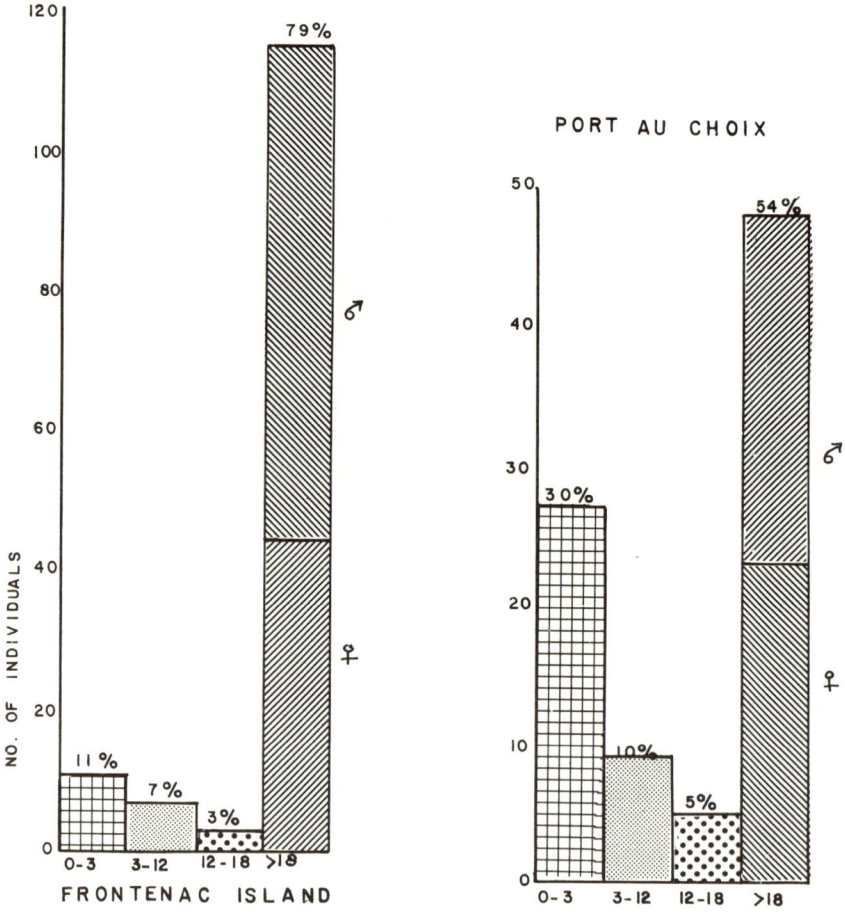

Figure 1. Population composition of sites, by age, class, and sex

The sex ratio is different at the two sites; the female:male ratio at Port au Choix is 17:23, while at Frontenac Island it is 45:71—a striking difference even allowing for some error in sex identifications. At Frontenac Island there were more male adult burials than those of other single age-sex group. At Port au Choix, the cemetery was open equally to adults of either sex and to newborns and infants. This may imply a different status niche for children at Port au Choix than at Frontenac Island, or it may imply a more cohesive society in which it was an important mark of group membership to be buried in the cemetery.

A preliminary examination of grave furniture (discussed more fully below) gives some confirmation of the contrasts noted above. Almost everyone at Port au Choix (94% of females, 94% of males) received property at death, while at Frontenac Island graves have a lower rate of grave good inclusion (38% of females, 56% of males) much more typical of the proportion of individuals with grave goods in a series of 65 eastern North American mortuary sites (Rothschild 1975). Again, these figures can be interpreted in two ways: females at Port au Choix occupied a different status niche than those at Frontenac Island or the former society used the inclusion of grave goods (of whatever type) as a marker of group membership.

Burial Position and Orientation

Several variables related to the placement of the body were examined as potential indicators of status differentiation. These included degree of flexion (extended, partly flexed, etc.), deposition (back, left side, etc.), and orientation of the body.

Only at Frontenac Island does the degree of flexion distinguish females from males. Extended burial characterizes 62% of the males and only 21% of the females (Figure 2); of the females, more than 43% are partly flexed, compared to 20% of the male population positioned in this manner. Deposition is not totally independent of flexion. At the Frontenac Island site there is a preference for placement on the back (68% of total burials). Of flexed (partly and fully) females, 57% are placed on their right sides, while only 35% of flexed males are so placed. No distinctions occur among left-sided burials. Another weak male-female differential exists in orientation of the Frontenac Island burials. The dominant orientation for skeletons at the site is along a north-south axis (which incidentally represents the axis of the flat elevated portion of the island). However, 12% of the females are oriented toward the east, while no males are aligned this way (Figure 3).

In summary, the significance of the distinctions noted here is somewhat obscured by the observation that the subset of the population distinguished by each variable is not the same, although there is some overlap. This suggests that the variation may mark a diffusely "different" female status, distinguished by a variety of possible special burial treatments.

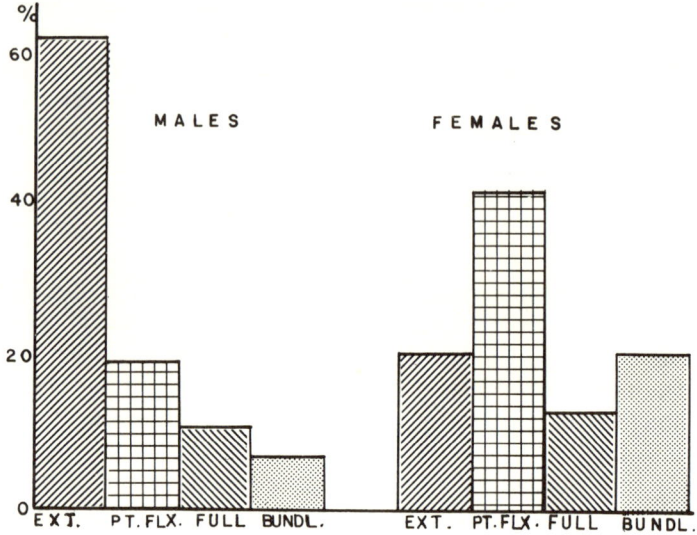
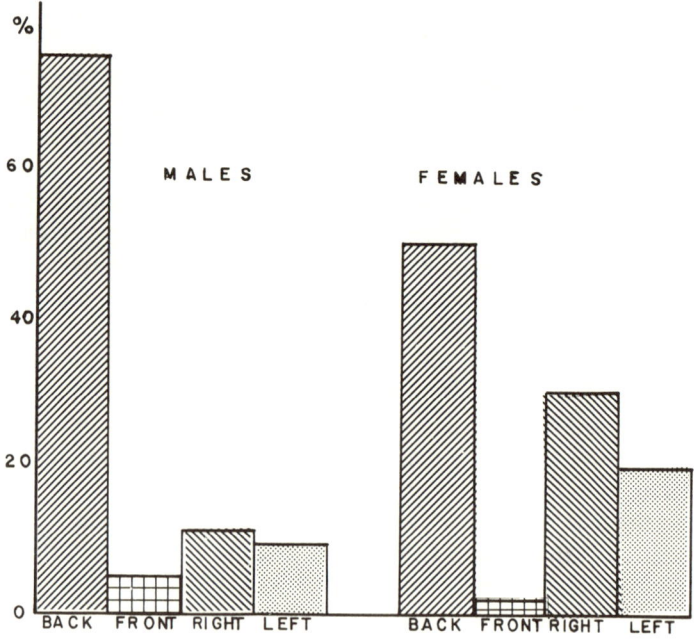

Figure 2. Body flexion and deposition type at Frontenac Island

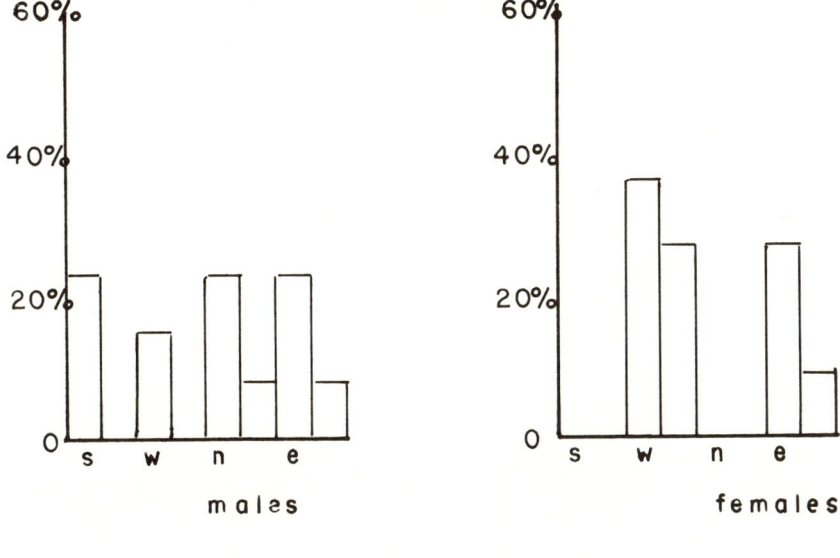

PORT AU CHOIX

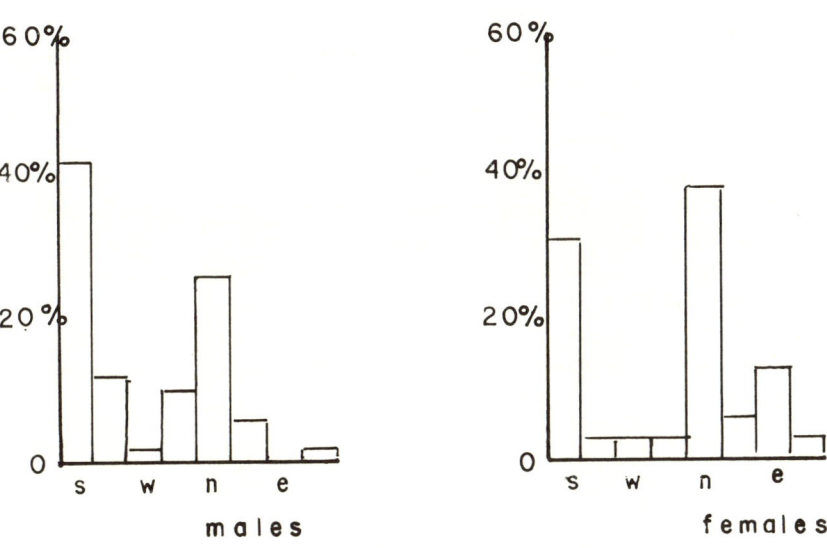

FRONTENAC ISLAND

Figure 3. Orientation of male, female graves at Port au Choix, Frontenac Island (in 45° increments)

As Port au Choix, only orientation among the attributes considered shows any male-female differences (Figure 3). Flexion and deposition are similar for both sexes. Unlike Frontenac Island there is no dominant axis of orientation at Port au Choix; the largest number of burials oriented in one direction is to the west, closest to the sea (25% of all burials), while east and west combined account for 38%. There is no clear expression of a cemetery-wide preference as there is at Frontenac Island, where 65% of all burials are oriented north or south. There is some distinction between male and female orientations, but the numbers are too small to interpret.

Grave Goods

Grave goods were examined in several ways. First, the presence or absence of certain classes of grave goods was analyzed. For this initial analysis, quantity of grave goods was ignored, and all burials associated with a certain artifact category were tabulated and then cross-tabulated against age and sex.

A number of predictive statements can be made, based on ethnographic knowledge and previous examinations of eastern Archaic sites: First, it would be expected that hunting, woodworking, and stone- and bone-working equipment would be associated with males, and hide-working equipment with females. Second, ceremonial artifacts, including musical equipment, would be expected to be found in association with males and ornaments in association with females. Finally, technomic artifacts would be expected to be associated with adults rather than children. A number of artifacts of unknown function (mammal and bird parts, quartz crystals, pebbles, concretions, and the like) were analyzed separately, with no predictions made about their association.

Chi-square was used to test the non-randomness of occurrence of these artifact associations (Table 1). In cases where there were no expectations as to the direction of association, two-tailed tests were used. Rather surprisingly, the initial analysis of the presence or absence of artifact classes yielded few statistically significant differences at Port au Choix: women are seen to have a disproportionate share of hide-working equipment, and adults have more than their predicted share of hunting, fishing, bone- and stone-working tools, bird parts, and quartz pebbles; at Frontenac Island, children have a greater than expected proportion of pendants and pins.

However, when quantities of artifacts, totaled for the age and sex class, were examined by a binomial test, almost all distributions varied from normal in the expected manner (Table 2). For example, males at both sites had disproportionate quantities of stone- and bone-working equipment and musical/ceremonial artifacts. Males at Port au Choix had more fishing equipment and at Frontenac Island they had more hunting and woodworking equipment and dog burials than expected. Females and children had more than their share of ornaments.

The interesting aspect of this analysis is the fact that in mortuary behav-

Table 1
Number of Graves with Various Artifacts

Artifacts	Males	Females	Adults	Children
Frontenac Island				
Hunting Equipment	19	9	28	4
Fishing equipment	6	1[a]	7	0
Hide-working equipment	8	3	11	2
Wood-working equipment	12	3	15	1
Stone- and bone-working equipment	10	5	15	2
Flutes, ceremonial	13	3	16	3[a]
Pendants, pins, beads	(too few to test)		5	6[ab]
Mammal parts, dog burials	11	2[a]	13	1[a]
Total number of graves	71	45	122	26
Port au Choix				
Hunting equipment	12	10	22	8[b]
Fishing equipment	8	4[a]	12	1[b]
Hide-working equipment	5	9[b]	14	6
Wood-working equipment	9	7	16	8
Stone- and bone-working equipment	12	5	17	6[b]
Tube, whistles	(too few to test)		5	4[a]
Pendants, pins	11	6	17	7[a]
Effigies, all types	7	3	10	4[a]
Shell beads	6	5	11	10[a]
Skate "beads"[c]	2	5	7	3[a]
Mammal parts	12	9[a]	21	12[a]
Bird parts	15	11[a]	26	6[ab]
Quartz pebbles	9	10[a]	19	4[ab]
Crystals	5	6[a]	11	3[a]
Concretions	4	7[a]	11	5[a]
Total number of graves	23	17	40	31

[a] = 2-tailed tests; all others are 1-tailed
[b] = Chi-square test significant at .05 level
[c] = these are fragments of skate skeletons

ior in both societies, the presence of an artifact type is *not* a discriminating characteristic, but the quantity of the artifact present *is*. At neither site is there an age or sex class distinguished by having richer accouterments than others; most distinctions seem to reflect role specialization according to a predictable division of labor. One readily visible and striking contrast between the sites is in the mean quantities of artifacts present in graves with artifacts. At Frontenac Island, these figures are 7.8 for males, 5.8 for females and 4.5 for infants, while at Port au Choix, males with artifacts have an average of 74.2 objects, females have 136.3 and infants 79.2.

It was suggested above that leadership, or importance, might be visible

Table 2
Quantities of Various Artifacts in Graves

Artifacts	Males	Females	Adults	Children
Frontenac Island				
Hunting equipment	65	19[a]	84	2[a]
Fishing equipment	39	37	76	0[a]
Wood-working equipment	16	6[a]	22	1[a]
Stone- and bone-working equipment	52	5[a]	57	1[a]
Flutes, tubes	10	0[a]	10	0
Ceremonial equipment	33	4[a]	37	3
Ornaments	3	8[a]	11	30[a]
Dogs, mammal parts	49	2	51	1
Port au Choix				
Hunting equipment	53	24	77	49
Fishing equipment	12	5[a]	17	1[a]
Hide-working equipment	11	45[a]	56	19
Stone- and bone-working equipment	54	8[a]	62	12
Tubes, whistles	9	1[a]	10	17[a]
Shell beads	107	536[a]	643	665[a]
Skate "beads"[b]	7	218[a]	225	3[a]
Mammal parts	108	57	165	90
Quartz pebbles	486	1103	1589	386[a]
Concretions	8	17	25	9

[a] Binomial test significant at .05 level
[b] These are fragments of skate skeletons

in either a greater quantity or a greater variety of objects included in an individual's grave, representing the number of duty-status relationships the dead individual maintained during life. A number of individuals at both sites are distinctive because they have larger quantities and/or greater diversity (measured by the number of different artifact types in a grave) than others in the cemetery (Figure 4). Such individuals were more readily identified at Port au Choix because there were more artifacts for which the quantity present varied widely.

At Frontenac Island, three males, one female, and one "older child" had greater quantities of one or more objects, and relatively greater numbers of functional classes of artifacts than other individuals. These individuals were examined as a group, with the expectation that if they held different status positions from their fellows, there might be other correlates in their mode of disposal. However, there was no redundancy or other way in which they were marked as a group. Their flexion, orientation, and deposition all matched the norm for the site. Therefore, according to the requirements established above, there are no individuals of clearly special status at this site. We cannot say that

Recognition of Leadership in Egalitarian Societies 177

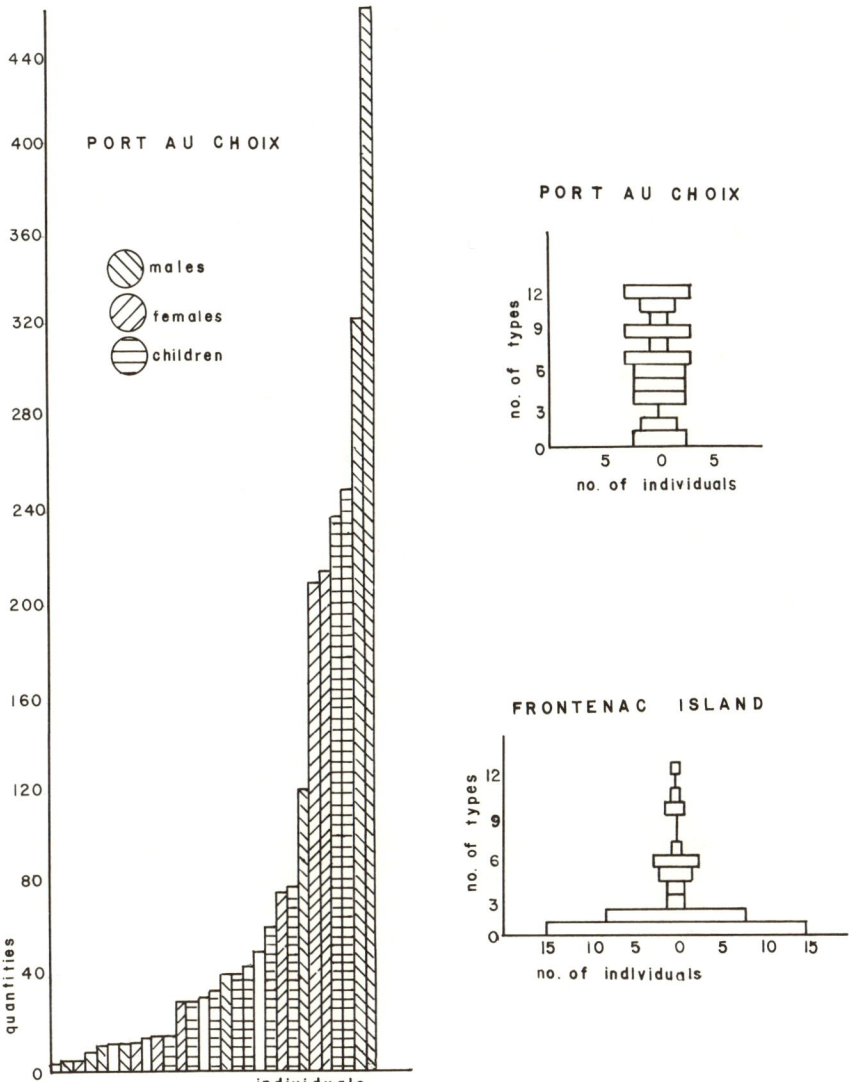

Figure 4. Bead quantities in graves at Port au Choix; number of different artifact types at sites

there were no individuals who had leadership or other important positions during life, but we can say that any such positions were not highly formalized.

At Port au Choix a rather different picture emerges. There are five males, five females, and four children with both large quantities of one or more artifacts and many artifact types. Five out of these ten adults are oriented toward the east, a non-dominant orientation at the site (seven burials are so oriented). These individuals fit the requirements for leaders because they are singled out by two parameters. It is interesting although not surprising that both males and females are represented. This distinctive orientation is not true of the four infants with greater quantities of grave goods; three of these four head west, the most common orientation.

In Tuck's (1976:89) analysis of the social organization of the site, he suggests that males, as a group, held higher-ranked statuses than females, although he examines the data from a perspective somewhat similar to the present analysis. I cannot explain our differing conclusions, but a situation of relative equality between the sexes seems to me both to better fit the data and what we know ethnographically about many hunting and gathering societies.

Spatial Organization

Additional evidence for a difference in organization between the two sites is suggested by their different use of space. At Frontenac Island there are no spatial divisions in the site. Ritchie (1945:10) suggests family burial plots, but I do not think such an interpretation is supportable; the distribution of burials seems close to random. At Port au Choix three groupings or clusters of burials are clearly separated. While there are some minor differences in the age-sex composition of these clusters, these are not sufficient to postulate areas of the cemetery reserved for one age or sex class. Further, there are no differences in the distribution of individuals with large quantities of artifacts among clusters; they are rather evenly spread among them. But a distinctive spatial segregation reinforces the idea of a more organized society (Saxe 1970).

Conclusions

A number of conclusions are suggested from this analysis: First, both sites represent the remains of egalitarian societies; that is, the variation on most of the attributes examined is clinal in nature. While differences exist within the sites, there are no individuals or groups qualitatively differentiated from the rest of the population. Most artifact associations followed an expected sex-based division of labor. Second, neither site presents an image of equal treatment for all members of society. Both populations excluded some children and adolescents from the cemeteries, indicating that age was a dimension of status. Both populations appear to treat the elder generation with special recognition.

The sites have a number of differences between them as well. First, sex and age are less clearly relevant factors of status at Port au Choix, both in access to the cemetery and in mortuary treatment (i.e., men, women, and children at Port au Choix have equally large quantities of grave goods). If, as Wobst (1976) suggests, societies in relatively richer environments tend to define social boundaries and group membership, perhaps this society defined its boundary by inclusion in the cemetery. Another possible boundary indicator at Port au Choix is the inclusion of hunting equipment with almost everyone. Second, at Frontenac Island some variation *between* age and sex classes in burial position and orientation and *within* classes in amount and variety of grave goods exist, but none of this variation is reinforced by another aspect of burial behavior. Finally, at Port au Choix a number of men and women are set apart from the majority by the quantity and/or diversity of grave goods and by a different orientation from the rest of the site. This latter group can be defined as leaders.

The difference between these northeastern Archaic egalitarian systems may be primarily related to the nature of their respective adaptations. Port au Choix exists in a coastal setting with a stable rich resource base that could support year-round base camps, or sedentism, as demonstrated by other coastal populations (Moseley 1975; Watanabe 1972). The large quantity of grave goods and the large number of infants at Port au Choix also may be evidence of this sedentism. Further, the efficient exploitation of caribou in large herds and marine mammals would call for a seasonally more organized group life and stronger leadership.[4] Frontenac Island seems to fit the more common Northeastern egalitarian model in which a seasonally mobile settlement pattern is the rule. It probably had a subsistence system in which a wide range of resources were exploited, none of them requiring major group organization.

Thus we see two societies that are alike in many important respects, yet one is more formally organized than the other in social and spatial terms, showing more differentiation within age-sex classes, more evidence of social affiliation, and expressing in several ways the presence of individuals who can be called leaders, linked possibly to environmental potential and the beginning of a stable, relatively densely settled population.

Notes

Acknowledgments. I am very grateful to James Tuck for providing me with generous access to unpublished data. I am also in debt to Robert Bettinger and Gregory Johnson for hours of discussion, and Anne-Marie Cantwell, Richard Jordan, Keith Kintigh, Steve Kowalewski, Eleanor Leacock, John Pfeiffer, Diana Rockman, Ed Rothschild, and Howard Winters for comments on earlier drafts of this work.

1. There are, of course, other possible statuses marked by unique mortuary treatment—for example, criminals, people who have died an unusual death, or other negatively sanctioned individuals. These people should be distinguishable from leaders as they are at the opposite end of the social spectrum.

2. It should be noted, however, that at least one other possible explanation for variation in the quantity or variety of grave goods exists: seasonal variation. In many so-called band societies there is a seasonal alternation of aggregation and dispersal (Helm 1972; Leacock 1969; Lee and DeVore 1968). Thus a person dying during a period of aggregation might receive more contributed objects than one dying in a period when people were more dispersed. Three attributes of disposal relating to seasonal variation were examined in the sites analyzed here. First, the ratio of bundle burials to other forms was examined, with the expectation that these might represent winter deaths. Second, orientation of the body was examined; in some societies where burials are oriented toward the rising (or setting) sun, orientations of the body vary within about a 60-degree range, following changes in the position of the sun on the horizon at dawn (or dusk) (Gruber 1971). Third, the presence of seasonally specific artifacts in graves was considered. None of these three traits provided data on season of death. Bundle burials and artifacts whose use could be clearly limited to one season were too rare to evaluate, and the range of orientations of bodies is greater than that of changes in the position of the sun.

3. Wobst (1976) has suggested that as population density increases, many types of social units become bounded, and such boundaries may be artifactually defined. (This insight, while coming from another perspective, is practically identical to one offered by Saxe [1970] in his Hypothesis 8). If we were able to discern artifactual or stylistic boundaries at Port au Choix, this might imply a more narrowly defined territorial base and an increased affiliation with a social unit.

4. Since this paper was written, Richard Jordan has convinced me that marine mammals rather than caribou are *the* important resource, also requiring group coordination for hunting. A recent study (Chisholm, Nelson, and Schwarcz 1982) suggests that it may be possible to determine the proportions of protein from marine and terrestrial sources directly from skeletal remains, and thus answer this question.

References Cited

Binford, Lewis R.
 1968 Post-Pleistocene Adaptation. *In* New Perspectives in Archaeology, Sally R. Binford and Lewis R. Binford, eds. pp. 313–341. Chicago: Aldine.
 1971 Mortuary Practices: Their Study and Their Potential. *In* Social Dimensions of Mortuary Practices, J. A. Brown, ed. pp. 6–29. Society for American Archaeology Memoir 25.
Braun, David P.
 1979 Illinois Hopewell Burial Practices and Social Organization: A Re-examination of the Klunk-Gibson Mound Group. *In* Hopewell Archaeology: The Chillicothe Conference, David S. Brose and N'omi Greber, eds. pp. 66–79. Kent: Kent State University Press.
Chisholm, B. S., D. E. Nelson, and H. P. Schwarcz
 1982 Stable Carbon Isotope Ratios as a Measure of Marine versus Terrestrial Protein in Ancient Diets. Science 216(4550):1131-1132.

Damas, David
    1972   The Copper Eskimo. *In* Hunters and Gatherers Today, M. C. Bicchieri, ed. pp. 3–50. New York: Holt, Rinehart and Winston.

Flannery, Kent V.
    1972   The Cultural Evolution of Civilizations *In* Annual Review of Ecology and Systematics, Vol. 3, Richard F. Johnston, Peter W. Frank, and Charles D. Michener, eds. pp. 399–426. Palo Alto: Annual Reviews.

Fried, Morton H.
    1967   The Evolution of Political Society. New York: Random House.

Gruber, Jacob W.
    1971   Patterning in Death in a Late Prehistoric Village in Pennsylvania. American Antiquity 36:64–76.

Helm, June
    1972   The Dogrib Indians. *In* Hunters and Gatherers Today, M. G. Bicchieri, ed. pp. 51–89. New York: Holt, Rinehart and Winston.

Johnson, Gregory A.
    1978   Information Sources and the Development of Decision-making Organization. *In* Social Archaeology: Beyond Subsistence and Dating, C. L. Redman et al., eds. pp. 87–112. New York: Academic Press.

Leacock, Eleanor
    1969   The Montagnais-Naskapi Band. *In* Contributions to Anthropology: Band Societies, David Damas, ed. pp. 1–17. National Museum of Canada Bulletin 228.

Lee, Richard B., and Irven DeVore
    1968   Man the Hunter. Chicago: Aldine.

Mauss, Marcel
    1967   The Gift. New York: W. W. Norton.

Moseley, Michael E.
    1975   The Maritime Foundation for Andean Civilization. Menlo Park, CA: Cummings Publishing.

Polanyi, Karl, Conrad M. Arensberg, and Harry W. Pearson, eds.
    1957   Trade and Market in the Early Empires. New York: Free Press.

Reynolds, Barrie
    1978   Beothuk. *In* Handbook of North American Indians. Vol. 15: Northeast. William C. Sturtevant and Bruce G. Trigger, eds. pp. 101–109. Washington: Smithsonian Institution.

Ritchie, William A.
    1945   An Early Site in Cayuga County, New York. Rochester Museum of Arts and Sciences Research Records 7.

Rogers, Edward S.
    1969   Band Organization among the Indians of Eastern Subarctic Canada. *In* Contributions to Anthropology: Band Societies, David Damas, ed. pp. 21–50. National Museum of Canada Bulletin 228.

Rothschild, Nan A.
    1975   Age and Sex, Status and Role, in Prehistoric Societies of Eastern North America. Ph.D. dissertation. Anthropology Department, New York University.

1979 Mortuary Behavior and Social Organization at Indian Knoll and Dickson Mounds. American Antiquity 44:658–675.

Sahlins, Marshall D.
1961 The Segmentary Lineage: An Organization of Predatory Expansion. American Anthropologist 63:332–345.

Saxe, Arthur A.
1970 Social Dimensions of Mortuary Practices. Ph.D. dissertation. Anthropology Department, University of Michigan.

Service, Elman
1962 Primitive Social Organization: An Evolutionary Perspective. New York: Random House.

Steward, Julian H.
1955 Theory of Culture Change. Urbana: University of Illinois Press.

Tuck, James A.
1971 An Archaic Cemetery at Port au Choix, Newfoundland. American Antiquity 36:343–358.
1976 Ancient Peoples of Port au Choix, Newfoundland. Memorial University of Newfoundland, Institute of Social and Economic Research, Social and Economic Studies, No. 17.

Watanabe, Hitoshi
1972 The Ainu Ecosystem. American Ethnological Society Monograph 54. Seattle: University of Washington Press.

Winters, Howard D.
1968 Value Systems and Trade Cycles of the Late Archaic in the Midwest. *In* New Perspectives in Archaeology, Sally R. and Lewis R. Binford, eds. pp. 175–221. Chicago: Aldine.
1974 Introduction, New Edition. *In* Indian Knoll, by W. S. Webb. Knoxville: University of Tennessee Press.

Wobst, H. Martin
1976 Locational Relationships in Paleolithic Society. Journal of Human Evolution 5:49–58.

Wright, Gary A.
1978 Social Differentiation in Early Natufian. *In* Social Archaeology: Beyond Subsistence and Dating, C. L. Redman et al., eds. pp. 201–223. New York: Academic Press.

14
Moundville: Late Prehistoric Sociopolitical Organization in the Southeastern United States

Christopher S. Peebles
University of Alabama
and
Instituut voor Prae- en Protohistorie
Universiteit van Amsterdam

Hernando de Soto's army of adventurers not only wreaked havoc among the Native American societies of the Southeast, but his expedition was both cause and witness to the end of indigenous sociopolitical evolution in the region. The Spanish quest for God, glory, and gold was the prelude to the imposition of European rivalries on the native peoples. The Spanish chronicles became the benchmarks from which all historic scholarship of Native American cultures of the Southeast must either begin or end. In the course of their four-year journey, from 1539 to 1543, de Soto's scribes recorded grand speeches in a form appropriate to the court of Charles V, made valuable, if idiosyncratic, ethnographic observations, and enshrined in prose a wide variety of minutiae that struck their fancy. Their records have been the subject of historical and ethnographic analyses (Bourne 1904; Varner and Varner 1951; B. Smith 1866; Swanton 1939; Wilkinson 1960), and these texts are now yielding to combined archaeological and ethnohistoric analyses (Phillips, Ford, and Griffin 1951; Brain, Toth, and Rodriguez-Buckingham 1974; Lankford 1977; M. Smith 1976).

From the brief and highly variable original observations of Ranjel, Biedma, and the Gentleman of Elvas, plus the reminiscences collected by Garcilasco de la Vega, the societies encountered by the de Soto expedition can be grouped into three major classes: The first were the segmentary agricultural societies of the Coastal Plain proper. These groups, whom the Spaniards later noted had less food to loot than groups farther inland, rid themselves of their visitors either by promises of riches among faraway societies or through guerilla warfare. The second were the highly productive, complex agricultural societies of the Fall Line Hills and Piedmont, who lived in large palisaded towns. These societies confronted the Spaniards directly on the field of battle and, as often as not, defeated them. The third were a few bands of hunters and gatherers who lived in the interstices between the first two types of societies. These last groups had few problems with the Spanish, who passed through their territories with dispatch and in privation.

The de Soto expedition is a sociological example of Heisenberg's "uncertainty principle": because of the expedition's effects, much of what its members saw was not to be seen again. Even when the exaggeration and ethnocentric bias of their observations are taken into account, the societies of the Southeast they described were very different than those observed some 200 years later. By 1700 hunters and gatherers remained only in parts of Florida, and very complex societies persisted only in parts of the Lower Mississippi Valley. In the interior, the descendants of the complex chiefdoms seen by de Soto had been transformed into groups of segmentary, egalitarian communities: the Creek, Cherokee, Chickasaw, Choctaw, and Alabama.

Comparison of the archaeological record of the 11th through 16th centuries, the tantalizing bits of 16th century ethnohistory, and the riches of 18th century observations in the Southeast provide a fertile if frustrating ground for research. Compare, for example, the following selections from these three types of source:

First is the 16th century description of the chief Tastaluca by the Gentleman of Elvas:

> The cacique [Tastaluca] was at home, in a piazza. Before his dwelling, on a high place, was spread a mat for him, upon which two cushions were placed, one above the other, to which he went and sat down, his men placing themselves around, some way removed, so that an open circle was formed about him, the Indians of the highest rank being nearest his person. One of them shaded him from the sun with a circular umbrella, spread wide, and the size of a target, with a small stem, and having a deer-skin extended over cross-sticks, quartered with red and white, which at a distance made it look like taffeta, the colors were so very perfect. It formed the standard of the Chief, which he carried into battle. His appearance was full of dignity: he was tall of person, muscular, lean, and symmetrical. He was the suzerain of many territories, and of numerous people, being equally feared by his vassals and neighboring nations. [B. Smith 1866:80-81]

Moreover, when the Spaniards asked for bearers to carry their equipment, Tastaluca was reported by Beidma to have said that "he was not accustomed to serving any one, but it was rather for all others to serve *him*" (B. Smith 1866:242).

Second is an 18th century summary of the government of the Southeastern Indians, the Creek, Chickasaw, Choctaw, and Cherokee, by Adair (1775:427):

they have no words to express despotic power, arbitrary kings, oppressed or obedient subjects. The power of their chiefs is an empty sound. They can only persuade or dissuade the people either by the force of good-nature and clear reasoning or colouring things so as to suit their prevailing passions.

Third is Larson's (1971a:67) summary of the social dimensions of the mortuary ritual at Etowah, a large 15th-century ceremonial center in northwest Georgia:

the burials constituting the group associated with the final construction phase of [Mound C] have been interpreted as representing a descent group set apart from other such groups in the society in that they are accorded a particular mortuary treatment. The suggestion is that they control trade in certain exotic materials and the objects that are used by them to express and validate their social position. It is also suggested that this social position is inherited. Therefore within the total society there existed stratification and within the descent group there was internal ranking.

It is clear that, in general, Larson's analysis of the 15th-century archaeological data and the observations of 16th-century adventurers are far closer to one another than either one is to the 18th-century summary by Adair. It likewise is apparent why the de Soto chronicles have served as an attractive model for the analysis of the archaeological remains of the late prehistoric societies in the Southeast.

In effect, the ethnohistoric record for the 16th century gives a brief glimpse of the complex societies of the Southeast, but by the time further records are available these hierarchical societies have been transformed into essentially egalitarian societies made up of independent communities knit together into loose confederacies. As a result, the social and political dimensions of the growth, florescence, and decline of these complex societies can be best approached through their archaeological remains, the 16th-century documents serving as a shaky but necessary foundation for such research. These documents can be used as highly distorted geographies subject to correction by matching archaeological sites with locations and groups mentioned in the text, as imperfect histories of native American groups in the Southeast, and as a source of data from which to construct models of social organization and political process to be tested with archaeological remains.

Integrated archaeological and ethnohistoric research into the social organization of complex chiefdoms has been undertaken in only a few areas of the Southeast. Notable among such research projects are the work of Brain (1978) in the Lower Mississippi Valley, Larson (1971a, 1971b, 1972), Seckinger (1977), and Hatch (1976) in the Ridge and Valley province of Georgia and

Tennessee, Brose and Percy (1978) and Goggin and Sturtevant (1964) in Florida, and Sears (1958, 1961), B. Smith (1978), and Hudson (1976) in the Southeast as a whole. In addition, there has been a decade of intensive research on the development and decline of the Moundville phase in west-central Alabama (Jenkins 1975; Sheldon 1974; Cailup B. Curren, personal communications; Steponaitis 1978, 1980; Peebles 1971, 1974, 1978, 1979, ms.; Peebles and Kus 1977; Walthall 1977). Some aspects of this research will form the substance of this paper.

Moundville: A.D. 900 to 1550

The Moundville site is central to the study of prehistoric social and political evolution in the Black Warrior River Valley. It is also a site that has served a number of roles during the millennium of its existence. First settled in the 10th century A.D., its growth as a ceremonial center began in the 11th century. From the 12th through 15th centuries its massive mounds and 100-acre plaza were a focus of the economic, political, and ritual life not only for its own inhabitants but also for the inhabitants of minor ceremonial centers and villages in a 240-square-mile area of the Lower Black Warrior River Valley as well. To 19th-century plantation owners Moundville's plaza was a level field for cotton and its mounds were a place of refuge for their animals during floods. For slaves and sharecroppers of the same era, the flanks of Mound R served as a cemetery for their dead. To C. B. Moore, who excavated at the site in 1905 and 1906 (Moore 1905, 1907), its artifacts were the zenith of Indian artistry in the eastern United States. When excavated by David DeJarnette and Walter B. Jones of the Alabama Museum of Natural History in the 1930s, Moundville absorbed the energies of hundreds of unemployed workers and gave in return wages, dignity, and one of the finest, best-documented, and best-preserved archaeological collection in the Southeast (Peebles 1979).

The data collected between 1905 and 1941, the results of recent excavations at Moundville by the Alabama Museum of Natural History and by the University of Michigan, and information from survey and testing programs at related sites hold the answers to a wide variety of questions about the social organization of the communities that made up the Moundville phase. Three aspects of these data will be used here: the ceramics, which provide the foundation for the chronology of the Moundville phase and which demonstrate the development of craft specialization at the Moundville site (Hardin 1981; Steponaitis 1980; Van der Leeuw 1981); the burials, which, if viewed from the perspective of mortuary ritual, can be seen as reflecting the terminal social status of the deceased (Brown 1971; Buikstra 1976; Saxe 1970; Peebles 1974; Rothschild chapter 3, this volume; Goldstein 1976; Tainter 1978), and, if viewed from the perspective of human biology, serve as indicators of health and diet (Buikstra 1976; Schoeninger 1980); and the intra-site distribution of

Moundville

dwellings, other features, and artifacts, which illustrates the ways in which space was divided, utilized, and symbolized (Fletcher 1977; Kus 1979).

Most of the data used in the analyses of the Moundville phase come from sites shown in Figure 1. On the basis of the ceramic chronology developed by Steponaitis (1980), some of the sites in Figure 1 can be assigned to the

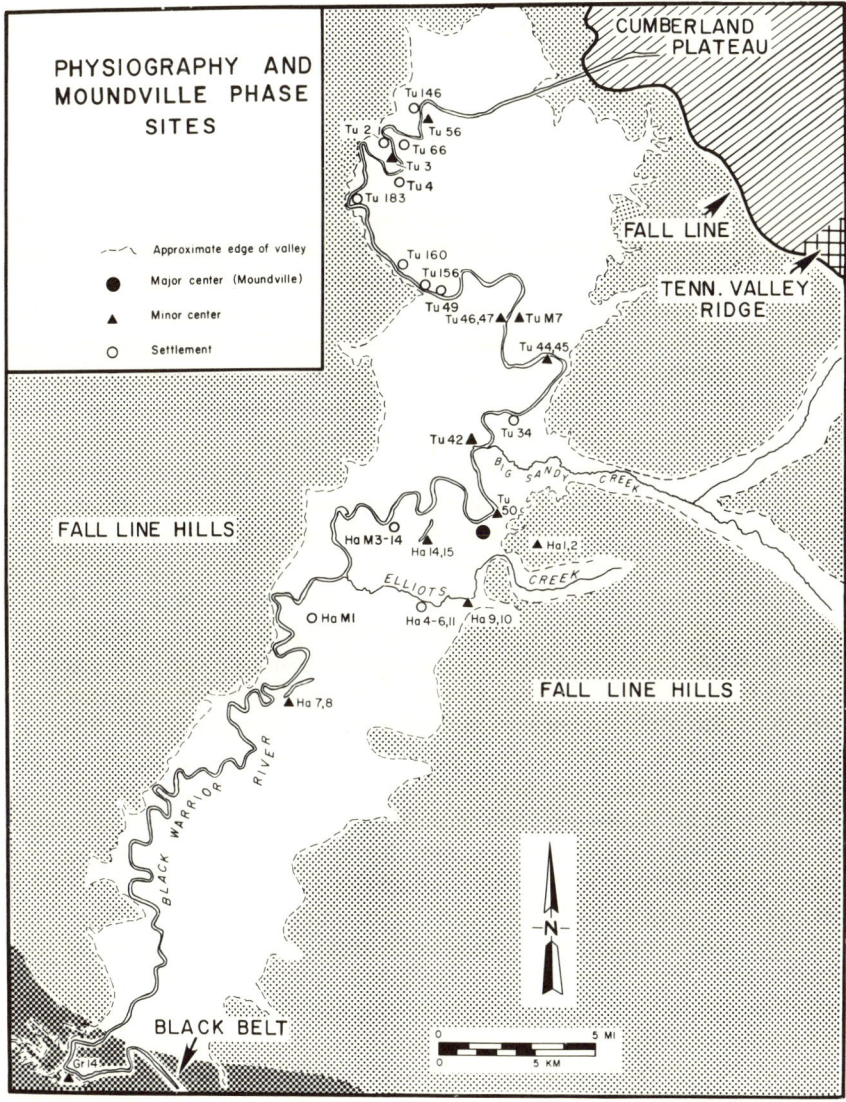

Figure 1. Moundville Phase sites in the Black Warrior River Valley, Alabama

Early Mississippian West Jefferson phase (A.D. 900–1050); almost all the sites were occupied during the Mature Mississippian Moundville phase (Moundville I A.D. 1050–1250, Moundville II A.D. 1250–1400, Moundville III A.D. 1400–1550); a few sites were occupied during the Late Mississippian Alabama River phase (A.D. 1550–1700). Analyses presently being conducted by T. K. Bozeman, Vincas Steponaitis, and P. D. Welch will refine considerably both the temporal limits of these periods and the assignment of archaeological sites to various of these chronological divisions. Nonetheless, there are sufficient data to make provisional cultural-historical judgments.

West Jefferson Phase

Although by no means the first occupation of the Black Warrior River Valley, the settlements of the West Jefferson phase are of interest here because they present a picture of the foundation from which the Moundville phase developed. Most of the sites of this phase are large (over one-hectare) settlements situated on relict river terraces. Included among these sites are the Ha 4,5,6, and 11 complex, an extensive component on the western margins of the Moundville site itself, and Tu 66. Smaller West Jefferson phase sites have been located near the mouth of Big Sandy Creek and in other parts of the Black Warrior River Valley, but like so many of the smaller sites from all periods, most have been missed thus far by archaeological survey. The surface collections from these and other West Jefferson phase sites show little differentiation either between the sites themselves or between various areas within these sites.

Excavation of West Jefferson phase sites located in the upper reaches of the Black Warrior and Cahaba Rivers (Jenkins 1975) showed that the basic residential unit in these settlements was a circular structure with a floor area of approximately 19 sq. m. Storage pits and food-processing facilities were situated in a band around these structures. The refuse that was used to fill these pits indicates that, although some corn was cultivated and eaten, most of the diet came from wild foods.

To date no burials from this phase have been identified in the collections from Moundville, and other sites in the Black Warrior River Valley having components from this period have not been excavated. It seems likely that the egalitarian society indicated by the undifferentiated nature of the dwellings and other areas that made up these settlements also will be reflected in an essentially egalitarian treatment of individuals after death.

Moundville I Period

By the beginning of this period, that is, by A.D. 1050, corn had become a dietary staple (Scarry 1981). Several minor ceremonial centers, each with a single truncated pyramidal mound, had been constructed. These single-mound, minor ceremonial centers that can be assigned to this period include Moundville, Tu 50, and Tu 56, probably Tu 44, and perhaps Ha 9. These minor ceremonial centers served as the foci for "provinces" that endured as territorial units for the next 400 years.

Limited evidence from Moundville, and corroborative data from the Bessemer site (DeJarnette and Wimberly 1941) located in the upper Black Warrior drainage network, shows that space and persons now were differentiated on bases other than subsistence pursuits, other household activities and roles stemming solely from age, sex, and personal achievement. The distinction between mound and village is one aspect of this differentiation, but at Moundville a further distinction is that between the residential area, the single platform mound, and a small burial mound set off from all the rest.

Ascriptive, hierarchical ranking of persons can be seen in the mortuary remains from Moundville and other sites of this period, and at least one political office is evident in the mortuary ceremonialism. There are two classes of burials evident in the Moundville I period. One class of burials, which can be associated with the superordinate, chiefly lineage, contains burials of all ages and both sexes. Burials of this class have been found near to and in Mound O, the first platform mount constructed at Moundville, and in a low, rounded mound south of Mound M. Generally, burials of this class have imported shell, metal, and stone artifacts as part of their grave goods. A few adult males were buried with distinctive circular copper gorgets and engraved stone discs. These latter items are not only indicators of high status but, because of their consistent context among several communities within and without the Moundville phase, also mark political or ritual office.

The other class—the vast majority of the burials from this time period—have grave goods which, in form and material, parallel divisions of age and sex: domestic items with adult women; industrial and hunting implements with adult males; ceramic bottles with adults of both sexes; plain bowls and jar with individuals of all ages and both sexes; "toy" vessels and "playthings" with children, and a wide variety of one-of-a-kind items with burials of all ages and both sexes. The individuals who comprise this class are interred away from the mounds, in the village areas and in cemeteries near the village areas.

In the first class of burials status—as defined by mortuary ritual and grave goods—cross cuts age and sex, and this fact indicates that superordinate status was dependent on the station into which an individual was born, that is, high status was determined primarily by ascription. Moreover, membership in this class was a prerequisite, along with age (adult) and sex (male), for accession to high office. In the second class status seems to have paralleled divisions of age and sex and, in addition, was dependent on the accomplishments of an individual throughout a lifetime. In effect, achievement, as manifested in part by mortuary ritual and grave goods, was constrained by age and sex.

Moundville II and III Periods

In the middle third of the 300 years spanned by these two periods of the Moundville phase, the zenith of social complexity in the Black Warrior River Valley was reached. The Moundville site reached its full size of 120 hectares and became the central ceremonial focus for the valley. The settlements in the several "provinces" show growth in population. There also were shifts in the location of the minor ceremonial centers. For example, "provincial" foci moved from Tu 56 to Tu 3, from Tu 44 to Tu M7 and then to Tu 46, from Tu 50 to Tu 42, and perhaps from Ha 9 to Ha 14. Ha 7 was constructed during this period, and Gr 14 may also be assigned to the Moundville II and III periods. Some of these minor shifts in settlement location north of Moundville may have been in response to minor changes in the flood pattern of the river (L. S. Alexander, personal communication). The construction southward from Moundville may have been the result of population expansion and redistribution within the Black Warrior Valley. The population of the valley as a whole probably was more than 10,000 persons, of whom approximately 3,000 were resident at Moundville.

The complexity of the Moundville community can be seen in Figure 2. Twenty large mounds define a 30-ha. plaza. An imaginary north-south line through the center of the plaza divides the site into symmetrical halves, the arrangement of mounds, buildings, artifact distributions, and burials as one half being virtually a mirror image of the other. Moundville gives every evidence of being a planned community, and the underlying structure is evident in a bilateral symmetry of spaces and activities.

Nineteen mounds were constructed during this period, and the pattern of mound size and use shows an alternation of small and large mounds along the eastern and western sides of the plaza (Figure 2). The small mounds contained high-status burials and "sacrificial" interments of skulls, decapitated skeletons, and infants; the large mounds served only as substructures for buildings. There are "public" buildings located near the northwest and northeast corners of the plaza (Figure 2: I, V). Caches of skulls and paints were found in pits near these buildings. Nearby were cleared areas that, to judge from the numerous "discoidals" found there, served as grounds for the "chunkee" game. Just inside the southern margin of the plaza, a charnel house (Figure 2: VI) and a sweathouse (Figure 2: VII) were found. Residential areas, made up of house clusters (Figure 2: IV, VIII) were located away from the plaza, and an "elite" residential area was found northeast of Mound E (Figure 2: III). Finally, the colors associated with burials underscore the division of the site into halves. All the black pigments and most of the red and yellow pigments were found in the eastern half of the site; all the white pigments in the western half.

The distribution of artifacts indicates that various industrial and ritual activities were carried out in particular areas of the site. The residential areas

Moundville 191

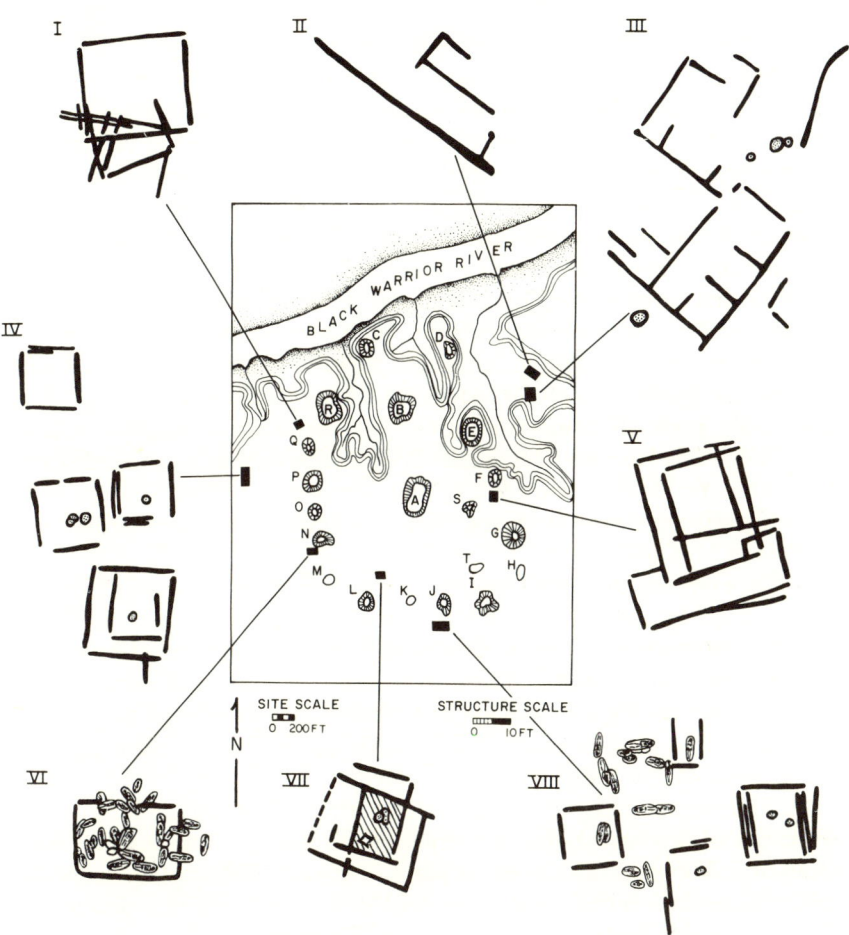

Figure 2. Distributing selected structures from Moundville

yielded food-processing tools and other items associated with household maintenance; the elite residential area produced discards from working copper and grinding pigments. Beadworking, hide processing, and pottery production seem to have been restricted to limited areas within the site. Analysis of the Moundville ceramic assemblage by Vincas Steponaitis, Margaret Hardin, and Sander van der Leeuw indicates that the Moundville II–III transition is marked by increasing specialization of ceramic manufacture at the site. Furthermore, there is limited but growing evidence that vessels manufactured at Moundville were exported to other sites in the Black Warrior River Valley.

An analysis of over 2,000 burials (Peebles 1974) showed that mortuary ritual divides the Moundville population into two clear-cut social strata. Approximately 5% of the population were buried with copper and stone items associated with the "Southern Cult" and were interred either within or near the mounds. Key artifacts and symbols, such as copper ear spools and the oblong copper gorget said to symbolize a scalp are found with men and women, children and adults of this group. Within this group there are two classes of adult male burials. One class, found only in the mounds, is composed of burials containing large copper axes and the remains of infants and skulls in the grave fill. The second is composed of burials from both the mounds and the cemeteries near the plaza that have engraved or plain stone palettes and paint pigments. These patterns of mortuary ritual suggest that ascription defined high rank, and that the individuals who held high political office were drawn from this stratum of society.

The mortuary ritual associated with the remaining 95% of the burials closely paralleled age and sex divisions within this population. This is not to say that there were no differences among these burials. There were artisans buried with their tools, children interred with their toys, and one woman placed in the grave with a burned corn cob stuffed in her mouth. The point to be made, however, is that once the elite stratum is removed, the variability in mortuary ritual seems to have been based on personal qualities and achievement rather than on ascriptive criteria.

There is evidence for a difference in diet that parallels the two major divisions in mortuary ritual. Ethnographic descriptions of chiefdoms (see references in Peebles and Kus 1977) all indicate that the chief and his lineage had a qualitatively and quantitatively superior diet. French accounts of the Natchez point to the fact that the Great Sun and his family had first choice of all large game and constant access to other foods (Swanton 1911:70-71, 118, 121). The relative amount of meat in the diet can be measured indirectly from the amount of strontium in bone mineral (Schoeninger 1979, 1980). Analysis of a small sample of Moundville burials (N=136) suggests that the "elite" group had significantly more meat in its diet (Schoeninger and Peebles 1981).

The information from other sites in the Black Warrior River Valley suggests that social complexity increased within these communities during this period as it did at Moundville. However, the data on these sites are sufficient only for an impressionistic, not a detailed, analysis.

The Alabama River Phase

Sometime between A.D. 1500 and 1600 the cultural edifice called the Moundville phase collapsed. The social and settlement hierarchy ruptured, and the organization associated with the mound and plaza complex and the symbols of the Southern Cult dissolved. There was continuity of settlement at some sites, and several new villages were established, but Moundville was almost totally abandoned. There seems to have been no major change in crops grown, animals hunted, or numbers of people in the population (Sheldon 1974). Only the symbols and the hierarchical organization faded from the scene. What remained was a collection of egalitarian communities that evidenced little internal variation and no evidence of intercommunity ranking.

By A.D. 1700 the Black Warrior River Valley had become a buffer zone between the Upper Creeks on the east and the Choctaw and Chickasaw on the west. The struggle in 1560 for the fealty of the Napochies, a Choctaw-speaking group resident in this area, by the Coza, an Upper Creek group (Swanton 1922:230–240), may signal the beginning of this spatial disengagement. The archaeological record certainly does not show a large population in the Black Warrior River Valley after 1700, and the documents are specific in their narrative of conflicting claims over the valley and warfare between the Lower Creeks and Choctaw.

Discussion

At least in outline, the development and decline of complex forms of social organization in the Moundville phase are clear. Undifferentiated communities evolved into a complex settlement system with Moundville at its center. The size and location of villages and hamlets was regulated by the productivity of adjacent agricultural soils (Peebles 1978), but the size and location of the minor ceremonial centers probably was dictated by administrative factors. As Steponaitis (1978) has shown, the location of these minor ceremonial centers minimized the "costs" of movement of goods and information from the several regions to Moundville. In addition, these minor centers were always spatially interposed between nearby villages and Moundville.

The growth in the complexity of social organization closely paralleled that of the settlement system. The elite segment of society grew from less than 1% of the population in the early part of the Moundville phase to approximately 5% of the population by the early part of Moundville III period. A single political or ritual office seems to have increased to two and perhaps three well-defined hierarchically ranked offices during the same span of time.

The nascent agricultural economy of the West Jefferson phase became a fully agricultural adaptation by the beginning of the Moundville I phase. By the end of the Moundville II period some productive specialization was evident, and intersocietal exchange seems to have been a monopoly of the elite stratum of society. In addition, trace element analysis of bone by Margaret Schoeninger suggest that these "elites" had more meat in their diet than did the population as a whole (Schoeninger and Peebles 1981).

This pattern of development can be explored from a number of conceptual vantage points. There is the almost axiomatic relationship between population growth and agricultural intensification. There is, in addition, Ford's (1977) cogent observations that increased agricultural dependence led to increased risks from the reliance on one or two crops. He argued that increasing social complexity was the buffer by which these risks were counteracted. Susan Kus and I (Peebles and Kus 1977) explored the relationships between social organization, the ability to process information, and environmental fluctuations. We concluded that not only agricultural management but also warfare was important in the growth of social complexity at Moundville.

> On the one hand as the dependence on agriculture increased, the risk of catastrophic crop failure increased, and the risk of local hostilities decreased. On the other hand, as local units were integrated into large political units, the risk of hostility from equally large neighboring politics increased and insecurity again increased. This left either alliance or large-scale preemptive raids as one strategy to eliminate the unpredictable element in a society's environment. Therefore, the regulatory functions of the chief were to make alliances, or war, as well as to buffer against the possiblity of crop failure.
>
> Such a view might explain the fact that a part of the iconography of the Southern Cult is related to warfare (Brown 1976), and that it served as well as a common set of symbols among several societies. It symbolized the equality of leaders among allies, equals among enemies, and it emphasized rank within a single polity. Such a view also goes far toward the understanding of warfare among chiefdoms. Such societies engaged in massive raids, but they generally did not take and hold the territory of the group over which they were victorious. Instead they contented themselves with uprooting crops, destroying stored food, taking captives, and generally disrupting their enemies. If warfare was the least predictable element in a chiefdom's environment, and if it could not be rendered predictable by an alliance, then complete disruption of the enemy group would remove it from contention for at least one seasonal cycle. It seems from the ethnohistoric record of the Southeast that warfare was of this nature and not the result of the territorial ambitions of one group for another's land. [Peebles ms.]

The decline and eventual demise of the Moundville phase presents conceptual problems not encountered in the investigation of its evolution. The easy solution is to point to de Soto, rapine, pillage, and European diseases. This explanation, however, does not fit the data neatly. The decrease in social and settlement complexity seems to begin before 1539. A more complex set of propostions would relate the costs of ritual regulation to productivity, surplus, and the benefits of such regulation in relation to changing social and natural environments. The cyclical model for the development of ranked societies proposed by Friedman (1975) seems applicable, at least in principle, to this problem.

Note

Acknowledgments. All of my work at Moundville is built upon the rich intellectual heritage created by David L. DeJarnette. In addition, the Department of Anthropology, Office of Archaeological Research, and Alabama Museum of Natural History at the University of Alabama have made this work both possible and productive. Much of the research reported here is supported by the National Science Foundation (BNS-7807133 A01) and represents the collective efforts of Vincas Steponaitis, Margaret Schoeninger, Margaret Scarry, Paul Welch, Tandy Bozeman, and students from the Universities of Chicago, Alabama, Michigan, Delaware, and Frankfurt am Main. My thanks to all.

References Cited

Adair, James
   1775   The History of the American Indians. London: Edward and Charles Dilly.
Bourne, Edward Gaylor
   1904   Narratives of the Career of Hernando De Soto. 2 vols. New York: A. S. Barnes.
Brain, Jeffrey
   1978   Late Prehistoric Settlement Patterns in the Yazoo Basin and Natchez Bluffs Region of the Lower Mississippi Valley. *In* Bruce G. Smith, ed. pp. 331–368. New York: Academic Press.
Brain, Jeffrey, P. Alan Toth, and Antonio Rodriguez-Buckingham
   1972   Ethnohistoric Archaeology and the De Soto Entrada into the Lower Mississippi Valley. Conference on Historic Site Archaeology Papers 7:232–289.
Brose, David S., and George W. Percy
   1978   Fort Walton Settlement Patterns. *In* Mississippian Settlement Patterns, Bruce D. Smith, ed. pp. 81–114. New York: Academic Press.
Brown, James A.
   1971   (ed.) Approaches to the Social Dimensions of Mortuary Practices. Society for American Archaeology Memoir 25.
   1976   The Southern Cult Reconsidered. Midcontinental Journal of Archaeology 1:115–135.
Buikstra, Jane M.
   1976   Hopewell in the Lower Illinois Valley: A Regional Study of Human Biological and Prehistoric Mortuary Behavior. Northwestern Archaeological Program Scientific Papers, No. 2. Evanston: Northwestern University Press.
DeJarnette, D. L., and S. B. Wimberly
   1941   The Bessemer Site. Geological Survey of Alabama Museum Paper 17.
Fletcher, Roland
   1977   Settlement Studies. *In* Spatial Archaeology, David Clarke, ed. pp. 47–162. London: Academic Press.
Ford, Richard I.
   1977   Evolutionary Ecology and the Evolution of Human Ecosystems: A Case Study from the Midwestern U.S.A. *In* Explanation of Prehistoric Change,

James N. Hill, ed. pp. 153–184. Albuquerque: University of New Mexico Press for the School of American Research.

Friedman, J.
  1975 Tribes, States, and Transformations. *In* Marxist Analyses and Social Anthropology, M. Block, ed. pp. 161–202. New York: Wiley.

Goggin, John M., and William C. Sturtevant
  1964 The Calusa: A Stratified, Nonagricultural Society. *In* Explorations in Cultural Anthropology, Ward H. Goodenough, ed. pp. 179–219. New York: McGraw-Hill.

Goldstein, Lynne G.
  1976 Spatial Structure and Social Organization: Regional Manifestations of Mississippian Society. Ph.D. dissertation. Anthropology Department, Northwestern University.

Hardin, Margaret
  1980 The Recognition of Individual Hands in the Context of Standardized Craft Production: Implications of the Technological and Stylistic Development of Moundville Engraved Ceramics. Southeastern Archaeological Conference Bulletin 24:108–110.

Hatch, J. W.
  1976 Status in Death: Principles of Ranking in Dallas Culture Mortuary Remains. Ph.D. dissertation. Anthropology Department, Pennsylvania State University.

Hudson, Charles
  1976 The Southeastern Indians. Knoxville: University of Tennessee Press.

Jenkins, N. J.
  1975 Terminal Woodland-Mississippian Interaction in Northern Alabama: The West Jefferson Phase. Paper presented at the Annual Meeting of the Southeastern Archaeological Conference, Tuscaloosa, Alabama.

Kus, Susan M.
  1979 Archaeology and Ideology: The Symbolic Organization of Space. Ph.D. dissertation. Anthropology Department, University of Michigan.

Lankford, George E., III
  1977 A New Look at De Soto's Route through Alabama. Journal of Alabama Archaeology 23:10–34.

Larson, Lewis H., Jr.
  1971a Archaeological Implications of Social Stratification at the Etowah Site, Georgia. Society for American Archaeology Memoir 25:52–67.
  1971b Settlement Distribution during the Mississippi Period. Southeastern Archaeological Conference Bulletin 13:19–25.
  1972 Functional Considerations of Warfare in the Southeast during the Mississippi Period. American Antiquity 37:383–392.

Moore, C. B.
  1905 Certain Aboriginal Remains of the Black Warrior River. Journal of the Academy of Natural Sciences of Philadelphia, 2nd ser. 13(2):124–244.
  1907 Moundville Revisited. Journal of the Academy of Natural Sciences of Philadelphia, 2nd ser. 13(3):334–405.

Peebles, Christopher S.
  1971 Moundville and Surrounding Sites: Some Structural Considerations of Mortuary Practices, II. Society for American Archaeology Memoir 25:68–91.

1974 Moundville: The Organization of a Prehistoric Community and Culture. Ph.D. dissertation. Anthropology Department, University of California, Santa Barbara.
1978 Determinants of Settlement Size and Location in the Moundville Phase. *In* Mississippian Settlement Patterns, Bruce D. Smith, ed. pp. 369–416. New York: Academic Press.
1979 Excavations at Moundville, 1905–1951. Ann Arbor: University of Michigan Press.
ms. Moundville: The Form and Content of a Mississippian Society. *In* The Emergence of the Mississippian, Stephen Williams, ed. Albuquerque: University of New Mexico Press. In press.

Peebles, Christopher S., and Susan M. Kus
1977 Some Archaeological Correlates of Ranked Societies. American Antiquity 42:421–448.

Phillips, Philip, James A. Ford, and James B. Griffin
1951 Archaeological Survey in the Lower Mississippi Alluvial Valley. Peabody Museum of Archaeology and Ethnology Papers, No. 60.

Saxe, Arthur A.
1970 Social Dimensions of Mortuary Practices. Ph.D. dissertation. Anthropology Department, University of Michigan.

Scarry, C. Margaret
1981 Plant Procurement Strategies in the West Jefferson and Moundville I Phases. Southeastern Archaeological Conference Bulletin 24:94–96.

Schoeninger, Margaret J.
1979 Dietary Reconstruction at Chalcatzingo, A Formative Period Site in Morelos, Mexico. University of Michigan Museum of Anthropology Technical Reports, No. 9
1980 Changes in Human Subsistence Activities from the Middle Paleolithic to the Neolithic Period in the Middle East. Ph.D. dissertation. Department of Anthropology, University of Michigan.

Schoeninger, Margaret J., and Christopher S. Peebles
1981 Some Notes on the Relationship between Status and Diet at Moundville. Southeastern Archaeological Conference Bulletin 24:96–97.

Sears, William H.
1958 The Wilbanks Site (9 CK-5). Georgia Bureau of American Ethnology Bulletin 169:129–194.
1961 The Study of Social and Religious Systems in North American Archaeology. Current Anthropology 2:223–246.

Seckinger, Ernest W., Jr.
1977 Social Complexity During the Mississippian Period in Northwest Georgia. M.A. thesis. Anthropology Department, University of Georgia.

Sheldon, Craig
1974 The Mississippian-Historic Transition in Central Alabama. Ph.D. dissertation. Anthropology Department, University of Georgia.

Smith, Bruce D.
1978 Variation in Mississippian Settlement Patterns. *In* Mississippian Settlement Patterns, Bruce D. Smith, ed. pp. 479–503. New York: Academic Press

Smith, Buckingham, transl.
   1866 Narratives of the Career of Hernando De Soto in the Conquest of Florida. New York: Bradford Club.

Smith, Marvin T.
   1976 The Route of De Soto through Tennessee, Georgia, and Alabama: The Evidence from Material Culture. Early Georgia 4:27–48.

Steponaitis, Vincas
   1978 Location Theory and Complex Chiefdoms: A Mississippian Example. *In* Mississippian Settlement Patterns, Bruce D. Smith, ed. pp. 417–454. New York: Academic Press.
   1980 Ceramics, Chronology, and Community Patterns at Moundville, A Late Prehistoric Site in Alabama. Ph.D. dissertation. Anthropology Department, University of Michigan.

Swanton, John R.
   1911 Indian Tribes of the Lower Mississippi Valley and Adjacent Coast of the Gulf of Mexico. Bureau of American Ethnology Bulletin 43.
   1922 Early History of the Creek Indians and Their Neighbors. Bureau of American Ethnology Bulletin 73.
   1939 Final Report of the United States De Soto Expedition Commission. Washington: Government Printing Office.

Tainter, Joseph A.
   1978 Mortuary Practices and the Study of Prehistoric Social Systems. Advances in Archaeological Method and Theory 1:105–141.

Van der Leeuw, Sander
   1980 Analysis of Moundville Phase Ceramic Technology. Southeastern Archaeological Conference Bulletin 24:105–108.

Varner, John, and Jeanette Varner, transls.
   1951 The Florida of the Inca. Austin: University of Texas Press.

Walthall, John A.
   1977 Moundville: An Introduction to the Archaeology of a Mississippian Chiefdom. Tuscaloosa: Alabama Museum of Natural History.

Wilkinson, Warren H.
   1960 Opening the Case against the U.S. De Soto Commission's Report and Other De Soto Papers. Jacksonville Beach: Alliance for the Preservation of Florida Antiquities.

15
The Analysis of Prehistoric Political Organization

Fred Plog
and
Steadman Upham
New Mexico State University

Although the archaeological record theoretically contains all of the data necessary for completely reconstructing extinct cultural systems (Binford 1962), archaeologists are rarely able to accomplish such a feat; certain social subsystems are more easily inferred than others. For precisely this reason, the study of prehistoric political organization is still in its nascent stage. Not until comparatively recently did archaeologists begin to address fundamental questions about prehistoric social organization (Binford 1962; Longacre 1964; Hill 1970). Now, a few studies have described prehistoric political organization using burial data (Brown 1971; Hatch 1976; Rothschild 1975; Saxe 1970; Peebles and Kus 1977; King 1978; G. Wright 1978), settlement data (Johnson 1973, 1975; Grebinger 1973; Steponaitis 1981; Upham and Rice 1978), and data on exchange systems (Wright and Johnson 1975; Renfrew 1975; Johnson 1975; Webb 1974; Dalton 1977; Earle 1977, 1978). But, although these works are a badly needed addition to more traditional time-space studies, they are sometimes marred by their lack of attention to specific variables, and the relation of these to ideal types. A cogent summary of this problem is that of Earle (1977, 1978), who successfully demonstrates that redistribution as an exchange type is not necessarily a correlate of chiefdoms, a political type.

Most archaeological studies of political organization are based on either Service's (1962) or Fried's (1967) typology. The use of these typologies to interpret the prehistoric past necessarily involves four major problems. First, if some key attribute in the typology is used in classifying the political organization of a particular site or region, the range of explanatory statements that can then be explored is either sharply curtailed or the arguments become hopelessly circular. When, for example, the size of the largest settlement is used to identify state organization, it is impossible to explore the relationship between state organization and population aggregation since the latter was used to define the former.

The second and third problems stem from the fact that the typologies are based on ideal types. As Fried (1967:14) has observed, ideal types are advantageous because by treating complex continua as simpler categories key aspects of variation and key patterns of covariation may be more easily studied. The usefulness of such simplification in the search for structural regularities is not to be doubted. However, the difficulties they create in the study of prehistory are two. First, in the study of social evolution, the complex patterns of variation are crucial for understanding why the most typical outcomes of evolutionary processes are the relatively few ideal types. The range of variation must be explored in order to understand why relatively few outcomes are typical. Second, if the claim that one goal of archaeology is the identification of behavioral and organizational patterns not found in the ethnographic and ethnohistoric records is to be taken seriously, then conceptual strategies must be employed that allow for the possibility of patterns of variation and covariation not found in the present. Thus, in both these respects, an approach to the archaeological record using continuous variables is desirable.

A fourth problem arises when ideal types are injudiciously used by archaeologists, ethnographers, or both. We do not question the utility for some discussions, arguments, and syntheses of applying terms such as "band" and "tribe," "egalitarian," and "stratified." But there are limits to the utility of such terms for detailed comparative and evolutionary studies. They mask important variation in particular institutional, status, and authority patterns. Perhaps more important is that they foster a too quick summary judgment about a particular case and hence ignore evidence of variation over space and time. The Southwestern Pueblo are a case in point. In virtually every summary classification, the modern Pueblo are characterized as tribal and egalitarian. As a result, analyses of Puebloan prehistory typically assume these same patterns. Yet the evidence suggests non-egalitarian organizations and behaviors among the Pueblo (Brandt 1976; Upham 1982).

Political Concepts: A Re-evaluation

We suggest that it is currently close to impossible to effectively utilize in a prehistoric context and in the absence of written records concepts such as social control, sanction, reinforcement, power, authority, custom, and law. Archaeologists sometimes find evidence that bears on such ideas. But such evidence occurs so infrequently that it makes little sense to imagine that one could effectively analyze or compare, for example, systems of social control. Certainly assumptions can be made about how the above correlate with particular organizational forms, but such assumptions are at best tenuous.

A beginning point in exploring directions that such studies might take is Fried's definition of political organization and related concepts. Fried (1967:21) defines political organization as "those portions of social organization that specifically relate to the individuals and groups that manage the affairs of public policy or seek to control the appointment or action of those individuals or groups." At a general level, we have no quarrel with this definition. But for archaeological puposes, emphasis must be placed on evidence of the manner in which affairs were *managed*, since evidence of specific efforts to control action is rare in prehistory. For this reason, archaeological data are difficult to analyze using the status- and role-based classification that Fried develops for ethnographic groups.

Although status and role are pertinent concepts for the study of political systems, the archaeological record, to the extent that it reflects political organization at all, is the product of managerial decisions broadly construed. In any society, the most basic of those decisions involve access to space, access to human and natural resources, and access to social resources including statuses, organization, and symbols. Across societies access to space, natural resources, and social resources varies in the extent of its restriction to particular individuals or groups and whether the restrictions are consensual or cooptative. Clearly, demonstrating that particular patterns of decision making are likely to leave particular patterns in material remains is critical to the success that archaeologists are likely to have in studying political organization in the past.

While we will discuss below limitations of access in regard to each of the above domains and briefly mention the manner in which access may be limited, we realize that the former and the latter are connected. For example, one might logically argue that all limitations of access are economically motivated, even though the way that access is limited may in some cases be linked to status differences within a population and in other cases to differential access to resources within a territory. We do not dispute such connectedness and hope to be able to define more clearly the specific archaeological data (rather than correlates) pertinent to each topic or set of topics.

We would again emphasize the importance to studies of evolution in spatially and temporally disparate societies of avoiding the assumption that the limitation of access or the decision-making process that underlies it are necessarily the same from one domain to another. For example, limitation in access to the production of specific craft goods does not require (although it may very well lead to) restricted access to social statuses. Restricted access to exchange items does not necessarily imply restriction of access to naturally available resources. When each such domain is treated independently, it is possible to explore the direction and nature of causality and to define in greater detail the continuum that lies between egalitarian and stratified societies.

Access to Space

In recent years, a large body of literature has appeared concerning human territoriality (see references in Lee and DeVore 1968 and Dyson-Hudson and Smith 1978), but there is little agreement about definitions of territoriality in these studies. Furthermore, as Dyson-Hudson and Smith (1978:21) point out, "the territoriality controversy in anthropology has primarily focused on hunter-gatherers." One major point of controversy has revolved around the question of whether territories are best viewed as fixed or flexible. King (1975, 1976) and Peterson (1975) are recent examples of a long line of anthropologists (e.g., Radcliffe-Brown 1930; Service 1962; Williams 1974) who argue that some form of fixed territorial band is the optimum pattern of spatial organization for hunter-gatherers under all or most ecological conditions. Other authors (e.g., Lee and DeVore 1968; Damas 1969) have argued that a more flexible pattern of spatial organization and resource utilization is typical of hunter-gatherers.

In attempting to use the concept of territoriality in studies of societies with different political organizations, Dyson-Hudson and Smith argue that both fixed and flexible patterns are possible but will occur under different circumstances. Fixed patterns, including explicit defense of an identified territory, are likely to occur only when "critical resources are sufficiently abundant and predictable in space and time, so that costs of exclusive use and defense of an area are outweighted by the benefits gained from resource control" (Dyson-Hudson and Smith 1978:21). We would extend this analysis by noting the articulation of "fixed" and "flexible" patterns with the common anthropological distinction between proprietory and usufruct rights. At any level of social organization—the family, village, clan or cultural group—individuals and groups may seek to "fix" access by claiming proprietary rights over space. Yet such a proprietary claim is neither necessary nor necessarily common, but only likely to arise given certain conditions.

This formulation is particularly useful for archaeological purposes because it forces upon us a clear distinction between the observation that a particular group of people occupy space and the claim that they either exclusively own or will defend an explicit territory. In all probability, the situation, especially prior to the existence of state-organized societies, was quite complex. There was almost certainly a great deal of fluidity in the spatial domain that a given hunting-gathering band occupied. In all likelihood occupied space and the degree to which it was defended changed in response to the growth and decline of a group, similar processes operating in those around it, and short- and long-term fluctuations in climatic patterns. However, at the other extreme there are and were groups that routinely defend territories with complex political coordination and specialists, soldiers. Many combinations are possible in between. Important variation also existed in the specific organizational entity that asserted proprietary rights over space: households within villages, villages, clans that are either within or crosscut villages, can all claim and defend rights to space.

Given this potential complexity, what evidence of the waxing and waning of territorial behavior can archaeologists expect to discover? There are at least five classes of evidence:

Distributions of Material Traits. It is tempting to define the spatial zones controlled using material trait distributions as indicators of such territories. Unfortunately, our growing understanding of the manner in which such boundaries are generated by interaction and exchange provides little support for the notion that such distributions reflect actual territories. Regardless of whether such zones were occupied by particular ethnic groups or were produced by particularly intense interaction or exchange, there are no grounds for the assumption that the spatial entity so defined was consciously perceived as an exclusive territory, much less used as such.

Boundary Markers. Shrines, cairns, petroglyphs, and even small scatters of broken sherds have been identified ethnographically and ethnohistorically as territorial markers. While it is not possible to say precisely what limitations of access were intended by such markers, some degree of restriction of access was symboled. Thus, to the extent that the use of such devices varied in time and/or space, differing concerns with access to space may be indicated.

Warfare. While it is tempting to take evidence of warfare such as mutilated bodies, as evidence of territoriality, it is apparent that, especially prior to the advent of state-organized societies, warfare and raiding had no necessary connection with actual defense of territory.

Architectural Features. Architectural features such as forts, defensive walls, garrisons, or signal towers are also not necessarily evidence of territoriality. Nevertheless, it seems reasonable to assume that when a society made a major labor and material investment in defense, territory was likely to have been at least relatively fixed. Unfortunately, spatial analyses indicating, for example, that such features bound a spatial unit or occur at key passes between different valleys have rarely been undertaken.

Art. Representational art can provide clues to the existence of more or less formally defined groups of warriors, which, like evidence of warfare or architectural features, may indicate a concern with defense of territory.

Access to Human and Natural Resources

Inferences regarding variation in the restriction of access to natural resources, goods, and labor present conceptual and analytical problems similar to those with territoriality. For example, apart from iconographic depictions of slaves, precisely what evidence can be used to infer the appropriation of human labor is problematical. A similar difficulty occurs in the case of primary resources since many of these are perishable and leave little trace in the archaeological record.

It should be noted that the distribution of most primary resources is highly localized; that within regions, there are likely to be many resources having a patchy distribution. To the extent that resources occurring naturally in only one area are found in others, exchange can be inferred. But, whether the exchange involved an exchange of items or the exchange of access to the resource location is uncertain. Similarly, limitation of access to one resource does not indicate restriction of access to others. It is far more probable, for example, that prehistoric peoples in the American Southwest sought to restrict access to good agricultural land rather than to piñon trees. Annual variability in the productivity of the latter is so great that conceptualizing the resource as a free one, available for exploitation by a number of nearby groups, would have been essential. Otherwise, a particular group would have had piñon available only one year out of every seven to fifteen. And again there is the problem of our limited ability to see restrictions operating at different levels: within villages, clans within villages, etc.

Perhaps the best basis for an initial assessment of differential access to resources is a simple economic one. If a resource is relatively free, one would anticipate heavy use in localities where it is abundant and a gradual or clinal decline as one moves away from the center of availability. Sharp gradients in a distributional pattern indicate some cultural or natural restriction of access.

Several different classes of data are useful in studying restrictions of access to human and natural resources:

Natural Resources

As noted earlier, a major problem in the study of natural resources is that many important ones are perishable and, therefore, are rarely, although occasionally, preserved (Minnis and S. Plog 1976). One traditional focus of such studies is raw materials used in manufacturing chipped and ground stone artifacts; studies of obsidian exchange are more common (e.g., Sidrys 1977; Findlow and Bolognese 1978) than those of more mundane materials (Green 1975). Renfrew (1975, 1977) has described a number of models useful in analyzing the manner in which access to these materials is restricted by different exchange patterns. To date, few other raw material distributions have been analyzed in sufficient detail to permit a description of the degree to which access to them was controlled.

Osteological analyses provide an indirect means of studying variation of individual and intra-settlement access to critical resources and raw materials (Shimkin 1973; McHenry and Shultz 1976; El-Najjar et al. 1976). Harris lines and other measures of nutritional stress, measures of stature, and the measures of incidence of disease among different segments of a population may be indicative of varied access. However, relatively few studies have been undertaken.

Craft Goods

Our understanding of the distributional patterns characteristic of craft goods and restrictions of access to them are substantial. To illustrate this productive avenue of analysis, we will use the case of Southwestern ceramic vessels. Wobst (1977) has argued that stylistic characteristics of material items can serve as important social boundary markers. In the American Southwest, such studies have been most successful in the case of black-on-white pottery. Drawing on the earlier work of Cronin (1962), Longacre (1964), Hill (1970), Tuggle (1970), and Wobst (1977), S. Plog (1977) has developed a new framework for design studies. Essentially, the premise of this work is that ceramic designs carry information and that stylistic variation on artifacts differentiates social groups, personal or group ownership, or religious or political identities. It follows that the distribution of particular stylistic elements can be used to delimit the distribution of particular groups or group affiliations and that stylist elements function in the process of boundary maintenance (Wobst 1977:330). Using this approach, it has been possible to delimit spatial units within which access to ceramic vessels carrying particular style elements was relatively unrestricted (see S. Plog 1977; Lightfoot 1978).

While many earlier design studies suggested that the distribution of style elements on black-and-white pottery was determined by residence rules, later work indicates that these styles were distinctive of groups occupying a relatively large area. The types of decisions that produced these distributions are, at this point, unclear. However, we do know that in the central and northern Southwest, regional black-on-white ceramic styles become spatially most distinctive during periods of high population growth, indicating some restriction of access to both material items and the painted symbols on them. The emergence of design style distributions that are more homogeneous locally and more varied regionally reflect the growing autonomy of local groups and the developing organizational complexity of prehistoric Southwestern cultural systems.

For example, working from the concept of minimum equilibrium size groups as developed by Wobst (1974) for Paleolithic cultural systems, Fred Plog (1979) demonstrates that during Pueblo II and III times (A.D. 900–1300) the Western Anasazi area can be subdivided into eleven major contiguous spatial units. Each of these units is between 10,000 and 15,000 square km. and contains artifactual remains that are substantially homogeneous. There is no evidence to indicate that particular ethnic groups occupied these territorial units. However, distributions such as these, especially when they are characterized by sharp boundaries, suggest restriction of access to one or more categories of material items.

At the local level, there is now preliminary evidence that some later Southwestern ceramic traditions were subject to restrictions of access such that they could be held only by the inhabitants of particular settlements or perhaps even particular individuals within them. Polychrome ceramics are a case in point (Martin and Plog 1973; Upham 1978). Although there is only preliminary evidence, important changes in the distribution of Southwestern ceramics began at about A.D. 1100 (and apparently culminate during the 14th century). During this time access to black-on-white pottery did not change substantially, although the greater variety of black-on-white pottery made prior to A.D. 1100 decreased. In contrast, access to polychrome ceramics appears to have been limited to a select portion of the population. Almost invariably, these types appear on the largest sites, in special use or ceremonial contexts, and/or in high-status burials. Although the relationship of many specific variables has yet to be delineated, at a very general level what is seen in the archaeological record is a shift from unrestricted to highly restricted distributions of particular types of ceramic vessels with only the residents of particular kinds of sites and, potentially, only a few individuals within them having access to certain forms.

Architecture and Settlement Patterns

Although we rarely think of architectural and settlement patterns as evidencing access restrictions, they clearly do so. References to "elite residential units" clearly imply that some members of a society had access to quantitatively and qualitatively different living quarters. Similarly, centers in a site hierarchy defined on the basis of size, architectural features, or the presence of exotic craft goods were settlements whose residents had access to domains of material culture not available to residents of the hinterland area. The Near Eastern villages with cone architecture described by Johnson (1975) had higher quantities of exchange items than surrounding settlements. Great kiva sites and sites with other distinctive architectural traits in the American Southwest often prove to have ceramics brought from a great distance, polychrome ceramics, shell, turquoise, beads, and other items that are not characteristic of typical settlements in the surrounding area.

The case of monumental architecture is an especially problematical one. Archaeologists have assumed that monumental architecture is a certain indicator of a complex society. Clearly, monumental architecture represents an enormous social investment in labor, materials, and organization. It is tempting to view such architecture as the product of coopted, if not forced, labor. Yet the construction of European cathedrals by casual volunteer labor over periods of many decades provides a warning against so easy an assumption. Studies of the magnitude of architecture and the speed of construction that are generally associated with different patterns for organizing human labor are clearly warranted if evidence of monumental architecture is to be correctly interpreted. Furthermore, there is no necessary correlation between monumental architecture and, for example, participation in far-flung exchange networks.

Access to Social Resources

While it is clearly possible to describe differential individual and group access to particular institutions, statuses, and symbols when living peoples are studied, we have great reservations about the feasibility of parallel prehistoric studies. In the preceding sections, we discussed restrictions of access to natural and material resources. These restrictions as they are reflected in the material patterns of different groups and time periods are used by archaeologists in making inferences concerning status, organization, and symbol systems. Thus, the only means of making inferences concerning access to social resources involve correlations with access to natural and material ones. If the latter provide the only means of knowing the former, no new information results from the inference in question. Two examples illustrate the problem.

We mentioned earlier increasingly detailed descriptions of variation in burial practices. In some excavated cemeteries, individuals were interred in roughly equivalent fashion while in others there were marked differences in the quantity and/or quality of goods used as grave furniture. Similarly, in some cemeteries infants and juveniles are buried with the "common" assemblage of grave goods, while in others a distinctive and generally smaller assemblage was used. In still others a few infant burials contain grave goods characteristic of high-status adult burials. This variation allows us to distinguish between societies in which all social groups had equivalent abilities to marshall material items for the burial ceremony and societies in which one or more social groups had markedly greater abilities to marshall those goods. The variation also allows a distinction between cases in which that ability was ascribed and cases in which it was achieved.

We disagree with those archaeologists who have argued that burial practices are unrelated to social status. A common line of reasoning in this regard is that grave goods are offered by the living and, hence, have little or no direct bearing on the social, political, or economic importance of the deceased. We would argue, as other archaeologists have suggested (Binford 1971; Peebles and Kus 1977), that cemeteries in which there is substantial variation in the quantity and quality of grave goods within burials indeed reflect social differentiation. However, quantities of burial goods are but one data set bearing on this issue. The diversity of grave offerings, the presence of "sociotechnic" artifacts, burial position, orientation and location within the cemetery, grave architecture, degree of custodial care of the osseous remains, correlations between age-sex distributions and individual inventories of grave goods, and nutritional and osteological studies relating to stress and stature can provide data to the archaeologist about ascribed statuses, systems of social ranking and economic privilege evidenced by restriction of access to particular resources and commodities. Thus, while variation in access to material goods is clearly indicated, the social aspects of that variation are not directly indicated by the archaeological data.

However, problems arise when inferences are made concerning the status held by a particular individual or the means used by the social group undertaking the burial to marshall the burial goods. Instances where particular burials have been interpreted as chiefs, kings, magicians, priests, etc. are suspect for a number of reasons. First, they presume the exclusivity of each such role when, in fact, political, religious, and economic statuses sometimes are and sometimes are not differentiated. Furthermore, burial treatment may reflect the last status held by an individual, the aggregate of statuses held, or both. Finally, while social groups do vary in their ability to command resources, the means they use to obtain and legitimize their access and the nature of the power they hold is quite variable.

Monumental architecture is a second case in point. There are certainly circumstances in which relatively rapid construction of substantial structures by a large labor force can be documented. In such instances, the existence of an institution capable of commanding and coordinating a large force of human labor is clearly indicated. It is equally clear that many societies had no such institution and among those societies that did there was great variation in the degree of control involved. Such differences again reflect the differential ability of social groups to mobilize resources. In such an example, it is very difficult to establish precisely what religious, political, or economic institution was responsible for the control, how power was legitimized, and in how many different areas of social life that power was exercised. Equally problematical is the absence of monumental architecture in societies that assessed over other criteria, appear to be politically complex. The absence of such forms may simply mean that power was invested in other pursuits.

Thus, we are arguing that, given the great variety of social forms that are used in human societies to structure power relationships, it is unlikely that one specific form can be identified on the basis of material culture patterning. At the same time, stratification and the complexity of political organization can be read directly from this patterning. While the use of ethnographic concepts for particular statuses and institutions may provide the appearance of insight and communication, such names provide little in the way of substance. Their relation to the material patterns with which archaeologists work is too tenuous to provide a serviceable basis for clear communication between archaeologists and ethnographers working within similar analytical and theoretical domains.

Consensus and Cooptation

For all of the reasons discussed in the preceding section, we are dubious that archaeologists can genuinely distinguish between situations in which differential access to resources was a product of consensus as opposed to differential power and will discuss this distinction only briefly. Humans are capable of rationalizing situations in which they find themselves in a very great number of ways. It is clear that there are societies in which members of lower-status groups are capable of convincing themselves or being convinced by others that they do not want access to resources and statuses, or that they actually have such rights in principle and choose not to exercise them. Equally clearly, differences in material welfare that are solely a product of individual or familial achievement can be and are rationalized as the product of cooptative behavior. Discussions of such cognitive issues are beyond both the interests and capabilities of most archaeologists.

Conclusion

While the tone of this essay may seem somewhat negative, our intention is not to argue that archaeologists have no bases for the exploration of variability in political organization. Our argument is only that such efforts are most successful now and will improve in the future, to the degree that we are sensitive to the material reality underlying our inferences. The pattern of material culture, variation within sites, between sites, and within and between larger spatial entities provides direct evidence of varying social stratification and political complexity. The presence of groups with quantitatively and qualitatively different material assemblages, the number of such groups, and the rigidity/fluidity of the boundaries that separate them indicate variation in the actual access that individuals and groups had to different domains of material and human resources. This spatial structure is itself more or less complex, more or less stratified, and more or less varied through time and space. Understanding that structure is the source of our understanding of political and social organization.

References Cited

Binford, Lewis R.
- 1962 Archaeology as Anthropology. American Antiquity 28:217–225.
- 1971 Mortuary Practices: Their Study and Their Potential. *In* Social Dimensions of Mortuary Practices, James A. Brown, ed. 6–29. Society for American Archaeology Memoir 25.

Brandt, Elizabeth A.
- 1976 On Secrecy and the Control of Knowledge through Speech. Paper presented at the Southwest Anthropological Association Meetings, San Francisco.

Brown, James A., ed.
- 1971 Approaches to the Social Dimensions of Mortuary Practices. Society for American Archaeology Memoir 25.

Cronin, Constance
　1962　An Analysis of Pottery Design Elements Indicating Possible Relationships between Three Decorated Types. *In* Chapters in the Prehistory of Eastern Arizona: I, Paul S. Martin et al. pp. 105–114. Fieldiana: Anthropology, Vol. 53.

Dalton, George
　1977　Aboriginal Economies in Stateless Societies. *In* Exchange Systems in Prehistory, Timothy Earle and J. Ericson, eds. pp. 191–212. New York: Academic Press.

Damas, David, ed.
　1969　Contributions to Anthropology: Band Societies. National Museum of Canada Bulletin 228.

Dyson-Hudson, Rada, and Eric Alden Smith
　1978　Human Territoriality: An Ecological Reassessment. American Anthropologist 80:21–41.

Earle, Timothy K.
　1977　A Reappraisal of Redistribution: Complex Hawaiian Chiefdoms. *In* Exchange Systems in Prehistory, Timothy Earle and J. Ericson, eds. pp.213–229. New York: Academic Press.
　1978　Economic and Social Organization of a Complex Chiefdom: The Halelea District, Kaua'i, Hawaii. Museum of Anthropology, University of Michigan, Anthropological Papers, No. 63.

El-Najjar, M., D. Ryan, C. G. Turner, and B. Lozoff
　1976　The Etiology of Porotic Hyperostosis among the Prehistoric and Historic Anasazi Indians of the Southwestern United States. American Journal of Physical Anthropology 44:477–489.

Findlow, Frank J., and Marisa Bolognese
　1978　An Initial Examination of Prehistoric Obsidian Exchange in Southwestern New Mexico. Unpublished manuscript.

Fried, Morton
　1967　The Evolution of Political Society. New York: Random House.

Grebinger, Paul
　1973　Prehistoric Social Organization in Chaco Canyon, New Mexico: An Alternative Reconstruction. The Kiva 39:3–23.

Green, Margie
　1975　Patterns of Variation in Chipped Stone Raw Materials for the Chevelon Drainage. M.A. thesis. Anthropology Department, State University of New York at Binghamton.

Hatch, James W.
　1976　Status in Death: Principles of Ranking in Dallas Culture Mortuary Remains. Ph.D. dissertation. Anthropology Department, Pennsylvania State University.

Hill, James N.
　1970　Broken K Pueblo: Prehistoric Social Organization in the American Southwest. University of Arizona Anthropological Papers, No. 18.

Johnson, Gregory A.
　1973　Local Exchange and Early State Development in Southwestern Iran. Museum of Anthropology, University of Michigan, Anthropological Papers, No. 51.

1975 Locational Analysis and the Investigation of Uruk Local Exchange Systems. *In* Ancient Civilization and Trade, J. A. Sabloff and C. C. Lamberg-Karlovsky, eds. pp. 285–339. Albuquerque: University of New Mexico Press for the School of American Research.

King, Glenn
1975 Socioterritorial Units among Carnivores and Early Hominids. Journal of Anthropological Research 31:69–87.
1976 Society and Territory in Human Evolution. Journal of Human Evolution 5:323–332.

King, Thomas F.
1978 Don't That Beat the Band? Nonegalitarian Political Organiza-tion in Prehistoric Central California. *In* Social Archaeology, Charles Redman et al., eds. pp. 225–248. New York: Academic Press.

Lee, Richard B., and Irven DeVore, eds.
1968 Man the Hunter. Chicago: Aldine.

Lightfoot, Kent G.
1978 Multi-site Communities in the Prehistoric Southwest: An Example from Pinedale, Arizona. Manuscript on file Department of Anthropology, Arizona State University, Tempe.

Longacre, William A.
1964 Sociological Implications of the Ceramic Analysis. *In* Chapters in the Prehistory of Arizona: II, Paul S. Martin et al., eds. pp. 155–167. Fieldiana: Anthropology, Vol. 55.

Martin, Paul S., and Fred Plog
1973 The Archaeology of Arizona: A Study of the Southwest Region. Garden City: Doubleday Natural History Press.

McHenry, Henry M., and Peter D. Shultz
1976 The Association between Harris Line and Enamel Hypoplasia in Prehistoric California Indians. American Journal of Physical Anthropology 44:507–513.

Minnis, Paul, and Stephen Plog
1976 A Study of the Site Specific Distribution of Agave Parryi in East Central Arizona. The Kiva 41:299–308.

Peebles, Christopher, and Susan M. Kus
1977 Some Archaeological Correlates of Ranked Societies. American Antiquity 42:421–448.

Peterson, Nicolas
1975 Hunter-Gatherer Territoriality: The Perspective from Australia. American Anthropologist 77:53–68.

Plog, Fred
1979 Prehistory: Western Anasazi. *In* Handbook of North American Indians. Vol. 9: Southwest, William C. Sturtevant and Alfonso Ortiz, eds. pp. 108–130. Washington: Smithsonian Institution.

Plog, Stephen
1977 A Multivariate Approach to the Explanation of Ceramic Design Variation. Ph.D. dissertation. Anthropology Department, University of Michigan.

Radcliffe-Brown, A. R.
1930 The Social Organization of Australian Tribes. Oceania 1:34–63.

Renfrew, Colin
  1975 Trade as Action at a Distance: Questions of Integration and Communication. *In* Ancient Civilization and Trade, J. A. Sabloff and C. C. Lamberg-Karlovsky, eds. pp. 3-60. Albuquerque: University of New Mexico Press for the School of American Research.
  1977 Alternative Models for Exchange and Spatial Distribution. *In* Exchange Systems in Prehistory, Timothy K. Earle and J. E. Ericson, eds. pp. 71-90. New York: Academic Press.
Rothschild, Nan A.
  1975 Age and Sex, Status and Role, in Prehistoric Societies of Eastern North America. Ph.D. dissertation. Anthropology Department, New York University.
Saxe, Arthur A.
  1970 Social Dimensions of Mortuary Practices. Ph.D. dissertation. Anthropology Department, University of Michigan.
Service, Elman R.
  1962 Primitive Social Organization. New York: Random House.
Shimkin, Demitri B.
  1973 Models for the Downfall: Some Ecological and Culture-Historical Considerations. *In* The Classic Maya Collapse, T. P. Culbert, ed. pp. 269–300. Albuquerque: University of New Mexico Press.
Sidrys, Raymond
  1977 Mass-Distance Measures for the Maya Obsidian Trade. *In* Exchange Systems in Prehistory, Timothy K. Earle and J. E. Ericson, eds. pp. 91-108. New York: Academic Press.
Steponaitis, Vincas
  1981 Settlement Hierarchies and Political Complexity in Nonmarket Societies: The Formative Period in the Valley of Mexico. American Anthropologist 83:320–363.
Tuggle, H. David
  1970 Prehistoric Community Relations in East-central Arizona. Ph.D. dissertation. Anthropology Department, University of Arizona.
Upham, Steadman
  1978 Final Report on Archaeological Investigations at Chavez Pass Ruin, Coconino National Forest, Arizona: The 1978 Field Season. Report submitted to the U.S.D.A. Forest Service, Coconino National Forest, Flagstaff, Arizona.
  1982 Polities and Power: An Economic and Political History of the Western Pueblo. New York: Academic Press.
Upham, Steadman, and Glen E. Rice
  1978 Up the Canal without a Pattern: Modeling Hohokam Interaction and Exchange. Paper presented at the 44th Annual Meetings of the Society for American Archaeology, Tucson.
Webb, Malcolm C.
  1974 Exchange Networks: Prehistory. Annual Review of Anthropology 3:357–383.
Williams, B. J.
  1974 A Model of Band Society. Society for American Archaeology Memoir 29.

Wobst, H. Martin
  1974 Boundary Conditions for Paleolithic Social Systems: A Simulation Approach. American Antiquity 39:142–178.
  1977 Stylistic Behavior and Information Exchange. *In* Papers for the Director: Research Essays in Honor of James B. Griffin, Charles E. Cleland, ed. pp. 317–342. Museum of Anthropology, University of Michigan, Anthropological Papers, No. 61.
Wright, Gary A.
  1978 Social Differentiation in the Early Natufian. *In* Social Archaeology, Charles L. Redman, ed. pp. 201–224. New York: Academic Press.
Wright, Henry T.
  1978 Recent Research on the Origins of the State. Annual Review of Anthropology 6:379–398.
Wright, Henry T., and Gregory A. Johnson
  1975 Population, Exchange, and Early State Formation in Southwestern Iran. American Anthropologist 77:267–289.

16
Some Simple Measures for the Study of Prehistoric Political Organization

Frank J. Findlow
Anacapa Research Associates

and

Neil J. Goldberg
Columbia University

In this paper we offer archaeologists three measures that will allow them to evaluate prehistoric political organization directly from settlement pattern data. The three measures illustrated are based on aspects of Central Place Theory commonly referenced by archaeologists in their analyses of prehistoric settlement patterns. Our approach, however, is novel insofar as the use of Central Place Theory by archaeologists is concerned. Rather than use Central Place Theory as a means of explaining variation in prehistoric settlement systems, we use those aspects of Central Place Theory that relate the political organization of a society to the spatial arrangement of its settlements in order to develop measures of prehistoric political organization based on settlement pattern data. Each of the measures illustrated is on a continuous scale and consequently should offer the archaeologist a high degree of accuracy in evaluating the relative political organization of prehistoric societies. The three measures are closely related theoretically and they all make use of two forms of data commonly available to archaeologists: relative population density and the organization of settlements. Consequently, it should be possible for archaeologists currently analyzing regional settlement pattern data to apply these measures without the need to collect any additional data.

Central Place Theory and the Measurement of Prehistoric Political Organization

Although Central Place Theory involves a complex body of interrelated principles, many of which are not directly relevant to the study of prehistoric political organization, certain of its concepts are of great importance because they concern the interrelationship between the distribution of human settlement and the cost of various political relationships. Most important in this regard are those portions of Central Place Theory that relate to the general administrative costs of political control. In the following list we summarize the most important of these principles.

1. All administrative aspects of political organization can be minimized if settlements are placed as close as possible to all of the population administered from them. In short the relative efficiency of any form of political organization can be measured in the degree to which such indirect costs such as movement, communications, and transport are minimized (Christaller 1933; Zipf 1949; Berry, Barnum and Tennant 1962; Wright and Johnson 1975).

2. The more complex a political function becomes the greater must be the support population that directly administers it. Consequently, larger communities always possess the potential for more complex political and administrative organization than smaller ones (Berry 1960, 1967; Berry and Garrison 1958; Bogue 1949; Forge 1972).

3. Increasing community size necessitates more complex forms of indirect communication and control. As a result of this larger settlements within a single cultural system must always have more complex forms of these factors than smaller ones (Berry 1960, 1967; Berry and Garrison 1958; Olsson 1965a, 1965b, 1966; Forge 1972; Carniero 1967).

4. With increasing community size the physical area needed to support a community will increase exponentially rather than linearly. Consequently, the territories dominated by larger centers will always be disproportionally large when compared to areas controlled by smaller settlements within the same cultural systems (Christaller 1933; Losch 1954; Berry 1960, 1967; Berry and Garrison 1958; Johnson 1972).

5. Because the various costs connected with distance (i.e., primarily communications and movement costs) increase exponentially with increased distance, the density of habitation around all communities has a tendency to decrease in a negative exponential fashion with increased distance from the center proper. For this reason the cost of extending administrative control outward throughout a settlement's hinterland will always increase exponentially as population decreases. The actual slope of the increase in administrative costs is determined by the simultaneous effects of the distance costs involved and the technological capabilities available to overcome them (Bogue 1949; Zipf 1949; Clark 1951; Losch 1954; Hodder and Millett 1980).

Without providing a formal proof for these principles, it should be sufficient for the purpose of this discussion to say that each is based on the idea that simple geometry must place physical limits on the range in settlement variation that can occur for any society with a given set of demographic characteristics and technological capabilities (Christaller 1933; Losch 1938, 1954; Zipf 1949; Olsson 1966).

On a still more general level these five points can be derived from a single principle that underlies all aspects of Central Place Theory and that relates the general morphology of settlement systems to the cultural behavior of the societies that use them. Specifically, underlying each of these five points is the general theoretical assumption that a settlement system's form is simultaneously a function of three elements: the nature of the available technological system, the size and organization of the population to be integrated by it, and the strength of all selective pressures that would favor a reduction in communications, movement, and distance costs (Losh 1938, 1954; Zipf 1949). For the purposes of this paper the five points outlined and the more general theoretical principle that supports them are important because they describe the connecting links between settlement patterns and aspects of political behavior.

Measures

The three measures illustrated here are all based directly on the aspects of Central Place Theory discussed in the preceding section. Although closely related theoretically, each measure evaluates a slightly different area of prehistoric political behavior, and each makes use of slightly different aspects of archaeological settlement pattern data. All measure prehistoric political behavior on a continuous scale, and when consistently applied each should provide a reliable means for making accurate cross-cultural comparisons of political behavior between prehistoric societies.

Population Gradients as a Measure of Prehistoric Political Organization

One of the universal characteristics of all settlement systems is the interrelationship between the organizational structure of centers and the clinal distribution of population within their hinterlands (Bogue 1949; Clark 1951; Berry, Simmons, and Tennant 1963). Basic to this relationship is the fact that population density within a specific center's territory always falls off in a negative exponential fashion with increased distance from the center proper (Clark 1951; Berry, Simmons, and Tennant 1963). Specifically, in those cases where a community possesses strong administrative and political control over the population around it the organization of the hinterland population tends to assume patterns that facilitate administrative efficiency. With a constant technological regime this will lead to population distribution patterns that reduce all movement-related costs (Berry, Simmons, and Tennant 1963). In almost every case increased administrative efficiency and/or stronger political control produces a general flattening of the fall-off in population density (Bogue 1949). Likewise, in those cases where political control is weaker the hinterland population will be less focused upon the community and the fall-off in population density will become steeper (Bogue 1949; Hodder 1972, 1974).

The above relationship between a settlement and the population around it can be modeled mathematically using the following simple expression:

Some Simple Measures

$$Pd = T(Pce^{-\beta D}) \qquad (1)$$

Where: Pd = the population density at distance D from the settlement studied

T = a constant reflecting the level of technology within the society examined

Pc = the population density of the community analyzed

β = the slope.

As the nature of the population fall-off within a hinterland reflects the degree of administrative and political control exerted by the focal community, the relative steepness of the fall-off slope can be used directly as a simple measure of the overall administrative and political efficiency of the community's government. Consequently, when the above model is fitted to data representing the population fall-off around a specific settlement, the value of beta becomes a measure of the overall organizational complexity of the community and its surrounding hinterland population. In an even more specific sense the value of beta can be interpreted as follows:

1. When beta is in the range 0 to -0.5, the population around a community is highly organized and focused on the center. In such cases all transport, communications, and other movement-related costs are minimized between any point in the hinterland and the center. Movement point to point in a direction other than toward or away from the focal community is always relatively inefficient. In such cases political control is near peak efficiency and the government of the primary settlement has the potential for complete control over the political and economic behavior of the hinterland population.

2. When beta is in the range -0.5 to -1.0 movement toward or away from the center is still more efficient than other point-to-point movement within the hinterland although it is less efficient than when beta assumes lower values. This sort of pattern is most likely to develop when movement from community to community occurs hierarchically through a series of intermediate points. An example of this would be those cases where movement to a center was funneled through a series of satellite communities. In cases like this a center would exert considerable political control over its hinterland population. However, such control would be considerably weaker and more inefficient than that found in communities with population gradients like those found under #1 above.

3. In situations where beta falls between -1.0 and -2.0, movement point to point within a hinterland around a community is equally efficient in all directions. As beta approaches -2.0, the pattern of population distribution becomes essentially random with respect to the center. In such cases the control of a community over the population around it would be very weak under the best conditions.

4. Finally, in cases where the above model does not fit a population fall-off regime in a statistically significant fashion, it can be assumed that the

community in question did not exert any direct control over the population in the territory around it.

It should be clear that, where technology is a constant, the value of beta will vary continuously with variation in political organization. The partitioning used in this discussion is designed to clarify the nature of the changes produced by variation in the value taken by beta and does not reflect any real breaks in political organizational complexity.

A Measure of Relative Political Centrality

The coefficient outlined in this section expands upon each of the five principles discussed earlier and uses the nature of their interaction in the formulation of a simple measure of political centrality within a settlement system. Simply stated this coefficient relates the distribution of population within a settlement system and the degree to which the system is hierarchically arranged. As discussed earlier the relative complexity of political administration varies directly with the aggregate size of a community (Christaller 1933; Losch 1938, 1954; Berry 1967; Carniero 1967; Forge 1972). Consequently, the frequency with which centers higher in the settlement hierarchy contain smaller communities within the population gradients around them is a measure both of the degree to which higher centers politically dominate lower ones and the overall focus of political organization within a regional settlement system (Losch 1938, 1954; Christaller 1933; Berry 1967). This interrelationship between the size of communities, relative political dominance, the characteristics of local population gradients, and the specific hierarchical arrangement of communities within a settlement system makes it possible to devise a measure of the degree to which political and administrative functions were centralized within a settlement system. Specifically, with information on the bifurcation ratio between community size modes within a settlement system and a measure of population density it is possible to measure relative political centrality using the following expression:

$$PC = [(D(K_1^{\beta_1-1}))/(D(K_1^{\beta_1-1})+D(DK_2^{\beta_2-1}))] \qquad (2)$$

Where: PC = the degree to which a settlement system was politically and administratively centralized
D = a measure of population density
K = the bifurcation ratio for a specific hierarchical level
β = the number of the hierarchical level above the base level 0

The values obtained through the use of this coefficient will vary between 0 and 1.0 depending on the degree of political focus within a given settlement system. The higher the value the more centralized the system. In the absence of any sort of hierarchical arrangement of communities this coefficient will always be 0. A value of 1.0 will result when a settlement system is perfectly hierarchically arranged and every settlement except the largest is contained within the hinterland of the community immediately above it in the hierarchical ordering of communities.

A Measure of Relative Political Power

As was discussed in a previous section, the cost of extending political control from any settlement throughout its hinterland is a direct function of the combined effects of population and distance (Losch 1938, 1954; Berry 1967). Rephrased this relationship can be used both to determine the optimal boundary of a prehistoric polity and its relative political power. Using a simple example, the general principles involved can be outlined as follows. If the cost of political organization within a community has some value (OC; organizational cost), then the cost of extending that organization outward from the center must be that value plus all of the combined costs associated with movement and distance (KT; where K is a measure of distance and T represents all movement costs). The simple relationship OC+KT then summarizes the total cost of extending political control outward from a community (Figure 1). Further, since distance costs are closely tied to population density and population density falls off in a negative exponential fashion around settlements, it follows that the cost of extending political control must increase in a manner that closely mirrors the fall-off in population density (Bogue 1949; Clark 1951; Berry, Simmons, and Tennant 1963). If it is assumed that the implementation of political control is at least partially a function of its cost, then the rate of implementation must also fall off in a negative exponential fashion with increased distance away from a community. Figure 2 provides an illustration of this relationship between the cost of political control and its actual implementation around a center. Finally, as is shown in Figure 3, the cost of extending political control and the fall-off in the actual rate at which it is implemented form two gradients that must eventually cross. At the point at which these two gradients meet, a boundary is defined beyond which the cost of extending political control would become icreasingly inefficient. This point can be viewed as marking the limit of effective political control from the community for which it was calculated.

As was discussed in the section on population gradients there is a considerable body of empirical evidence that allows population fall-off around communities to be modeled. Since the actual rate at which political power can be implemented is perfectly correlated with a fall-off in population density, it follows that it can be modeled using the same expression that was used to model population gradients around centers:

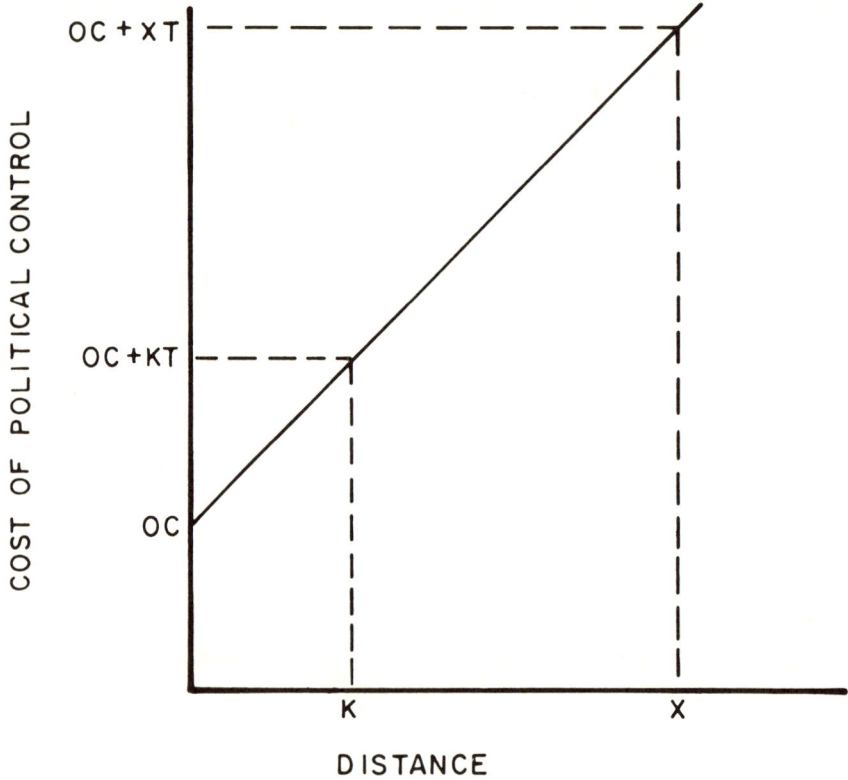

Figure 1. Distance and the cost of extending political control outward from a center. Where OC is the cost of political organization at the center, KT is the product of transport, movement and communications costs at distance K, and X is a distance K + X.

$$APID = T(Pce^{-\beta D}) \qquad (3)$$

Where: APID = the rate of implementation of political power at distance D from the center
  T = a constant reflecting the level of technology within the society examined
  Pc = the population density of the community analyzed
  β = the slope

Since the cost of movement and distance are negatively correlated with the fall-off in population density and the rate at which political power can be implemented, it follows that such movement and distance costs can be initially modeled using the following expression:

Some Simple Measures

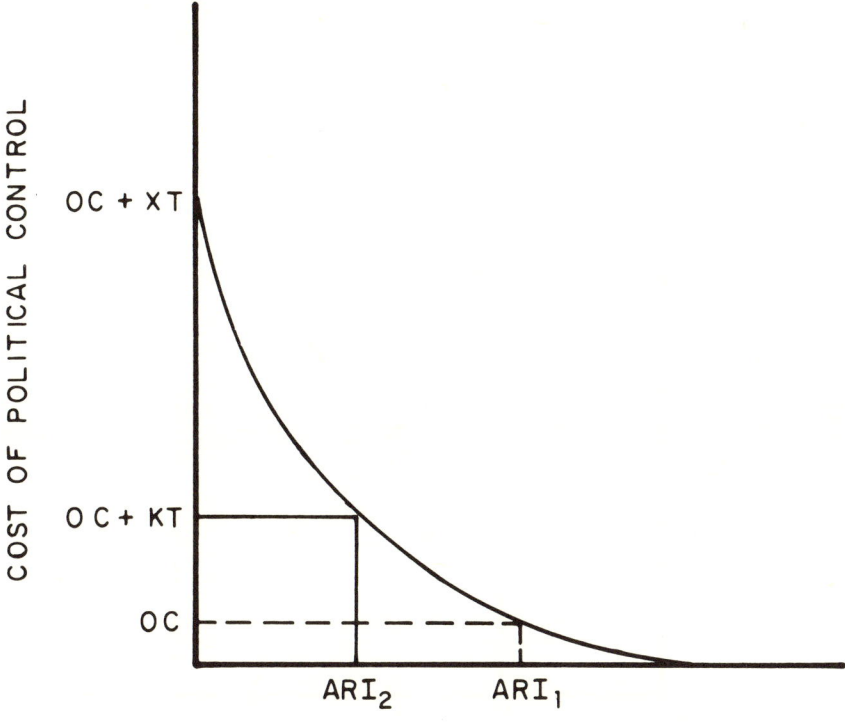

Figure 2. The actual rate at which political control can be implemented within the hinterland of a center (ARI). Where OC, XT, and KT are the same as in Figure 1.

$$CPCD = T(Pce^{\beta D}) \qquad (4)$$

Where: CPCD = the movement and distance costs associated with the extension of political power
T = a constant reflecting the level of technology within the society examined
Pc = population density of the community analyzed
β = the slope

Given the actual slope for these two related models and the equilibrium point defined by their intersection, it is possible to view a prehistoric polity as a center surrounded by a continuous boundary formed of such equilibrium points. Since a circle is the most efficient approximation of any unknown two-dimensional shape, a prehistoric polity might initially be seen as a circular

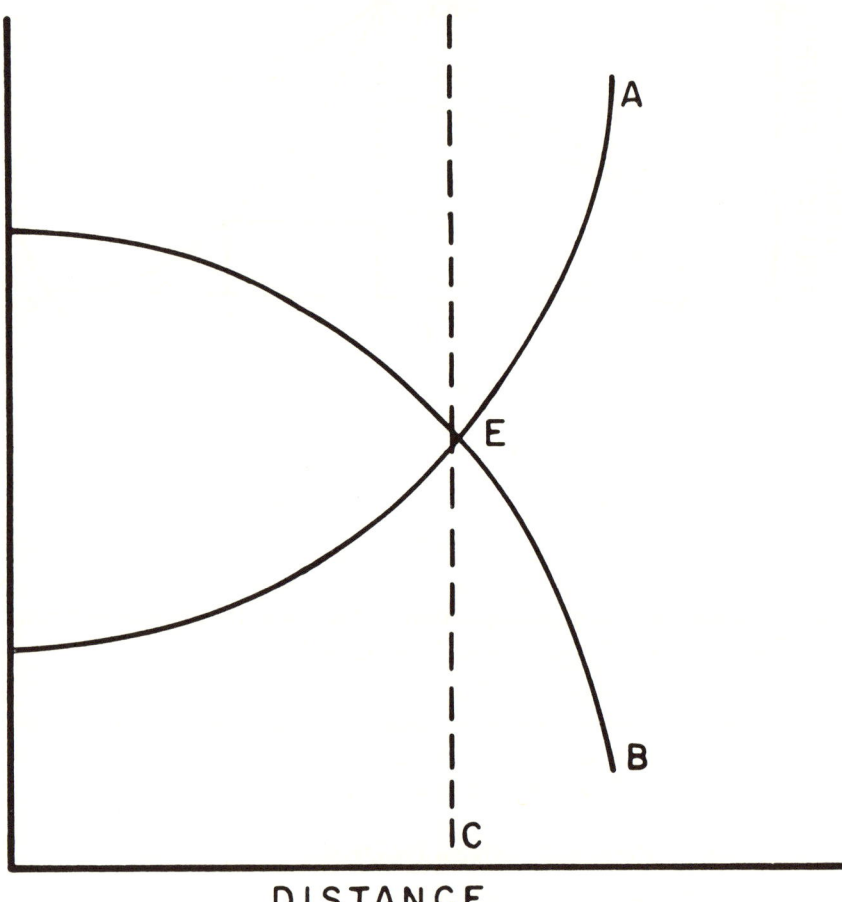

Figure 3. Limits on the extension of political control outward from a center. Where A represents all movement, communications, and transport costs associated with distance, B represents the decline in the actual rate of implementation of political control outward from a center, E is the intersection point, and C is the equilibrium point defined by the two gradients.

territory with a radius equal to the distance from the center to the average equilibrium point. Further, as the implementation of political power within this hypothetical prehistoric polity must fall off in a negative exponential manner from the center to the average equilibrium point, it is possible to add a second dimension to this model and view the polity as a cone-shaped structure in which relative political power is represented by the vertical dimension and area by the horizontal (Figure 4). Using this model the relative political power

Some Simple Measures

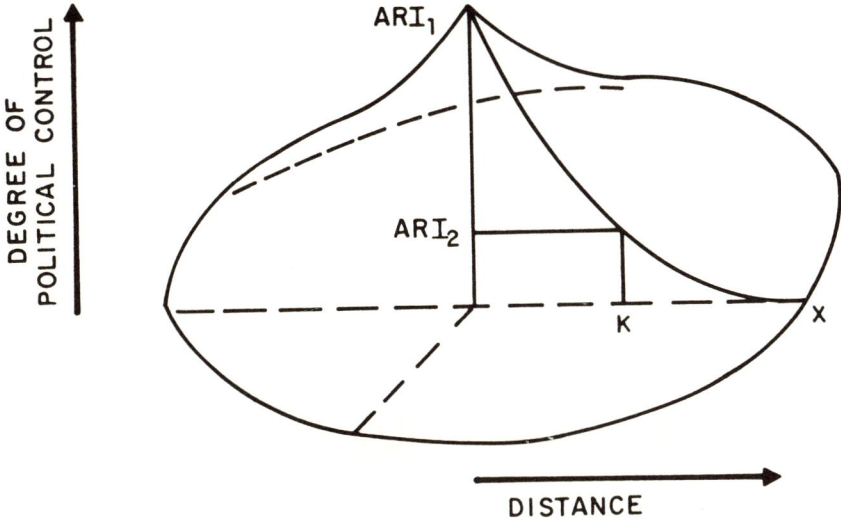

Figure 4. This figure represents a physical model of political power viewed as a form of a demand cone. Here the vertical dimension represents the actual rate of implementation of political control (ARI), and the horizontal dimension distance. X and K are the same as in figure 1.

of this hypothetical prehistoric polity could be measured as the integral of the area under the surface of this cone. Mathematically this measure of relative political power could be expressed using the following model:

$$RPP = PD \int_0^{2\pi} [\int_0^{K=X} f(OC+KT)KDK]d \qquad (5)$$

Where: RPP = relative political power
         PD = population density
         OC = the cost of political organization at the center
         KT = the product of all distance and movement costs
         X = the distance to the average equilibrium point.

While this measure provides an initial estimation of the size and power of a prehistoric polity, it can be greatly improved by taking into specific account the effects of environmental, movement, and distance costs. For example, if distance costs are measured not as simple linear distance, but as a function of the unique characteristics of local topography, a more realistic approximation of a prehistoric polity can be achieved. Such changes can be incorporated into expression 5 as follows:

$$RPP = PD \Sigma_0^{2\pi} [\int_0^{\lambda=X} ((T(Pce^{\beta\lambda}))\lambda d\lambda) - (\int_0^{\lambda} f(s)ds)] \qquad (6)$$

Where: RPP = Relative political power
   λ = linear distance
   X = the equilibrium point
   Pc = population density at the center
   S = a function reflecting the costs engendered by local relief and other topographic factors
   PD = population density
   T = a constant reflecting the level of technology within the society examined
   β = the slope

As outlined in expression 6 the measure should provide an accurate estimate of the political power available to a single prehistoric community. With the following modification the measure can be expanded to encompass the relative political power of entire prehistoric settlement systems:

$$RPP = \Sigma_1^N [\Sigma_0^{2\pi}[\int^{\lambda=X}((T(Pce^{\beta\lambda}))\lambda d\lambda)-(\int_0^\lambda f(s)ds)]] \qquad (7)$$

Where: RPP = relative political power within a settlement system
   N = the number of communities in the uppermost size mode in the settlement hierarchy
   λ = linear distance
   Pc = population density at the center
   S = a function reflecting the costs engendered by local relief and other topographic factors
   T = a constant reflecting the level of technology within the society examined
   β = the slope

The three measures illustrated in this section are all designed to have wide applicability in archaeological research. Consequently, there should be no difficulty in applying them to any body of archaeological settlement pattern data. Since each measure examines a slightly different area of prehistoric political behavior, it is advisable to use all three simultaneously to obtain the maximum amount of information. Likewise cross-cultural comparisons of prehistoric societies will be improved if all three measures are used.

Conclusions

In this paper the interrelationship between settlement patterns and political organization was investigated in an effort to illustrate the ways in which their interdependence might be used in the development of measures capable of analyzing prehistoric political organization. Specifically, in this study several aspects of Central Place Theory were used to support the development of three measures of prehistoric political behavior. Although these measures were limited to the measurement of relative centrality, relative complexity, and relative power within prehistoric polities, they are of more general importance because they demonstrate that it is not only possible to measure prehistoric political organization using settlement pattern data, but also because they demonstrate that Central Place Theory can supply the theoretical underpinning for the development of measures of prehistoric behavior normally thought to be beyond the scope of archaeological research.

References Cited

Berry, B. L. J.
    1960   The Impact of Expanding Metropolitan Communities upon Central Place Hierarchies. Annals of the Association of American Geographers, pp. 112–116.
    1967   Geography of Market Centers. Englewood Cliffs, NJ: Prentice-Hall.

Berry, B. L. M., H. Barnum, and R. J. Tennant
    1962   Retail Location and Consumer Behavior. Regional Science Association Papers and Proceedings 9:65–106.

Berry, B. L. J., and W. L. Garrison
    1958   A Note on Central Place Theory and the Range of a Good. Economic Geography 34:304–311.

Berry, B. L. J., J. W. Simmons, and R. J. Tennant
    1963   Urban Population Densities: Structure and Change. Geographical Review 53:389–405.

Bogue, D. J.
    1949   The Structure of the Metropolitan Community: A Study of Dominance and Subdominance. Ann Arbor: Horace H. Rackham School of Graduate Studies, University of Michigan.

Carneiro, R. L.
    1967   On the Relationship between Size of Population and Complexity of Social Organization. Southwestern Journal of Anthropology 23:234–243.

Christaller, W.
    1933   Die zentralen Orte in Süddeuntschland: Eine ökonomisch-geographische Untersuchung Über die Gesetzmässigkeit der Verbreitung und Entwicklung der Siedlungen mit städtischen Funktionen. Jena: G. Fischer.

Clark, C.
    1951   Urban Population Densities. Journal of the Royal Statistical Society, Series A, 114:490–496.

Forge, A.
    1972   Normative Factors in the Settlement Size of Neolithic Cultivators. *In* Man, Settlement and Urbanism, P. J. Ucko, R. Tringham, and G. W. Dimbleby, eds. London: Duckworth Press.

Hodder, I.
 1972 Locational Models and the Study of Romano-British Settlement. *In* Models in Archaeology, D. L. Clarke, ed. pp. 887–910. London: Methuen.
 1974 A Regression Analysis of Some Trade and Marketing Patterns. World Archaeology 6:172–189.

Hodder, I., and M. Millet
 1980 Romano-British Villas and Towns: A Systemic Analysis. World Archaeology 12:69–76.

Johnson, G.A.
 1972 A Test of the Utility of Central Place Theory in Archaeology. *In* Man, Settlement and Urbanism, P. J. Ucko, R. Tringham, and G. W. Dimbleby, eds. pp. 769–785. London: Duckworth Press.

Lösch, A.
 1938 The Nature of Economic Regions. Southern Economic Journal 5:71–78.
 1954 The Economics of Location. New Haven: Yale University Press.

Olsson, G.
 1965a Distance and Human Interaction: A Review and Bibliography. Philadelphia: The Regional Science Research Institute.
 1965b Distance and Human Interaction: A Migration Study. Geografska Annales 47b:3–40.
 1966 Central Place Systems, Spatial Interaction and Stochastic Process. Regional Science Association Papers and Proceedings 18:13–45.

Wright, H. T., and G. A. Johnson
 1975 Population Exchange and Early State Formation in Southwestern Iran. American Anthropologist 77:267–289.

Zipf, G. K.
 1949 Human Behavior and the Principle of Least Effort. Cambridge: Addison-Wesley.